HORTON FOOTE

Getting Frankie Married—and Afterwards
and other plays

HORTON FOOTE

Getting Frankie Married—and Afterwards
and other plays

CONTEMPORARY PLAYWRIGHTS
SERIES

SK
A Smith and Kraus Book

A Smith and Kraus Book
Published by Smith and Kraus, Inc.
PO Box 127, Lyme, NH 03768

Copyright ©1998 by Horton Foote
All rights reserved
Manufactured in the United States of America
Cover and Text Design by Julia Hill
Cover photo © Keith Carter

First Edition: July 1998
10 9 8 7 6 5 4 3 2 1

The Library of Congress Cataloging-In-Publication Data
Foote, Horton.
[Plays, selections]
Getting Frankie married — and afterwards and other plays / Horton Foote. —1st ed.
p. cm. (Contemporary playwrights series, ISSN 1067-9510)
ISBN 1057525-136-1
I. Title. II. Title: Collected Plays. III. Series.
PS3511.0344A6   1996
812'.54—dc20   93-33306
                 CIP

CONTENTS

INTRODUCTION

I used to keep a hidden stash of Hershey chocolate bars in my pocket just in case I ran into my friend Horton. No one was supposed to know that I would occasionally pass a forbidden bar his way, but of course everyone knew and I knew they knew and Horton knew they knew, but we all pretended not to and in turn, had a good smile about it with each pass of one of the banned bars.

It's the little things that seem to be alive and kicking with my friend Horton, those things that as we step back seem to reveal themselves as a reflection of our very lives, our purpose, our essence. Horton Foote is a master of capturing the little bits that make up our complicated selves, those things that at a glance seem really nothing at all, except for the simple fact that they add up to everything.

Horton and I first met during the intermission of Romulus Linney's play, *The Sorrows of Frederick*. He had heard that his friend had the courage to put himself on the chopping block with an experiment, an entire season of his work at a new tiny theatre in New York, Signature Theatre Company. You see, Horton loves his friends and loves theatre. He didn't miss a production that year. Eagerly, he watched and applauded the daring and tenacity of his friend, Romulus.

In that first meeting I sat with then "Mr. Foote" and immediately felt a kinship that revealed a depth of character and goodness, igniting the light and fire of friendship. As we sat chatting, I recalled thinking of the scope of Horton's work, including his remarkable nine-play cycle, *The Orphan's Home*, which explores the intimate canvas of family, friendship, and the difficult daily choices that define our lives. I thought of his dusty, breathtaking adaptation of Faulkner's *Tomorrow*, his exquisite screenplays *Tender Mercies, The Trip to Bountiful,* and *To Kill a Mockingbird,* and his fifty-year journey as a writer passing through time with a consistent vision and integrity. It was in that reflective moment when I suggested to Horton we should do a season together, to which he responded with that certain Horton gleam in his eye, "Okay, Buddy. Anytime, I'm ready. Let's go!" Three years later we passed through the doors of the rehearsal hall to an astonishing season.

Our work together preserves a precious moment in time when all seemed well and I shared a year with my gentle friend. In addition to a curious wonder that lives in Horton, there is a fierce respect for the truth on stage that is absolutely intoxicating. He is relentless in his search for the quiet truths that define the common bond of our lives.

When I said Horton loves the theatre I wasn't kidding. I think Horton attended nearly every rehearsal and all but a handful of performances. He loves the craft, the art, the event itself. He thrives in the creative atmosphere of the rehearsal hall and theatre. His work is without a doubt a great passion, but at the very core of Horton is his family...his heart.

It is the marriage of work and family that brings to life the depth of the Foote experience. He pulls life's mysteries from a deep well of emotional, spiritual, and personal experience that is reflected in each moment of his work. He lives in the small simple house where he was born, surrounds himself with his children, Daisy, Hallie, Horton Jr., and Walter, as well as his extended family. I remember celebrating the announcement of his Pulitzer Prize for Drama in a room filled with family and friends, but it's at the opening of *The Young Man from Atlanta* on Broadway, a triumph for any playwright, where his admirable balance of the important things in life filled my heart. As we rode home in the provided limousine, my wife turned to a distracted Horton and asked him how he was feeling about his achievement. He turned with his soft, welling, gentle eyes and said, "I miss my wife, Lillian. I wish she were here." We all quietly spent the ride home thinking of their forty-eight years together and the weight of loss and love on that night of celebration as the Manhattan skyline passed before our eyes.

It is the collective experience of life's tiniest moments that communicates meaning and purpose. Embracing these flashes and seeing them as touch points of definition is what Horton Foote gives us with his grace, his heart, and his work.

You see before you some of Horton's treasured touch points. My advice to you is to quickly grab that chocolate bar and turn each page until you reach the end of this wonderful collection and discover yourself in the heart of the master and common man that is Horton Foote.

James Houghton
Founding Artistic Director
Signature Theatre Company

THE DAY EMILY MARRIED

ORIGINAL PRODUCTION

The Day Emily Married was originally presented at Silver Springs Stage, Silver Springs, Maryland, May–June 1997. It was directed by Jack Sbarbori with the following cast:

SADIE. . . . . Eugenia Sorgnit
LYD DAVIS "BELLE". . . . . Gay Hill
EMILY . . . . Stephanie Mumford
RICHARD MURRAY . . . . Bob Justis
ADDIE. . . . . Sunday Wynkoop
LEE DAVIS. . . . . Rob Peters
LUCY FAY. . . . . Elizabeth Lawrence
ALMA NASH . . . . Patty Richmond
MAUD BARKER . . . . Marilyn Osterman

PLACE
Harrison, Texas

TIME
Early summer, 1956

ACT I

SCENE I

A bedroom and back sitting room of the Lee Davis home. The bedroom stage right is a small room with a double bed, two chairs, and a dresser. A door connects it with the larger room, the sitting room stage left. The sitting room has gay floral wall paper and white ivory wicker furniture consisting of a couch, rocking chair and three straight chairs. There is a door upstage left of the room leading to the rest of the house. A door upstage left center leads into a closet. The walls of the sitting room are covered with family pictures of every description and size.

Lyd Davis, tall, thin, angular, erect of carriage and heavily corseted with handsome almost severe features, is sitting on a chair by the window, asleep. Emily Davis, her daughter, comes into the room through the screen door. She is simply but well dressed and has just driven sixty miles from Houston. She sees her mother sleeping, starts for the small room when Addie, a Black, comes in from the door, upstage right center.

ADDIE: Hello, Miss Emily. I was just coming in to check on Miss Lyd. I better wake her or she won't sleep tonight.

EMILY: Yes, I guess you'd better.

(She goes into the small room and closes the door. She lights a cigarette. Addie goes over to Lyd and gently shakes her.)

ADDIE: Miss Lyd. Miss Lyd. Wake up. Wake up now.

(Lyd opens her eyes and looks up at Addie.)

Miss Emily is home.

LYD: Did she get all her shopping done?

ADDIE: I guess so.

LYD: *(Whispering to Addie.)* Why on earth she wants to get married again is beyond me. *(Lyd closes her eyes and shakes her head.)* I liked Ben. He was a sweet boy. When they got up on the floor it was like a show to watch them waltz. People would give them the floor but he drank. He was sweet and a gentleman, but he drank.

ADDIE: *(Interrupting.)* Ben. Miss Lyd, what's Mr. Ben got to do with anything? Miss Emily's marrying Mr. Richard in four days.

LYD: *(Closing her eyes and shaking her head.)* Richard adores her. He doesn't want that child out of his sight. He's after her every second to marry him. The trouble is there's nothing for the young people to do here anymore. No one entertains the young people. When I was a girl, there were balls twice a week. They'd turn the whole courthouse over to us and they built the Opera House. That's condemned now.

(Emily comes into the sitting room. She is still smoking.)

EMILY: Are Richard and Daddy still out at the farm?

LYD: I think so. If you'd stop smoking, I bet Ben would stop drinking.

(Emily starts for the screen door.)

Where are you going now?

EMILY: To get some dresses from my car.

ADDIE: Want me to help you?

EMILY: No, thank you. I can manage.

(She goes out. Addie fans herself.)

ADDIE: It's been so hot.

LYD: Hot? I nearly froze to death all day. *(She pulls the shawl tight around her.)* *(Richard Murray comes in the door, upstage right center. He is good looking and aggressive. He is wearing work clothes.)*

RICHARD: Hello. Mr. Lee will be along in a minute.

LYD: Emily's home. She's getting some clothes from her car.

(He starts for the screen door.)

Have you been at the farms all day?

RICHARD: Yes, ma'am.

LYD: You must like walking around in those hot fields?

RICHARD: I don't mind it. We were surveying today. That's interesting.

(Emily comes in the screen door, her arms filled with dresses.)

Here, let me help you, honey.

(He takes the dresses and they go in the small room. She then shuts the door. Richard puts the dresses down on the bed. They kiss.)

Did you say goodbye to everybody at the boardinghouse?

EMILY: No, they were all gone to work, or downtown shopping by the time I got there. I looked around my room as I was packing and I thought to myself, how did I ever stand living here?

RICHARD: How did you?

EMILY: I don't know. I tried to come back here and live after my divorce from Ben, but I just couldn't. And I suppose I was too frightened, or lonely, or something, to live by myself, so I found this boardinghouse and moved there. There were five other women living there. I was the youngest. We ate breakfast and supper together every day of the week. Sometimes there was not a word said during the whole meal. One woman cried herself to sleep every night. The other women would come out into the hallway and stand outside her door wondering if they shouldn't go in to her, and ask her why she was crying, but they never did. The first night you came to call on me there, I said to myself, dear God, let him like me. He's handsome and I know he's had lots of girls and I don't know why it should be me he's chosen, but let it happen. Please, let it happen.

(Richard puts his arms around her.)

I was thinking as I drove back here, how we met this last time so by accident. It scared me. What would have happened if you hadn't been in Houston that day and we hadn't passed each other in the street? *(She starts hanging her clothes in the closet.)* I saw you that day half a block away. I didn't want to speak to you though, because I knew you were a friend of Ben's. I was sure you had seen me, and when I turned around after we had passed each other, and found you were looking at me, I was so embarrassed.

RICHARD: What did you think when I asked you for lunch?

EMILY: Oh, I didn't want to go at all. Not that I didn't like you, but I thought he doesn't know Ben and I are divorced and now I will have to explain all of that.

RICHARD: And I thought, she doesn't know I know she's divorced, and how can I tell her without embarrassing her?

LYD: *(Calling.)* What are you doing in there with that door closed?

EMILY: Nothing, Mother.

LYD: Well, open that door and come on out here. Lee would have a fit if he walked in here and found you in there with that door closed.

EMILY: You talk to Mother. That's what she wants. I'll finish unpacking.

(She continues hanging up her clothes. He goes out to the sitting room.)

RICHARD: Mind if I lie down on the couch for a while? I'm beat.

LYD: Go right ahead.

(He lies down.)

Do you have a nice room over in Victoria?

RICHARD: It's all right. Since I've been going with Emily, I'm never there anyway, except to sleep.

LYD: I guess that's the truth. You know the last time Alma Nash was home she stood me down that you and Emily met in Houston. I said you did not, you met right here.

RICHARD: No, Miss Lyd. We met in Houston. You remember, I only came here five weeks ago, when Emily started her visit. We've known each other at least five years. I met Emily first when she was still married to Ben.

LYD: Oh. *(A pause.)* How does it feel working for an oil crew and moving all the time from town to town, from state to state?

RICHARD: I'm tired to death of it. I believe I've lived at one time or another in every rooming house in Texas, Louisiana, and Mississippi. I know I've eaten in every greasy restaurant. I left home when I was fifteen, and before I ended up in the Army, I had been in six different states. The day I look forward to, is when I have my own house and can settle down and never leave my own yard.

LYD: Well, don't expect Emily to stay home with you. She was born restless, this child. She started driving a car at twelve and from then on Lee and I never saw her except at meal times.

(Lee Davis comes in through the screen door. He speaks slowly and quietly, but with a great deal of authority.)

LEE: Hello, folks. *(He goes over to Lyd and kisses her.)* Hello, Belle.

LYD: Hello, Daddy.

(Emily comes out of her room. He kisses her.)

LEE: Hello, girl. *(He points to Richard.)* I want to tell you something about this young man, Emily. There's not a lazy bone in his body. He knows right now more about my farms than I do. Today, he discovered five acres on my farm near the River Road that belonged to me and I'd forgotten were ever part of my farm. The man with the place next to mine had fenced it in and claimed it as his own. I would never have discovered it if he hadn't, on his own, this afternoon, taken a surveyor and decided to walk around my land.

LYD: Why, you don't mean it?

LEE: Yes, I do. Aren't you proud of him, Emily?

EMILY: I certainly am.

LYD: I just wish someone from Richard's family could come to the wedding.

EMILY: Mama, Richard has no family. I told you that.

LYD: Did you? Then I forgot. I'm sorry. Have you told me where you were born, Richard?

RICHARD: Yes, ma'am. I told you. I was born in Georgia. We moved to Louisiana then, when I was eight. To Beaumont when I was ten, and then on and on…My mother died when I was fourteen. The last relative I had was an aunt. She died two years ago.

LYD: Do you have a picture of your mother and father? I'd love to see them.

RICHARD: No, I don't. I have no family, and no pictures of a family.

LEE: Well, you have a family now, son.

RICHARD: Thank you.

LYD: I'd think you two were brothers, the way you get along. What do you talk about so much?

LEE: We have a lot to talk about, Belle.

(Emily gets up.)

EMILY: Excuse me. I'm going to wash up and change my dress.

RICHARD: I think I'll get into my suit, too.

(She goes into the small room. He goes out the door, upstage left center. Lee settles down in a chair. He rests his head against it.)

LYD: My God, I've never seen anything like the way he adores that child. He told me if she didn't marry him, that he hoped they would tie him to a car and drag him around the courthouse square until he was dead.

(Music is heard faintly from a highway cafe. Lee rocks back and forth quietly in his chair. Lyd sits up straight in hers.)

Daddy, is that window up behind me?

LEE: Yes, it is, Belle.

(He gets up and closes the window. Twilight is beginning outside. He turns the lamp on.)

LYD: Isn't that silly? Getting cold this way in the middle of July? Look at my hands. The palms are covered with perspiration.

(There is a pause. Lee rocks back and forth.)

Do you think that boy can support Emily, Daddy?

LEE: Yes, Belle, I do. He has a very good job. And he has no bad habits as far as I can see. He's well thought of, too. Thurman May told me he ran into Tom Carter in Houston.

LYD: Who?

LEE: Tom Carter.

LYD: The oil-millionaire?

LEE: Ex-millionaire now. He has been a millionaire twice. Anyway, he told Thurman May he knew Richard and thought very highly of him. *(He reaches over and takes his wife's hand.)* You're still my flapper, Belle.

LYD: Thank you, Daddy. You're still my jelly bean.

LEE: Here's a little something to buy you a dress for the wedding. *(He reaches in his pocket and gets a large bill.)*

LYD: I've got my dress already for the wedding.

LEE: Well, then buy yourself another dress.

LYD: What do I need clothes for? An old scarecrow like me?

LEE: There's no one around here as pretty as you are. I want to see you get dressed up. I want you to get something red. I've always liked you in red. While you're downtown, I wish you'd stop in the beauty parlor and have your hair touched up. I think it needs it. I like you to look like my flapper...

LYD: All right, Daddy. *(She begins to cry.)*

LEE: Don't cry, Belle. Please don't cry. I'll do anything you want, if you just won't cry.

(A pause. Lyd wipes her eyes.)

LYD: I'm sorry, Daddy. I'm so sorry. It's just that I feel so lonely. I get so lonely here by myself.

LEE: I know. Well, Emily's back home.

LYD: But she's leaving in four days. She'll be gone for good then. *(She gets up and goes to the wall and looks at the pictures.)* I was thinking about Papa the other night. Why, he wouldn't even recognize the town he was born in if he came back. The opera house is condemned, the 1915 storm got nearly all the frame stores, and what was left the fire took. I remember those beautiful trees Papa planted around the Courthouse Square, and when those men came to cut them down, he took his gun and stood there for two days and nights guarding those trees. They cut them down, though, when he died. They say we have to have progress. They've torn the courthouse down and put up that new one that looks like a block of sulphur, it's so ugly. All that Papa would recognize around the square is the statue of the sheriff that was killed by the desperado and the monument to the Confederate dead. A restaurant behind us, a filling station across the street, he wouldn't even recognize me with my face lined and my hair dyed. But my back's straight and I've tried to watch my figure like he said ladies should.

LEE: Belle...

LYD: Yes, Daddy.

LEE: We got an offer again for the house.

LYD: I remember you told me at dinner. Fifteen thousand?

LEE: No, twenty-five.

LYD: That's right. Twenty-five. I declare. Well, money isn't everything.

LEE: No.

LYD: It isn't as if we needed it. If we did, I'd feel we'd have to think about it. *(Lee has closed his eyes again.)* Daddy, you look tired. Did you work hard today?

LEE: Yes, I did.

LYD: Here, let me take your shoes off. *(She kneels down and starts to remove his shoes.)* You've been so good to me all these years. I want you to know, that I couldn't have asked for a nicer husband. I was talking to some ladies the other day, and they were bragging about their husbands, and I said, "Ladies, are you all through?" *(She puts the shoes down. She sits beside Lee and takes his hand.)* They said, "Yes," and I said, "I have a husband who has never said a cross word to me and every morning of my life has brought me two slices of bacon and a poached egg and toast and coffee to my bed and kisses me and says, "Eat your breakfast," and they said, "Well, you can't beat that," and I said, "When God made Lee, he threw the pattern away."

(Lee has his eyes closed again.)

Daddy. Daddy. You're falling asleep in your chair. Come on. Lie down on the couch, Daddy.

LEE: I'm not asleep, Belle. I was only thinking. We're neither of us getting any younger. What would you think of Emily and Richard living here with us after they're married. You're not feeling well so much of the time, if anything happened to me...

LYD: Daddy, don't say that.

LEE: Well, if it did, Belle, you and Emily would have a lot of responsibilities. You know the money is all spent now from the land we sold fifteen years ago.

LYD: I don't want to think about it. I've only one request of God and that's that he take me first. I don't want to hear you talk about such things.

LEE: Belle, we have to be practical.

LYD: No, I don't. I don't want to talk about it at all.

LEE: All I'm saying, Lyd, is that since everything we have here will belong to Emily someday, why shouldn't she stay here with her husband?

LYD: Whatever you want to do, Daddy, would suit me fine. I just don't want to talk about our leaving each other anymore. That's all. If we ever have to be separated I want God to take me first.

LEE: I want to sell the rest of the farms and set Richard up in business. He has a fine head on his shoulders. People like him. He'd do well in business here.

(Emily comes back into the small room. She changes her dress.)

LYD: Daddy, if you sold our land, wouldn't you miss farming?

LEE: I'd like to rest, Belle. I'm very tired. I've been tired for a long, long time.

LYD: Are you, Lee?

LEE: Yes.

LYD: Then whatever you say, Daddy. Whatever you want to do. *(She laughs again, softly to herself.)* Yes sir, I wish you could have seen those ladies faces. I just sat there and listened and I said, "Ladies, are you all through?" and they said, "Yes." And I told them, "When God made Lee, he threw the pattern away."

(Emily comes to the door of her room.)

EMILY: Daddy, can I see you for a minute?

LEE: Certainly, kid.

(He gets up and goes into her room. She closes the door.)

Getting excited about the wedding?

EMILY: Yes, I am, Daddy.

LEE: I think you're going to be very happy, kid. I think it's going to be all different this time.

EMILY: I think so, too. *(A pause.)* Richard spoke to me last night about his working with you, and our living here after we're married.

LEE: He said he would. It occurred to me it was the wise thing to do.

EMILY: It was very sweet of you to suggest it, and we both appreciate your thinking of us and asking us to stay.

LEE: It would certainly give us great pleasure. Like I told Richard, I've never had a son.

EMILY: Daddy, we can't stay here.

LEE: You can't?

EMILY: No. I told Richard I would think about it and talk it over with you, but I don't want us to.

(Lee seems badly disappointed.)

I'm sorry, Daddy.

LEE: Your mother would like you to stay. Richard told me he would.

(A pause. Emily doesn't answer.)

I wouldn't ask him to farm. He must have told you that.

EMILY: Yes, he did.

LEE: I'd sell the farm and invest in a business for him. I was going to suggest re-doing the whole house for you.

EMILY: No, why should you spend money on that, when you know in a few years you'll sell it for a filling station anyway. I wish you'd sell it now, while you can get such a good price for it.

LEE: I asked your mother again about selling it. She doesn't want to.

(Richard comes into the sitting room from upstage left center. He goes to the screen door and stands looking out.)

EMILY: If we stay, I'd want to do the cooking, and take care of the house.

LEE: That would have to be up to your mother, Emily. After all, this is Belle's house. Of course, we could never let Addie go, and it seems to me it would be foolish having Addie here with nothing to do. I just thought if we all made a special effort to get along, I'm sure there would be enough to keep you and Addie both busy...

EMILY: I know it just won't work, Daddy. I told Richard I'd think about it and talk it over with you, but I really don't think we should stay.

LEE: Belle gets so lonesome when you're not here.

EMILY: I'm sorry.

(A pause. He looks at Emily.)

LEE: Well, all right, kid. If you feel that way, we'll say no more about it. *(A pause. He reaches in his pocket and gets a check.)* Use this on your honeymoon.

EMILY: No, thank you. You can't afford to do this. You've done enough for me.

LEE: You'll hurt me very much, if you won't take it. I want you to have it, Emily.

(She sees he is very hurt.)

EMILY: Oh, all right. *(She kisses him.)* I think you're the sweetest and most generous person in the whole world.

LEE: I think you're pretty nice yourself. I wouldn't trade you for anything I've seen yet. I know that. I think I'll take your mother for a little ride before supper. She hasn't been out the house all day. It will be good for her to get out. *(He goes into the sitting room.)* Would you like to go for a little ride, Belle?

LYD: Aren't you tired?

LEE: No, I rested while I was sitting up in the chair.

LYD: All right.

(She gets up and starts for the screen door. Lee follows. Emily comes into the sitting room. Richard is looking at the pictures on the wall.)

EMILY: Could you hear us talking in there?

RICHARD: No.

EMILY: We both decided that it was wiser if you and I didn't come back here to live. I know that Daddy was disappointed at first, but then I think he realized what I said was true...

RICHARD: What did you say?

EMILY: Just that we shouldn't live here together. *(A pause.)* Daddy gave me this check to spend on our honeymoon.

RICHARD: He can't afford to do that.

EMILY: I know, and I didn't want to take it, but he looked so hurt that I accepted it anyway.

RICHARD: Give it to me. I want him to take it back. I don't want him giving us things whether I stay here or not.

(She gives him the check and he puts it in his pocket.)

EMILY: You're disappointed we're not staying, aren't you?

(Richard doesn't answer.)

I was afraid you would be. I know that you think living in one place, having a family around you, is the most wonderful thing in the world. *(A pause.)* Honey, it was a mistake that Ben and I ever lived here.

RICHARD: Emily, I've told you and told you I don't want to hear about Ben Lacque. I can see him drunk any day in the week on West Milam Street in Houston. I know all about him. I'd like to punch him in the face for the way he treated you. I knew Ben before you did. He was no good then. He's no good now. I don't want ever to hear about him again. *(A pause.)* I'm sorry. I don't know why I got so excited. *(A pause.)* What did you want to tell me?

EMILY: Nothing.

RICHARD: Yes, you did. Something about you and Ben…

EMILY: It doesn't matter. *(A pause.)* When I was a girl I used to hate coming into this room. It seemed like a museum with all Mother's pictures around. I could never somehow think of them as my family, but only as Mother's. I used to dream of them one day coming home and finding all the pictures gone. Even now, I'd like to turn the faces of every one of them to the wall.

RICHARD: Why, Emily?

EMILY: Because they remind me of how unhappy I was, growing up here. In my ballet costume. In my party dresses. Mother and Daddy were forty when I was born. I was the only child. They hovered over me. Mama was determined to make me the belle of the ball, the most popular girl in the town. But the more she told me what to wear and what to do to make myself popular, the more awkward and ill at ease I became. I tried to talk to Mama about it, but she got upset and said I was making the whole thing up, that I was popular and I was attractive. They sent me away to boarding school, but I got homesick and let me come back after six weeks. At fifteen they bought me a car. I can remember the years by the cars I've had. A yellow Buick, a green Chevrolet, a red Ford. I'd get up at eleven and ride with whatever girl I was friendly with at the time. Round and round the square I'd ride; and then I met Ben. He sold burial insurance and Mama and Daddy couldn't bear that, so he gave it up, but they didn't like his next job, either, collecting laundry, so he gave that up, and Daddy told him if he didn't drink for six weeks, he would buy him a business. We sat here in this room and watched and waited to see if he would pass the test. Well, he didn't. He stopped it for three weeks and then came home drunk and he and Daddy had a fight and we had to leave.

RICHARD: Emily, do you think anybody—your father, your mother, anybody—is going to boss me or run my life or tell me what to do? Do you think I'm Ben? Do you think I'm weak?

EMILY: No, but maybe I am. *(A pause.)* I don't want to live here with them. Is that so wrong? Oh, I want to be alone with my husband. I don't want my mother and father with me every minute of the day.

RICHARD: Emily...

EMILY: I want my freedom. I want my own home.

RICHARD: You'll have your own home someday. The finest house anyone has ever had. I'm going to get you a lot of things before I'm through. Clothes, jewels, fur coats...

EMILY: I don't care anything about fine clothes, or a fine house.

RICHARD: But I do. I wouldn't feel like a man or a decent husband if I can't get these things for my wife. I don't want them for myself, but I want them for you. And I'm going to get them. Here is my opportunity, Emily. There are wonderful possibilities here. I want your father to go into the oil business with me. It's what I'm ready to do now. I've spent twelve years working hard in the oil fields. Studying, learning. I've investigated every independent setup on this Gulf Coast, and now I know I'm ready to go out on my own. I know some wildcatters that started with only three or four thousand dollars. They leased a little land, sold their leases for a profit. They got their start that way. Others got their start by getting some money together and joining in with someone of more experience, who's working with a good geologist. That's how I'd like us to begin. I know a lot of men in the business that respect me and that I respect. I know one man that has leased some land, and I agree should pay off handsomely. He's trying to finance the developments of it now.

EMILY: Who is he?

RICHARD: Tom Carter. I admire him as much as any man I know of. I think he knows more about oil and where it can be found than any man in this state.

EMILY: I thought he was broke?

RICHARD: He is. That's why I thought we could make a good trade with him now. He needs cash, and he'd be easy to bargain with. We could get a lot for our money.

EMILY: Have you and Daddy talked about all this?

RICHARD: *(Laughing.)* Yes. That's all we've talked about this last week, whenever we've been together. He's asked to meet Tom Carter. There's also an insurance business for sale around town that he's asked me to look into and I've agreed.

EMILY: Richard, it might be six months before the farms are sold. How will we support ourselves?

RICHARD: No, it won't. Your Father knows of three men right now who want to buy his land. All we have to do is draw up papers. That couldn't take more than a month. I'll keep working with the crew over in Victoria until that's done, and we have a business to go into.

EMILY: All right. Let's say you and Daddy do go into business. Why do we have to live here?

RICHARD: For their sake. *(He takes her hand.)* Emily, I've tried every way I know how to keep from worrying about this, but you're going to have to know. Your Daddy isn't well.

EMILY: What do you mean?

RICHARD: He's had two heart attacks. The doctors have told him that if he doesn't slow down soon, he'll just fall over dead one of these days.

EMILY: Oh, honey.

RICHARD: He told me about it when he asked me to live here.

EMILY: Why hasn't he told me?

RICHARD: Because he didn't want you to be worried. He had his last attack when you were still living in Houston.

EMILY: Well, he's going to stop working right this minute. He's going to sell the farms and this house…

RICHARD: Your mother says he can't sell the house.

EMILY: I'll tell Mother just how sick he is, and then she'll have to let him.

RICHARD: And have her kill herself from worrying over him? The worst thing you can do is to tell her.

(A pause.)

EMILY: I suppose.

RICHARD: We're just both going to have to help them now, Emily. Your daddy has confided a lot in me. The money he had when he sold off that first piece of land is all gone now. Do you realize that if he died tomorrow, Miss Lyd would get along all right because he has some insurance, but that he hasn't saved a penny for his own old age? When he sells the rest of the farms, he'll have to invest in a business in order to live. I've looked at his books. I know exactly how things are. It's a shame. Hard as he's worked all his life.

EMILY: I know.

RICHARD: What gets me is the money he's loaned out through the years that he never collected. Do you realize that your Uncle Davis died owing him ten thousand dollars? There were four or five others that the same thing happened to.

EMILY: I'm sure. Uncle Davis and all of Daddy's relatives and Mother's relatives...

RICHARD: Jack Barker has been borrowing money from him over a fifteen-year period. He let him have it at three percent interest. He just pays the interest back year after year and doesn't even try to pay anything back on the debt.

EMILY: Well, he has no money.

RICHARD: I know, honey. But your father doesn't either now. He can't afford to do business like this any longer. Jack Barker has farms and he's agreed that if he can't pay him back, that it's time he protects himself by taking his land.

EMILY: D...

RICHARD: And what about your Mother. What's going to happen to her? I haven't said anything, I hate to spoil your father's hopes, but I think she gets worse every day. She turns on gas stoves in the middle of summer and forgets to light them. She sits around in the hottest weather with a coat or a shawl on, saying she's cold. She's wandered to the river twice and Addie has to be sent to get her back. She needs help.

EMILY: We've sent her to every doctor in town.

RICHARD: The doctors here aren't equipped to help her. She needs a specialist, or a sanitarium. Your father was worrying about her the other day when I was here and I discussed with him the possibilities...

EMILY: *(Crying.)* I'm sorry.

RICHARD: Now come on, Emily.

(A pause. She wipes her eyes.)

EMILY: I'm sorry. *(A pause.)* Honey, I'm too upset to talk anymore. I don't know what's the best thing to do. I'd do anything in this world to help them, but I don't know honestly if our staying here is the solution.

(Lyd comes in.)

LYD: It's too windy out in that car for me. *(She goes to her chair and pulls the shawl around her.)*

EMILY: Where'd Daddy go?

LYD: He'll be along in a little while. He said he had some business to attend to. I saw Alma Nash as I was getting out of the car. She hollered across the street and said she was coming over to tell us hello.

(Addie comes in.)

ADDIE: I need some milk for supper.

RICHARD: I'll get it for you.

(He goes out the door upstage left center.)

ADDIE: If I have supper in about fifteen minutes, will that please everybody?

EMILY: Yes, Addie.

(She goes out. Emily goes over to her Mother and hugs her.)

LYD: What's that for?

EMILY: Because I love you.

LYD: I love you too, honey.

(Alma Nash comes in the screen door.)

ALMA: Hey, I'm here for the wedding. *(She gives Emily a hug and kiss.)*

EMILY: Mama told me you were in town. What time did you get in?

ALMA: Late last night.

LYD: Sit down, Alma.

ALMA: Thank you. Estelle Marshall is coming by for me any minute. *(She turns to Lyd.)* Cousin Lyd, you look so good. Is that a new shade you're dying your hair?

LYD: No, it's the same old shade. Only I have to get somebody to drive me to the beauty parlor and it fades a little between trips. Where've you been?

ALMA: Well, I was in New Orleans and then I stopped back by Houston and swung over to Corpus and then back by Victoria for a week.

EMILY: Alma, I'm trying to decide which of two dresses to wear at my wedding and on the trip afterwards. Come look at them, will you, and tell me which you like?

ALMA: I'd love to.

(They go into the small bedroom.)

Where are you going on your honeymoon?

EMILY: New Orleans. *(She picks up two dresses.)* Here they are. Which do you like?

ALMA: They're both pretty. But I think I like this one best.

EMILY: Do you like this one, Mother?

LYD: Yes, I think I do.

EMILY: Then I'll keep this one. Mama, would you please go and get Alma a Coke?

LYD: Certainly. Do you want one?

EMILY: No, thank you.

(Lyd goes out.)

ALMA: What time is the wedding?

EMILY: Four on Monday. We may live here, Alma. Richard may work with Daddy. I was opposed to the whole idea at first, but Daddy isn't at all well, and Mother needs me, and Richard wants to stay and go into a business.

ALMA: Well, I think it's a good idea. You know, running around the way I do, I'm thrown with all kinds of people, and Emily, I think you'd be miserable following around after an oil crew. I met a lot of people that Richard has to work with in Victoria and I don't think much of them. They're not your kind at all.

(Addie comes in.)

ADDIE: Your cook's on the phone, Miss Alma. There's a lady come to call over at your house.

ALMA: Did she tell you her name?

ADDIE: Yes'm. A Miss Lucy Douglas, I think she said.

(Alma gets up and peers out of the window.)

ALMA: Oh, Lord. She's the last person in the world I want to see. Go tell her to say that I'm not here.

ADDIE: Yes'm. *(She goes out.)*

ALMA: I met her at a party in Victoria the other night. She was with some old rancher that everybody said was the richest thing in that part of the country. He had a beet-red face, wore cowboy boots, and talked all the time. He got drunk as a dog and she kept right up with him. The next day when I was downtown shopping I met her again, and she spoke to me, and she said the next time she was passing through on her way to Houston she was gonna stop by and see me. Well, you know how you do, I said oh, I hoped she would, not meaning a word of it, and certainly not expecting her to, but while I was in the bathtub this morning, didn't my front doorbell ring and I got out of the tub, and put a robe on, and hollered who is it? "Lucy," this woman's voice called back just as sweetly. "Lucy who?" I said. "Lucy Douglas," she said. "I was on my way to Houston and I stopped by like I promised."

(Lyd comes in with the Coke.)

LYD: Here's the Coke, Alma.

ALMA: Thank you. *(She takes the Coke.)* And in she came and began to tell me the most intimate secrets of her life. Me. A perfect stranger. I was so embarrassed.

(Addie comes in.)

ADDIE: Miss Alma, excuse me. Your maid said she couldn't tell her that, because she can see you over here.

ALMA: All right, then tell her I'll be right there.

(Addie goes out.)

She told me about the rich rancher she was with. She said she had a terrible disappointment about him. She said his sister had suddenly appeared from California, while he was on a big drunk, and had declared him incapable of managing his money and had taken him back to California with her. She said the whole thing had...

(Lucy Douglas has come to the door. She is handsome and extremely well dressed. She knocks. Emily goes to the door.)

EMILY: Yes?

LUCY: I'm Lucy Douglas. I'm looking for Alma Nash.

EMILY: Oh, yes. Won't you come in? I'm Emily Davis.

LUCY: How do you do? *(Lucy comes into the room.)*

ALMA: I was just on my way home, Lucy.

LUCY: I know and I don't want you to bother. I told your maid to tell you that. I just stopped by for a second. I came by especially this morning to invite you to a party I'm giving Saturday, and halfway to Houston I remembered I hadn't asked you. I felt like such a fool. Can you come?

ALMA: I'll try.

LUCY: Emily, could you and Richard come?

EMILY: *(Laughing.)* Oh, no. You see, we're getting married Monday...

LUCY: Yes, I heard.

EMILY: And I have so much to do.

LUCY: Is Richard here now?

EMILY: No.

ALMA: Come on. I'll walk you over to my house. I'm waiting for a friend that's taking me to dinner.

LUCY: No, I don't want you to do that. I have to go right on to Victoria anyway. You stay right here.

LYD: Has everybody forgotten their manners? I haven't met the lady.

EMILY: Excuse me, Mother. Miss Douglas, this is my mother, Mrs. Davis.

LYD: How do you do.

LUCY: How do you do. *(She starts out.)* I hope I see you Saturday, Alma, and Emily, you tell Richard I was asking for him.

EMILY: I will.

LUCY: Goodbye, Mrs. Davis.

LYD: Goodbye.

(Lucy goes out of the door.)

ALMA: Do you think she's attractive?

EMILY: Yes, I do.

ALMA: Hard, though. I bet she's had a life. She has beautiful clothes. I bet she spends a fortune on her back.

LYD: I once made this child a lovely voile with a princess waist and when she walked down the street she stopped traffic.

EMILY: I wonder how she knows Richard?

ALMA: I guess because they met in Victoria. She seems very friendly with people that work on his oil crew. Oh, they're wild on those crews. It's just open season for the wives to hunt each other's husbands.

LYD: *(Laughing.)* I used to make every stitch this child put on her back. She looked like a queen when I made her clothes. The mothers used to all beg me to loan them the patterns. But one day she walked in, announced she wouldn't wear the clothes I made for her any longer. She didn't look modern enough, she said. I cried myself to sleep that night, I can tell you. The very next morning she gave all her clothes away and went downtown and bought all new outfits that made her look just like everybody else.

(Across the street someone honks a car. Alma looks out.)

ALMA: That's for me. I'll see you tomorrow. *(She goes running out.)*

LYD: I want to show you what I'm wearing to your wedding. *(She gets up and goes to the closet. She gets a brilliant red dress out. She takes it into the small room and changes into it.)*

(Richard comes in the door upstage left center.)

EMILY: Richard, I want to stay.

(He takes her into his arms. They kiss.)

RICHARD: I'm glad. I know you won't be sorry.

EMILY: I know.

RICHARD: Have you told your mother and daddy yet?

EMILY: No.

RICHARD: Don't you know they'll be excited? Where's your dad?

EMILY: Still downtown. Honey, who is Lucy Douglas?

RICHARD: A girl I used to go with. Why?

EMILY: She was here a few minutes ago to see Alma Nash. She asked to be remembered to you.

(Lyd comes in wearing a red dress.)

That's very becoming, Mother.

LYD: Thank you.

EMILY: Mother, we've decided to stay on.

LYD: In Harrison?

EMILY: Yes.

(Lee comes in the screen door.)

LYD: Daddy, they're going to stay. The children are going to stay.

EMILY: If you still want us.

LEE: You are very welcome. You're welcome as the flowers in May.

(Richard goes over to Lee and puts his arms around him.)

RICHARD: Hey, you look tired.

LEE: I am, a little.

(Richard gets a chair for him.)

LYD: Daddy, do you like the dress I'm wearing? It's for the wedding.

LEE: You look as pretty as a seventeen-year-old girl, Belle.

EMILY: You go change it now, Mother. You'll want it nice for Monday.

LYD: All right. *(She goes into the bedroom.)*

LEE: Emily, I was telling Richard that Miss Lena Cookenboo bought an established business for her boy that drinks. He's neglecting it so that she wants to sell it cheap. There's a nice small building they use that goes with it…

RICHARD: I told her all about that.

LEE: Did you tell her that we were also thinking about the oil business?

RICHARD: Yessir.

EMILY: What do you figure you can get for them, Daddy?

LEE: Roughly, I'd say forty thousand after taxes. Richard thinks I've sometimes been lax as a businessman by not collecting money that's owed me. And I guess I have.

(Lyd comes in.)

But you know it's sometimes harder to do the business-like thing, when you're dealing with member of your own family, or old friends like Jack Barker.

LYD: What's that about Jack Barker?

LEE: Business, Belle. Business.

LYD: I'm fond of Jack Barker and Maud. I'm responsible for that match. I played cupid there. I've played cupid a lot in my day. All the girls saw what a good job I did in picking my own husband that they used to come to me for advice. *(She sits by the window.)* You don't know how glad I am that you're going to stay, children. I told Lee today that I get so lonely here by myself. *(A pause.)* Richard, I was forty and Lee was forty-one when Emily was born. We had lost two children, and when she lived, it seemed like a miracle.

(Emily goes into the small room.)

When Emily found out that Lee and I were older than the mothers and fathers of the other children she knew, she was terrified that we would die and leave her alone. But I told her not to worry, we had waited too long to have her. We would never die and leave her alone. She was born in this very room at four o'clock on a Monday morning, and I was born here...

(Emily comes back into the room with a picture of Richard. She hands it to Lyd.)

What's this?

EMILY: Richard's picture. I think if we're going to live here, he should be up on the wall with the rest of us. Don't you?

LYD: I most certainly do.

(She takes the picture. She goes to the wall and is hanging it up as the curtain falls.)

SCENE II

A month later. A desk has been added to the sitting room. It is covered with papers and documents. Emily is in the small bedroom. It is occupied by her mother and father. She has a bureau drawer open beside her on the bed, and she is straightening that out. Richard comes in the screen door. He has a briefcase under his arm and puts it on the desk.

EMILY: *(Calling.)* Is that my husband?

RICHARD: Yes, ma'am.

(She goes out to him.)

EMILY: Everything all done?

RICHARD: Yes, it is. Your father just has to glance over the papers. I have them all here. Your dad not back yet?

EMILY: No.

(There is a knock on the door. Emily goes to answer it. Maud Barker, a nervous, intense woman with work-worn hands, is there.)

Hello, Miss Maud.

(She opens the door and Mrs. Barker comes in.)

Do you know my husband? Richard, this is Mrs. Barker.

MAUD: Oh, yes. How do you do.

RICHARD: How do you do.

MAUD: Is your father home?

EMILY: No, he's out at the farm with Mother.

MAUD: We'd heard he'd sold them.

EMILY: He has. He's out there now saying goodbye to the tenants. Will you wait for him?

MAUD: No, thank you. I can't, Emily. Will you tell him please I was by?

EMILY: I certainly will. How's Mr. Barker?

MAUD: He's been very well, thank you. This is our busiest month, of course. Cotton season is a busy time for all of us, I guess.

EMILY: It certainly is.

MAUD: It was very nice to have seen you, Mr. Murray.

RICHARD: Thank you. It was nice to have seen you.

MAUD: Goodbye, Emily.

EMILY: Goodbye.

(Maud goes out.)

RICHARD: I bet I know what she wants.

EMILY: What?

RICHARD: More time to pay their interest.

EMILY: I wouldn't be surprised.

RICHARD: According to the books, there have only been four years that they've paid on time.

EMILY: When's it due?

RICHARD: Not for a month. *(He picks up the papers on his desk.)* Did you ever study titles and deeds?

EMILY: No.

RICHARD: Well, they go on and on.

EMILY: Did you and Daddy go over and see about the insurance business this morning?

RICHARD: We looked at the building and we talked briefly to the lady that's selling. We made a date to all meet again next Thursday on my day off.

EMILY: Are you tired?

RICHARD: A little.

EMILY: I hope you're not trying to do too much. It's a shame you have to come here and work on your day off from the oil field.

RICHARD: This has been the hardest part. I just didn't realize what it meant to get a cotton crop in. The records that have to be kept. The bookkeeping. *(Lee and Lyd come in the screen door. Lyd has a hat on; she takes it off and goes to the window and looks out.)*

EMILY: Did you say goodbye to everybody out at the farm, Daddy?

LEE: Yes, I did, kid.

LYD: And we wished them good happiness and good fortune, and they wished us good happiness and good fortune. Didn't they, Daddy?

LEE: Yes, Belle.

(Richard goes over to Lee and puts his arm around him.)

RICHARD: Wasn't easy to say goodbye, was it?

LEE: No, it wasn't. *(A pause.)* I was twenty-three when I bought my first farm. Land was ten dollars an acre then, if you were willing to clear it up yourself, and I was. My first farm was nothing but a wilderness of oak and hackberry and ash and pecan and it rained that year and the men I hired to help me clear the land had to walk sometimes in water up to their knees. It took us nine months to clear sixty acres, but we got it done, and the next spring I planted my first crop, and I felt like a king and emperor, and I rode on horseback fifteen miles every day that summer to watch my crop grow and prosper. The cotton that year was higher than my waist and we got a bale and a half to the acre. *(A pause.)* Well, it's all passed me by. That's all. I don't really understand farming, anyway. Not anymore. Machines and fertilizers and crop curtailments. I leave it gladly to younger men.

LYD: Emily, you're changing this room so I can hardly recognize it, except for my pictures.

EMILY: Maybe someday you'll let me move them out of here into your bedroom?

RICHARD: No. Don't move them, honey. Leave them here. I like to look at them. They're my family too, now. I want them around me when I work. The grandfathers and the great grandfathers, the cousins and the uncles…

LYD: That's my mother and father up there, and my five sisters and two brothers. There are my mother's people, and these my father's. My father, Emily's grandfather, was a judge, his father, my grandfather, was the governor of this state. His plantation was so large he didn't know the extent of it. This cottage was his summer home. The big house was forty miles up the river. They lived like kings in those days. His table was set for company day and night. My grandmother fought the Indians. The men were all off to war, and she was in this very house alone with her children when some Indians came and wanted money. She took a gun and held them off. Single handed. He was a governor and I was his granddaughter.

LEE: *(Rising.)* What time is it?

RICHARD: Almost four.

LEE: I better get started looking at the papers. When are we due at the lawyers?

RICHARD: By five.

(Lee gathers up the papers at the desk.)

LYD: *(Laughing.)* Once when Emily was having a fight with her first husband, Ben, she got mad at me about something, and she threatened to burn all my pictures. She said she was going to have a bonfire right out in the backyard.

EMILY: Daddy, Mrs. Barker was here looking for you. She didn't say what she wanted. She said she'll be in touch with you, later.

LEE: All right.

EMILY: And we're planning early supper tonight. At six. I thought we'd all go out together afterwards to celebrate the sale of the farms.

LEE: That sounds fine to me. How would you like that, Belle?

LYD: Oh, I'd love it. I've got my good dress on now, and I was hoping I'd get a chance to wear it out again today.

(Lee goes into the little room, studying the papers as he goes. Richard goes back to work at the desk. Emily has started some sewing. She looks over and sees how lonely her mother seems, and she puts down the sewing and goes over to her.)

EMILY: How about a game of honeymoon bridge?

LYD: All right. I'll get the cards.

(She gets up and starts to look for them. Lee comes back in.)

LEE: Excuse me, Richard. Are you going into Houston to see Tom Carter this Sunday?

RICHARD: Yessir.

(Lee goes back into the small room. Lyd finds the cards and brings them down to Emily. Alma Nash comes in the screen door. She has a plate of cake in her hands.)

ALMA: Why are you so dressed up, Cousin Lyd? *(She goes over to Emily and Lyd.)*

LYD: I dressed up to go out and tell Lee's tenants goodbye. And now we're going out after supper to help celebrate the sale of the farms.

(The phone rings and Richard gets up to answer it. He goes out.)

My God, I never saw anybody work like Richard works. He's at that desk, morning, noon, and night.

ALMA: I brought you some cake for your supper.

LYD: Oh, thank you.

ALMA: Playing honeymoon bridge?

EMILY: Yes, if Mama ever makes up her mind about a bid.

LYD: Sh.

(Alma stands behind Lyd, peering at her cards.)

I bid no trump.

ALMA: You bid what?

LYD: A no trump. You heard me the first time.

ALMA: Oh, no, honey. I wouldn't bid that.

LYD: Well, I'm going to. I've been playing bridge before either of you were born and I know what I want to bid.

(Richard comes in from upstage left center and goes into the small room.)

RICHARD: Tom Carter just called from Houston. He can't see us Sunday. He has to leave town tomorrow morning on business. He said he could meet with us tonight.

LEE: Well… *(A pause.)* When's he coming back?

RICHARD: Not for a week.

LEE: Couldn't we see him then? It seems a shame to spoil our plans for tonight. I think it would be good for all of us to have a little time off.

RICHARD: He doesn't come back until a week from Friday. That means it will be a week from next Friday before I'll have the free time to go over there again.

LEE: Well, it's too bad. But certainly…

(Richard closes the door.)

RICHARD: Mr. Lee, I would like for us to see him tonight, if you don't mind. I just heard yesterday that my oil crew is moving in two weeks. I don't want Emily worried and I know she will be if we don't have a business started by the time I leave the crew.

LEE: Of course, I didn't realize that. What time does he want to see us?

RICHARD: I told him I'd call him back after I talked it over with you.

LEE: *(Looking at his watch.)* Well, if we leave here by five thirty, we should be in Houston by seven. We should be able to finish our supper and meet him by nine.

RICHARD: Yessir. I certainly appreciate your doing this, Mr. Lee.

LEE: That's all right. I look forward to meeting him.

(Richard goes out. Lyd puts her cards down.)

LYD: I'm tired of playing cards. Let's talk.

EMILY: We can't talk out here, Mama.

LYD: Why not?

EMILY: Because Cousin Lee and Richard are working. It would disturb them.

(Lee comes in.)

LEE: Belle, our plans are going to have to change.

LYD: Aren't we going out?

LEE: No. Richard and I have to talk to Mr. Carter tonight. He can't see us on Sunday.

LYD: Well, can you have supper with us? Addie fixed a special one.

LEE: I'm afraid not.

LYD: Well, can we ride into Houston with you?

LEE: It wouldn't be practical, Belle. This is a business trip.

(Richard comes in.)

Did you talk to him?

RICHARD: Yessir. He'll see us at nine.

LEE: Then I'd better hurry and finish. *(He goes back to his room.)*

(Richard goes back to work at the desk.)

LYD: Why don't you stay and eat with us, Alma?

ALMA: I can't. I made another date. I'm playing bridge tonight.

RICHARD: *(Calling over his shoulders.)* Alma, I ran into Lucy Douglas in Victoria one day last week, and she said to tell you she was sorry you couldn't get to her party.

ALMA: I know. Emily told me. I wrote her a note apologizing. I'd been on the run for three weeks and I just couldn't make myself drive those forty miles that night.

LYD: *(Whispering.)* Is that the girl you thought was so pretty?

EMILY: Yes, Mama. Play cards. Don't talk.

LYD: Well, they were talking. *(Lyd puts the cards down.)* I'm too restless to play cards. I'm so disappointed about not going out.

EMILY: I'll take you out. We'll go to the pictures.

LYD: That's very sweet of you. *(She gets up and goes into Lee's room.)*

ALMA: I've got to go. Say goodbye to Cousin Lyd for me.

EMILY: All right. Come back, Alma.

(Alma goes out. Lyd has been standing, watching Lee.)

LYD: What are you doing, Daddy?

LEE: Studying these papers.

LYD: I'm sorry you can't be with us tonight.

LEE: I am, too.

LYD: Emily is going to take me to the picture show after supper, though.

LEE: That's nice.

(He doesn't look up from his papers, but continues to work. Lyd goes out to Richard. She stands for a moment, watching him.)

LYD: What are you doing, son?

RICHARD: Getting these books in order.

LYD: I've never seen anyone work harder than you do. Don't work too hard. *(She points to a picture.)* This lady was a great aunt of mine. *(She sees he is trying to concentrate. She goes back to her chair.)*
(Lee comes in.)

LEE: It's all done. We'll take them over to the lawyers and get them signed and then be on our way to Houston.

RICHARD: Good.

(Lee goes to his wife and kisses her.)

LEE: Goodbye, Belle.

LYD: Goodbye, Daddy. Drive carefully.

(Richard kisses Emily.)

RICHARD: Goodbye, honey.

EMILY: I'll wait up for you.

RICHARD: No, don't do that. We might be all hours. We have a lot to talk about.

EMILY: All right.

LEE: Come on, Richard.

(They go out the screen door. In the distance a child can be heard practicing a piano. Emily goes back to her sewing. Lyd looks out of the window.)

LYD: That's Sybil Taylor practicing. She practices this same time every afternoon. I wish you'd kept on with your music, Emily. I used to love to play duets with you. What are you making?

EMILY: A scarf for the bureau.

LYD: It's pretty. I haven't sewn in so long, I bet I've forgotten how. *(She calls out the window.)* That's a pretty piece you're playing, Sybil Taylor. *(She gets the cards and begins to shuffle them.)* Do you know Richard told me he doesn't have a picture of his mother and father, and he wouldn't know where to find one? *(She puts the cards before her.)* Emily. Emily.

EMILY: What is it, Mother?

LYD: We're going to be rich. Look. The cards say so. *(A pause. She looks again.)* No. I'm sorry. I made a mistake. *(She picks a card up.)* That doesn't mean money. That means death.

EMILY: Death. Heavens, Mama. Shuffle the cards again quick.

LYD: Oh, the death card never worries me. You remember Cousin Etta was always turning up the death card and she lived to be a hundred and two.

(She holds up another card.) Here it is again. Here's the death card. *(A pause.)* The day Papa died, there was a dove that lighted on the roof of this house. Alma's Mama saw it. She told me she was sweeping off the sidewalk in front of the house, when she looked up and saw it light here. And she said to herself, there'll be a death over there today. And at three o'clock that very afternoon, Papa keeled over in front of Murray's Department Store while talking some business over with Mr. Jeff Tyler. He was dead before Mama had time to get to him.

(Lee comes back in.)

LYD: Did you forget something, honey?

LEE: No, I got very tired suddenly. I felt dizzy...

(Emily goes to him.)

Richard thought I should come back here and rest. He went on to the lawyers.

(He goes into the small bedroom. Emily goes after him.)

EMILY: I don't think you should try driving into Houston, tonight, Daddy.

LEE: That's what Richard says. He'll go and get some figures from Mr. Carter. He'll take me Sunday week.

EMILY: Would you like me to call a doctor?

LEE: No, I think I've just been working too hard, and maybe saying goodbye to the farms upset me a little more than I wanted to admit.

(Lyd comes in.)

LYD: Is my sweetheart all right?

LEE: Yes, Belle.

EMILY: Come on, Mother.

(They start out of the room.)

LEE: Emily, did Richard mention the insurance business any more to you?

EMILY: He told me you had been in today to look at the building, and you were to talk again on Thursday.

LEE: I see. I've made a lot of inquiries around town and everyone thinks it would be a good investment. We have a lot of friends here, I'm grateful to say, and I feel confident they would all give a lot of business to us.

EMILY: I'm sure they would. But I don't want you to be thinking of anything like this now. I want you to rest.

LEE: Emily...

EMILY: I mean it, Daddy. Rest.

(She closes the door. She and her mother resume their seats by the window. She begins her sewing again, as curtain falls.)

ACT II
SCENE I

Three weeks later in the early afternoon. Lyd is seated alone in the small bedroom with the windows closed and the shades drawn. She has a shawl around her shoulders, and the door between the bedroom and the sitting room is closed. The sitting room is empty. There are papers spread over Richard's desk. Emily comes into the sitting room, she goes to the screen door and holds it open.

EMILY: Come in, Alma.

(Alma comes in with zinnias. Emily takes them from her and puts them into two vases.)

Thank you. I hate to take your flowers but we didn't have a single one left in our yard. I thought we ought to have some flowers in the house for Mother's party. I want to plant some in our yard, now that I have the house in some kind of order.

ALMA: Made more changes in here, haven't you?

EMILY: A few. And I could do a lot more if we could afford it. But Richard says we should spend as little as possible until he and Daddy get some kind of business started and I agree with him. Thank goodness he'll be home for a change now. I hated to see the job in Victoria end, but I'm glad he's getting some time to rest.

ALMA: When are he and Lee settling on a business?

EMILY: I don't know. But I pray very soon. I think it's making us all very nervous being up in the air this way. But you know Daddy. He just can't be rushed. I try to explain that to Richard. This hasn't been an easy month, let me tell you.

ALMA: How's Cousin Lyd feeling today?

EMILY: Not well. You know she was just fine for about three weeks and then she had this spell. The doctor gave her some pills for her nerves and to make her sleep, but she won't take them. I can hear her wandering around the house all times of the night. As soon as there is a business, Richard and Daddy can have an office some place else and I think that will help. We are all just stumbling over each other now. Every time Richard comes in here and tries to work she comes in and wants to talk. He made the mistake once of telling her he was interested in hearing about our family, and now every five minutes she's trying to tell him about this one and that one. This morning he was nervous and he got mad and asked her not to talk, and she says he hurt her feelings and she went in there and locked the door.

ALMA: I'm having a table of bridge this afternoon. Why don't you come over and play while your mother is having her party?

EMILY: I'd better not. I'd better stay here and help Addie. Anyway, Richard will be home soon and I told him I would be here. *(Whispering.)* Daddy finally consented to let D. collect the money that Jack Barker owes him. He's over there now. So maybe we can get something settled about business. D's worried to death about the way they're spending money, everything going out, nothing coming in, and so am I. But Daddy just feels he has to take his time and be sure. And I suppose he does. Richard is certainly trying to do his part. He tries to be patient and considerate of us all, but you know for all the unhappiness I had with Ben, I still think Mama likes him better than Richard.

LYD: *(Calling.)* I can hear you talking about me in there.

ALMA: Come on out, Cousin Lyd.

LYD: It's too cold for me out there. Emily has all the windows up, because Richard likes it that way. And he's king around here now, in case you haven't heard.

EMILY: You see.

LYD: And furthermore, Ben Lacque came from a lovely family. He was a very sweet boy, and his only weakness was that he drank.

EMILY: He was also unfaithful and lazy and improvident and arrogant and cruel.

LYD: He was always sweet to me.

EMILY: I know. And Richard tells you off and makes you behave yourself, and you don't like that.

ALMA: Don't argue with her.

LYD: What's become of your friend, Alma, that you and Emily thought was so beautiful?

ALMA: My friend?

EMILY: Mama means Lucy Douglas. She tries to make me admit ten times a day that I don't think she's attractive.

ALMA: I don't know, Cousin Lyd. I saw her in Houston three days ago and she barely spoke.

LYD: She called here yesterday.

EMILY: Who, Mama?

LYD: Lucy Douglas.

EMILY: Where was I?

LYD: You'd gone to the beauty parlor.

EMILY: What did she want?

LYD: I don't know. Richard answered the phone. Richard hurt my feelings, Alma. He pretends to be so interested in my house and everything…

EMILY: Mama, he is interested. He just hasn't time to talk about it every minute of the day.

ALMA: I've got to go. If you change your mind about playing bridge come on over.

EMILY: All right.

(Alma goes out the screen door. Emily goes to the flowers and arranges them.)

LYD: *(Calling.)* Alma.

EMILY: She had to go, Mama.

LYD: What are you doing?

EMILY: Arranging flowers.

LYD: When you finish that come in and talk.

EMILY: You come on out here.

LYD: Richard doesn't want me out there.

EMILY: Now, he doesn't care if you come out here. It's just that he can't carry on a conversation while he's working.

(The front bell rings. Emily goes out of the room to answer it. Lyd gets up out of her chair, and comes out in the sitting room. She opens the closet door and takes out a small gas heater. She plugs it into the wall, turning it on but forgetting to light it. She then goes and shuts all the windows and the door. She goes to her chair by the window and sits drawing her shawl tight around her. Emily comes into the room reading a letter.)

LYD: Who was at the front door?

EMILY: It was a special delivery. *(She starts to look around the room.)* Mother, I smell gas. *(She sees the gas stove. She runs to it, and turns the handle off.)* Mother, how many times have I told you never to take this stove and connect it without permission.

LYD: I was cold.

EMILY: I can't help it if you were. You are not to go near the stove. Do you hear me?

LYD: Yes.

EMILY: You're always turning it on and forgetting to light it. You're going to kill us all one of these days. *(She notices the windows and door are shut. Emily opens them.)* And I want this window left up and the door open.

LYD: I'm freezing to death. There is a perfectly horrible draft right on my back.

EMILY: Then sit some place else, Mama. *(She puts the stove back in the closet.)*

LYD: Who was that special delivery for?

EMILY: Richard. Mama, was yesterday the only time Lucy Douglas called?

LYD: The only time I know of. Why?

EMILY: I just wondered.

LYD: I saw Maud Barker drive by about an hour ago. I wish I could drive a car. I wouldn't sit cooped up in this house all the time. I wish you'd take me visiting.

EMILY: Have you forgotten you're going to have a birthday party for Miss Lila Mae in exactly two hours?

(Lyd looks at her.)

LYD: Is this Thursday?

EMILY: Yes, ma'am.

LYD: Oh, my God. *(She gets up and starts to pick up around the room. She goes to Richard's desk and starts to pile papers up.)*

EMILY: Mother, don't bother any of those papers of Richard's. We'll pick them up in time. Maybe you should have the party in the living room, anyhow.

LYD: No, I feel like having my loved ones around me today. Will you be here for the party?

EMILY: Yes'm.

LYD: That's fine. It will do you good to mix with people for a change. You and Richard are going to drive yourselves crazy talking about money all the time. You should forget all about this getting rich for awhile. I declare, being around Miss Lila Mae is better than going to church. She is nearly ninety and she does all her own work and is always happy and bright and cheerful. And do you know why? Because she never thinks of herself, but spends her time doing for other people. I would think you and Richard would get tired of always talking money. What good is it? Can it get you friends? Can it make you happy? Can it get you to heaven? I'm rich. I'm rich in friends and happiness, spiritual things. *(Lyd shakes her head and looks out the window and then back at Emily.)* Emily, have you been crying?

EMILY: No. *(She lights a cigarette and starts to walk around the room. She looks up at pictures on the wall.)*

LYD: Do you know, Emily, I've noticed as you've grown older you look more and more like my sister Sadie. She was about your age when that picture of her was taken. She had cried all that day because she and her husband were having to move away. *(A pause.)* Are you nervous, Emily?

EMILY: No, I'm just restless.

LYD: I remember one day Sadie said to me...Emily, you aren't listening to a word I say.

EMILY: Yes, I am.

LYD: What did I say?

EMILY: Something about those pictures. *(She crosses over to them.)* Mother. Where is Richard's picture?

LYD: In the drawer over there.

EMILY: Did you take it down?

LYD: Yes.

EMILY: Why?

LYD: I told you. Because he hurt my feelings.

EMILY: Oh, Mother. *(She grabs a picture off the wall.)* And I don't want to ever see Ben's picture up there again. Is that clear? *(She takes the picture into the small room and puts it into a drawer. She comes back to her mother.)* Mother, I wish you'd let me take them all out of here and put them in your room.

LYD: You couldn't get them on the walls. There's not enough space for them in there.

EMILY: There would be if you put all the pictures of me away. That would be half of them.

LYD: As long as I live every one of those pictures are going to stay up there.

EMILY: I hate to look at those tacky old things.

LYD: I don't think they're tacky. They're my treasures.

EMILY: Mother, don't be so stubborn. Let me take them down. You know I have to live here too.

LYD: No, you're not. And I don't want to talk about it anymore, now. Sadie said to me...

EMILY: All right. But someday you're going to come home and find them all burned.

LYD: Don't you have any family sentiment?

EMILY: No.

(She goes to a chair and lights a cigarette. Lyd twists at her dress and looks as if she were ready to cry.)

LYD: I don't know what's wrong with me. I swear I'm having a chill.

(Emily takes the letter from her pocket and starts to read it.)

LYD: Emily? Is that bad news? I wish you wouldn't go on reading it that way and not telling me anything if it's bad news.

EMILY: It doesn't concern you, Mother.

LYD: Well, then put it away. It depresses me to look at it.

(Emily stuffs the letter back into her pocket.)

Sadie could be a devil, you know. She was the one that was never afraid of my father.

EMILY: Mother, I'm going to at least take the toe-dancing pictures of me down. They're ridiculous looking. They're so ugly and tacky I'm ashamed for Richard to see them.

LYD: They belong to me.

EMILY: Well, they're pictures of me and I don't want them up any longer. I've always hated them. *(She quickly takes seven or eight pictures down from the wall.)*

LYD: Don't burn them, Emily. Please don't burn them.

EMILY: I'm not going to burn them. I just don't want them up where people can see them. I'll put them away in your drawer.

(She goes into the bedroom and puts the pictures in the top drawer of the dresser. Richard comes in.)

RICHARD: Where's my wife?

EMILY: I'm in here. *(She comes in.)*

RICHARD: How about a cup of coffee?

EMILY: All right. Did you see them?

RICHARD: Uh huh.

(He points to Lyd, making a gesture of silence. Emily starts out.)

LYD: I thought there was a special delivery for Richard.

EMILY: No, it was for me. I only told you that to keep you from nagging me about reading it. *(She goes out.)*

RICHARD: Miss Lyd, I want to apologize to you for losing my temper this morning. I don't know what gets into me. I know it isn't easy for you having your house taken over this way. But if you'll be patient with me, as soon as Mr. Lee and I decide on a business, I'll have a place to work in and be out of your way.

LYD: I understand. Son, speak to Emily and tell her not to burn my pictures. They're one of the few things in life that give me pleasure.

(Emily comes in with two cups of coffee.)

EMILY: Will you have coffee, Mother?

LYD: No, thank you. *(She goes out.)*

RICHARD: I apologized to her. She said she understood.

(Emily closes the door after her.)

EMILY: I'm glad. Did you see Jack Barker?

RICHARD: I just left there.

EMILY: Was Miss Maud there?

RICHARD: If she was I didn't see her. Mr. Barker let me in and we sat down in the living room, and he asked me what I wanted and I told him that your dad had decided not to renew his note and he wanted to settle their debt immediately. And then he told me all the hard luck he'd had through the years and asked if I couldn't see my way clear to give him some more time.

EMILY: Did you tell him he's had ten years?

RICHARD: Yes.

(Lyd comes back in.)

EMILY: Mother, were you eavesdropping?

LYD: No. Why should I be? What do I care about your old secrets. I've got some of my own. I just wanted to remind Richard I'm having a birthday party for Lila Mae.

EMILY: He hasn't forgotten.

(Lyd begins to cry.)

Mother. Mother, what is it?

(Lyd shrugs her shoulders and won't answer.)

We're going to get this room ready in time, now, don't worry.

LYD: Are you going to burn my pictures? I know you won't do it unless you get mad at me. I'm so afraid you'll get mad and burn my pictures.

EMILY: I told you I wasn't. *(Emily goes to the bedroom and gets the pictures and brings them back into the room.)* Now here they are. Please stop crying. You're gonna get yourself all upset and you won't be able to enjoy the party.

LYD: Thank you. *(She takes them and then she reaches into the pocket for a handkerchief and wipes her eyes. She goes over to the chair and gets her shawl and puts it around her shoulders.)* I'm cold.

RICHARD: Now you can't be cold, Miss Lyd. It's very hot out. You must be imagining it.

LYD: I don't imagine it. I feel it. I'm cold. I'm trembling all over.

EMILY: Do you want me to call the doctor?

(Lyd shrugs her shoulders.)

LYD: They can't do anything. I've been to every doctor in town including the osteopath. They all think it's my imagination. Daddy took me twice to

Mineral Wells. It was a waste of money. *(She cries again.)* All I know is, I get so nervous I can't stand it.

EMILY: Honey, what am I going to do?

RICHARD: Shall I go get Mr. Lee? I saw him uptown.

EMILY: No. I don't want to worry him. Mother, honey, if you're not feeling well, maybe you should rest this afternoon and we can have the party tomorrow. Is that what you would like to do?

(Lyd shrugs her shoulders.)

What would you like to do?

(Lyd is trembling now and trying to control herself. She shrugs her shoulders and starts sobbing.)

Come on. I'd better take you to bed and you can rest. We'll have the party tomorrow. Richard, you go call Miss Rita and Miss Lila Mae and tell them Mother isn't well. They'll understand.

RICHARD: All right. *(He goes out.)*

LYD: I want to get well. I can't stand going on feeling this way. I don't know why I feel this way.

EMILY: I know, Mother. And you'll be better soon. Now, come on to bed. *(She helps her into the bedroom. She turns down the cover of the bed and helps her mother get into the bed, and covered up.)*

LYD: Thank you.

(She closes her eyes and Emily goes to the window and pulls the shade down and then quietly goes out of the room and softly closes the door behind her. Richard comes back.)

RICHARD: I called them. They said they were sorry, but they understand.

EMILY: I just don't know what will help Mother. I know she gets lonely, but I can't spend all my time with her.

RICHARD: Your father should be here soon.

EMILY: It's worse when he's here. He's gotten so moody since he quit farming. He just sits around and stares and sighs. I had to think of twenty excuses to keep him busy and out of the house today.

RICHARD: I know. It's like he's walking around in some kind of dream. If he isn't here, he's standing in front of the drugstore talking to the same old men. I know he'll be happier when he has something to do, but he keeps asking for more time to make his decision and that's all right with me, but I'm afraid if he doesn't make up his mind soon, we're going to lose out entirely as far as Tom Carter is concerned. *(A pause.)* I just think I'll have to insist on its all being settled today, Emily, one way or the other.

(He goes to the desk and starts to work. She quietly opens the door to the bedroom and sees her mother is asleep.)

EMILY: She's asleep. Well, that'll be good for her.

RICHARD: It's going to all work out fine. We just have to have patience, I suppose.

EMILY: Richard, Mother told me Lucy Douglas called here yesterday.

RICHARD: She did.

EMILY: What did she want?

RICHARD: She was trying to find Alma Nash. *(He goes back to work.)*

EMILY: Richard...

RICHARD: What?

EMILY: Nothing. Nothing.

RICHARD: What is it, Emily?

EMILY: Really, it's nothing.

(Richard looks at her.)

RICHARD: Now, come and tell me.

EMILY: I'm just a little blue. I'll tell you about it later.

RICHARD: Are you still worried about your Mother?

EMILY: Partly.

RICHARD: You know, that's another thing. Your dad asks me to go and see about this sanitarium in Houston and I make arrangements for him to talk to the doctors and inspect the place, and at the last minute he changes his mind and won't see them. Oh, well. We have made some progress. The farms are sold. I've been to see Jack Barker now...

(Addie comes in.)

ADDIE: I'm here for the party. Want me to clean in here?

EMILY: We called it off. She wasn't feeling well.

ADDIE: She get nervous?

EMILY: Yes.

ADDIE: Why don't you take her to a doctor, Miss Emily?

EMILY: I want to, but she won't go. She says they don't do her any good.

ADDIE: Well, I just hope I'm not around the next time she gets nervous and wanders off down to the river. And if I am, don't call on me to go and get her back. I can't stand it anymore. If you and Mr. Lee had ever gone down there to get her back, you'd do something.

(Lee comes in. Addie takes the coffee cups and goes out.)

LEE: What did you ask me to bring you from town?

EMILY: Soap powder, milk, and eggs.

LEE: I'd better go back. I got to talking to some of the men at the drugstore and I forgot until just this minute. I tell you it's funny. I used to see men standing around town down there and wonder what they were talking about. I never had time to really find out. Now I've gotten to talking to them, I forget everything else. It's a good thing I never started it before, what kind of a living would I have gotten made?

EMILY: Mother's not feeling well again.

LEE: Is she in the bedroom?

EMILY: Yes, but she's asleep.

LEE: Is she? Well, I'll go and get the groceries and come right back.

RICHARD: I'll go for you.

LEE: No, thank you, son. I'll get them. Did you see Jack?

RICHARD: Yes. He asked for more time. Like Emily said, he's had ten years.

LEE: He's always pressed for money. Has been, it seems to me, his whole life. He's to be pitied, I guess. He works hard. I just hope now Lyd doesn't hear about it. She's fond of Jack and Maud. It would upset her. *(He starts for the door.)*

RICHARD: Mr. Lee, I don't like to pressure you any more about Tom Carter, but I was explaining earlier to Emily...

LEE: That reminds me, Richard. I heard of a business on the highway that's for sale. It sounds very good to me. I think we ought to look into it. The owner has evidently been doing well, but his wife doesn't like this part of the country and they're moving. It's a freezing plant. You've probably seen it. He rents lockers to people here in town, and I thought since you didn't care for the insurance business.

RICHARD: I didn't say I didn't care for the insurance business. It was just that we agreed to wait on that until you made a decision on Tom Carter.

LEE: Yes, I know. Well, I have made my decision on that, Richard. I made it this morning. I've been talking to my friends here in town, and they've made me very wary of anything to do with the oil business.

RICHARD: May I ask why?

LEE: Certainly. Thornton Mays told me, for one, that he thought the oil business was extremely risky, so did Damon Thomas, and a number of others cautioned me about going into it. They all seem to think you should have a great deal of money, which, of course, I haven't got.

RICHARD: How much do they have?

LEE: They're not gamblers, son. And whatever they have, they hold on to. They're considered mighty sound businessmen. We could do a lot worse than follow their advice. I've often been grateful for their help in matters of business.

RICHARD: I'm sure these gentlemen mean well, but do they know Mr. Carter?

LEE: Not personally, I believe.

RICHARD: But you met him and talked with him. And didn't you tell me you liked him and were impressed?

LEE: Yes, I did. But my friends have always given me excellent advice.

RICHARD: Excuse me, Mr. Lee, but this is one time I think they're advising you wrong.

LEE: They felt I would need a great deal of money...

RICHARD: But you're willing to invest in other businesses...

LEE: I know, I know, but that's quite different. They're steady and sure...

RICHARD: Look, Mr. Lee. You know how I feel about you and the responsibility I feel toward you and this family. I would do anything rather than in any way cause you to make a mistake.

LEE: I know that.

RICHARD: But I have to say this. All my life, I've watched men here in this state get rich. Some of them did it slowly, working hard and accumulating, but most of them are rich today because they recognized an opportunity when it came along. They had faith in something other men couldn't see and wouldn't take a chance on. My dad was a plodder. He thought it was gambling and a sin to take a chance on anything. Once he had five hundred dollars saved up. It was in the early days of the oil business. A friend of his came to him, said we have some shares left open in a pool, come on, take a chance, put in your five hundred dollars. He didn't sleep all that night worrying about what to do. Finally he decided that he couldn't do it. He was afraid to take a chance. The men that invested in that pool are all big rich men today. Six months later my mother had to have an operation, and the poor devil's five hundred dollars had to go to the doctor bills, so he ended up losing his money anyway. He lived with nothing. He died with nothing.

LEE: I keep hearing you use the word rich lately, son. I don't know why you feel you're failing me unless you make me rich. If I've given you that impression, I apologize. It was not my intention. I have all I want, or will ever need. It was my wish, and it is still my wish, to start a small modest business for you and Emily, if you'd like me to. But I want to make it perfectly clear if I'm to invest my money at all, I want to invest it conservatively.

RICHARD: Excuse me, but now I think I'm confused. Did you say now you want to go into business to do me a favor? Am I crazy or didn't you tell me not more than six weeks ago, I would be doing you a favor if I came here. Emily…

EMILY: I'm staying out of this. *(She goes to the window and looks out.)*

LEE: You are doing me a favor, certainly, but…

RICHARD: Let me finish, please. Didn't you say that you wanted and needed me? That my opinions and advice meant something? They were of value…

LEE: They were. They were…I value your opinions most highly.

RICHARD: Then listen to me, please. Miss Lyd is always telling me how she came from Indian fighters. Do you know what Indian fighters mean to me? Not some old woman home protecting her home and children, because the men are off to war, but men who are not satisfied with what they have. Restless. Ambitious.

LEE: I wouldn't know anything about that, Richard. My people came here after the Indians fought. We got our land by peaceful means. By hard work and slow accumulation. We treated the land kindly and it treated us kindly. My father was content. I am content. We were never out to glut the land for greed.

RICHARD: I'm not greedy. For Christ sakes, don't call me greedy. But I'm a man and I want to do for my wife. And I want respect for myself, and you don't get respect these days by selling insurance or running a two-bit business out on the highway.

LEE: I'm sorry. I've made my decision. I'm not going into the oil business.
(Richard goes to the desk and grabs up some papers.)

RICHARD: Will you please look at these? I've gone over them by myself and studied the figures on your insurance business. Eight thousand a year is the most that's ever been made. The way money is spent in this house, do you think you could live on eight thousand a year without every year going into your capital?

LEE: We'd have to live on it. I'd insist we live on it. We'd own a business and if we worked hard, we'd make more money every year.

RICHARD: And in ten years, maybe we'd be clearing ten thousand. I made six thousand on the oil crew. You're asking me to lose money.

LEE: But we'd own a business. We have money in the bank. We have a house. I think on the contrary, it's a very good thing for all of us. Can you guarantee we'll make anything on oil? No, you can't. And that's why at my age, I have to be against it.
(A pause.)

RICHARD: And there's nothing I can do to convince you?

LEE: I'm afraid not.

RICHARD: O.K. *(He walks away from him.)*

LEE: I'd appreciate it if you'd tell Mr. Carter for me.

RICHARD: All right.

> *(Lee goes out the screen door. Richard goes to the desk and throws the papers down.)*
>
> What's come over him? What's gotten into him? I think I'm going crazy. Was this the man that gave me his every confidence? That told me he trusted me? Do you know how long eight thousand dollars would last in this house? I've been keeping the books. I know how money goes here. *(He turns to Emily.)* Why didn't you say anything?

EMILY: I have my own troubles.

RICHARD: I think you're scared of your father. That's what I think.

EMILY: I'm not scared of him. But I told you he can be stubborn. It's better not to argue with him at times like this. You just can't get anywhere with him once he's made up his mind. He's talked to some of his friends and they've made him cautious. You can't blame him. How much did you and Daddy discuss investing?

RICHARD: We never got around to that. I just always assumed he'd be willing to put in twenty thousand. That's what they were asking for the insurance business and building.

EMILY: Why don't you ask for just part of the money?

RICHARD: What are you talking about?

EMILY: Say a thousand dollars. Then if that pays off, you can invest the rest.

RICHARD: Who put that idea in your head?

EMILY: Nobody.

RICHARD: Come on. You didn't think that up by yourself.

EMILY: I tell you I know Daddy. I think I know why he's stalling. I'm sure it would be easier to handle if it were done this way.

RICHARD: What's the matter? Have you lost confidence in Tom Carter?

EMILY: No, I haven't. I like him fine. I told you that.

RICHARD: All right.

EMILY: But Daddy has gotten a lot of fears put into his head by these old friends of his. He's had a lot of time to think, and they've been working on him, and they're scaring him.

RICHARD: That's too damn bad.

EMILY: And if I know my Daddy, you'll be smart if you ask for a little to invest at first…

RICHARD: No. Do you hear that? If he has twenty thousand dollars to put in an insurance business, then he has it to invest in an oil well. I've been waiting all my life for an opportunity like this and I'm not going to throw it away.

EMILY: All right, Richard. All right. If you invest a thousand, that'll make us...

RICHARD: Peanuts.

EMILY: Well, what will you do if Daddy won't let you have the money? Have you thought about that? Just what will you do?

RICHARD: If he doesn't it's a stinking trick. He should have been man enough to have said so before. I had every right to think he would.

EMILY: Don't yell at me. I can't help it. It's his money.

RICHARD: Sure. Sure. It's his money. I do all the dirty work. I quit my job. I sell the farms for him. I go to Jack Barker, because I think he'll come in on this thing. I practically pledge my word to a man like Tom Carter that I'll deliver twenty thousand dollars...

EMILY: I wish you hadn't. I wish to God you hadn't.

RICHARD: Why? I had every right to do it, didn't I?

EMILY: No. Because I've always warned you, you couldn't be sure of Daddy until the papers were signed.

RICHARD: Well, I'm going to deliver. Now how do you like that? He's not going to get out of it.

EMILY: Think of Daddy. It would be awful if he lost that much money.

RICHARD: Tom Carter isn't in this for his health. He doesn't lose.

EMILY: Hasn't he lost two fortunes?

RICHARD: Well, he may take chances when he has money, but not when he's broke.

EMILY: I didn't say he would do it on purpose. But he's been wrong before and he could be wrong again.

RICHARD: Do you think I'd risk it if I weren't sure?

EMILY: Oh, I don't know, D. I don't know what to say. *(A pause.)* What do you want me to do about it?

RICHARD: I want you to help me make your dad come in on this...

EMILY: And I want to keep out of it. If I had my way we'd leave right now.

RICHARD: We're not going to leave. We're going to see this thing through.

EMILY: What if we can't? What if Daddy won't let us do anything we want? It's his money. We can't do anything about it.

RICHARD: We're going to do something about it.

EMILY: What will we do? What will we do?

RICHARD: I'll do something.

EMILY: What? It's his money. Why don't we go out and earn something of our own?

RICHARD: That's a nasty thing to say after all I've done around this god-damned place. That's a nasty thing to say. I gave up my job. Remember that. And your dad better remember. I gave up a good job. What a lousy thing to say.

EMILY: Is it?

RICHARD: Yes, it is. And I tell you right now. Listen to me. If I hadn't poured my heart's blood into this place, I would walk out right now.

EMILY: Am I included in that?

RICHARD: I don't want to talk any more. I'm too mad to talk.

EMILY: Richard, I asked you a question.

RICHARD: And I don't want to talk to you now, so shut up.

EMILY: *(Shouting.)* You will talk to me now. I asked you a question.

RICHARD: I told you to shut up. I don't want to talk any more.

EMILY: Does that include me?

(Richard starts for the screen door.)

RICHARD: I don't have to stay here and be shouted at.

EMILY: Is that why you married me? Just because of my father's property? Answer me, Richard Murray. Is that why you married me?

RICHARD: Listen here, lady. I don't have to take insults from you. You better watch what you say. You have no right to make accusations like that. I don't care how mad you are.

EMILY: Oh yes, I have. I have every right. I think it is. If you want to know why I've been so upset, read this.

(She takes the letter out of her pocket and throws it at him. She is crying. He goes to the letter, picks it up, and reads it.)

Why didn't you marry her? Or didn't she have enough?

(She continues crying. Richard has read the letter. He seems worried and concerned. He twists it up and lets it fall to the floor. He goes to Emily and tries to put his arms around her. She throws him off.)

Go away. Go away and leave me alone.

(There is a pause. He stands watching her.)

RICHARD: Emily...

EMILY: I don't want to hear anything you have to say.

RICHARD: You have to listen to me, honey. I need your help badly. I want to make you a good husband. I want us to be happy together. I know we can be, if you'll only help me.

(She doesn't answer.)

Don't you hear me? I need your help. Believe me, I'm sorry you've gotten hurt. I'd cut off both my arms before I'd see you hurt. I don't want to have anything to do with this woman, but she won't let me alone and I get involved before I know what is happening. *(A pause.)* Lucy Douglas sent that letter out of spite, to hurt you and me and try to break up our marriage. Are you going to let her get by with it? *(A pause.)* Emily, I was obligated to her. That's why I had to keep seeing her.

EMILY: How were you obligated to her?

RICHARD: I was. I just was. *(A pause.)* She loaned me a great deal of money once. I've never been able to pay her back. That's why I'm so anxious for the oil deal to come through, so I can pay her back. Every time I threatened to stop seeing her, she said she'd get in touch with you or your father and tell you the whole thing. Three days ago I made up my mind no matter what happened I wanted to stop living this way. I went to Victoria and told her. She told me if I did stop seeing her, she'd fix us and I guess this is her way of trying to do it. I should have come to you and explained everything right then, I know, but I thought why should you be hurt, unless, it's absolutely necessary. I never thought she would go through with her threats.

EMILY: Did you do it?

RICHARD: What?

EMILY: What the letter says. Did you get drunk and tell your friends you were marrying me because of my money?

RICHARD: What do you think? *(He hands her the letter.)*

EMILY: What are you giving me the letter for?

RICHARD: I want you to tear it up and forget that she ever existed.

EMILY: What good will that do now? *(She lets the letter fall back to the floor.)*

RICHARD: I'll do anything I can to make it up to you, if you'll just say you forgive me.

EMILY: I don't know. I love you, but I'm scared. *(A pause. She walks around the room.)* Go away for a while, and let me think.

RICHARD: I'm not going to leave you like this.

EMILY: Please, D. I want to be by myself now.

RICHARD: All right. But remember what I told you. I've already given her up, or you wouldn't have gotten this letter. *(A pause. He goes to her.)* You believe that, don't you?

EMILY: Yes, I believe that.

RICHARD: And I know I've done a rotten thing, and I'm not trying to excuse myself, but I promise I'll make it up to you. *(A pause.)* Would you kiss me before I go?

(She doesn't answer.)

Please, honey. Kiss me.

EMILY: I look so ugly. My eyes are all red and burning.

RICHARD: Come on.

EMILY: All right.

(She kisses him. He goes out the screen door. She begins to cry again. Addie comes in from the kitchen.)

ADDIE: Anybody decided what they want for supper? *(She sees Emily.)* What's the matter, Miss Emily?

EMILY: Nothing, Addie, nothing. *(She wipes her eyes.)* Would you get my compact, please.

ADDIE: Where is it?

EMILY: In Mother's room. On the dresser.

(Addie goes into the bedroom, gets the compact, and brings it to Emily. Emily powders her face.)

Was Mother awake?

ADDIE: Yes'm. Can I get anything for you?

EMILY: No. *(She begins to cry again.)*

ADDIE: Don't cry, Miss Emily. Don't let your mother hear you cryin'.

EMILY: I'm trying not to, but I can't help it. I can't help it.

ADDIE: What did he do to you?

EMILY: Nothing.

(She goes out the screen door. Addie shakes her head as she watches her go. She calls into the bedroom.)

ADDIE: Miss Lyd, come on out here. Are you going to spend the rest of your life on that bed?

(Lyd comes out clutching the pictures of Emily.)

It's dark as pitch in there. No wonder you were nervous.

LYD: What was the fightin' all about?

ADDIE: God knows.

LYD: Could you hear them?

ADDIE: How could I help but hear them? I bet they could hear them down at the courthouse.

LYD: It's worse today than when Ben was here. I thought when he left, we'd have some peace. When Emily starts fighting with her husband, there's no living with her. I remember from before. Did he take his clothes?

ADDIE: No'm.

LYD: Did he say he was going to?

ADDIE: I didn't hear him say he was.

LYD: When she fought with Ben, he'd always leave and she'd pack his clothes, but then he always came back. *(Lyd starts taking all the pictures down from the wall.)*

ADDIE: I thought you were so sick. Now what are you doin'?

LYD: I'm takin' my pictures down. They're in danger here. *(She hands some of them to Addie and continues taking the others down.)*

ADDIE: What kind of foolishness is this? I've got supper to fix, Miss Lyd...

LYD: Supper can wait. I want you to take my pictures to your house.

ADDIE: To my house? Why do you want me to take them to my house?

LYD: They're in danger here. Emily's threatened me with burning them again. If she's fighting with her husband, God knows what she might take into her head to do. Now, hurry before she gets back.

ADDIE: Miss Lyd, let me wait until after supper. I can't go through town in broad daylight carryin' these pictures. People will think I'm crazy...

LYD: No, they won't. Just say I asked you to. Now hurry...

ADDIE: I can't, Miss Lyd.

LYD: Yes, you can.

ADDIE: I can't. I'd be mortified.

LYD: I thought you cared about me.

ADDIE: I do. You know I do.

LYD: Then go ahead. Hurry.

ADDIE: I can't.

LYD: Why, Addie? Why?

ADDIE: Because you'd be all alone if I left now. I promised Mr. Lee never to leave you alone when you're nervous. I'll take them after supper.

LYD: I'll stay right here and wait for you.

ADDIE: But s'pose you get nervous and forget?

LYD: I won't. If you don't go, and they stay in this house another single minute, I'll get sure enough nervous. I'll be sick from nervousness. Poor Daddy, he has so much to bear now without my getting sick now that Emily and her husband are fighting.

(In the distance a child can be heard practicing a piano.)

ADDIE: You swear to me you won't leave that chair?

LYD: I swear, Addie.

ADDIE: All right. Give them to me. Now, you sit there.

LYD: I will. I will. Now you hurry and go.

ADDIE: Yes'm. I'll get my hat. *(She takes the pictures and goes out the door.)*

(Lyd calls after her.)

LYD: I'm gonna sit right by this window and listen to the music and watch the cars go by on the highway, like I've done all my life.

(She gets up and gets the shawl and puts it around her, and then comes back to her chair. She sits and watches out the window as the curtain falls.)

SCENE II

An hour after the preceding scene. Lyd is still seated by the window, listening to the child practice. After a moment she goes to the closet and takes down a banjo. She comes and sits again in the corner, holding the banjo in her lap. There is a knock on the door.

LYD: Come in.

(Maud Barker comes in.)

Maud—Maud Barker, what a surprise. What a sweet, pleasant surprise. Come in.

MAUD: I can't stay, Miss Lyd. You're alone, aren't you? I saw all the cars gone.

LYD: Yes. I'm alone. Sit down. Where have you been keeping yourself? It's been so long since you've been to see me. I think of you and Jack so much. Tell me about Jack. How is he?

MAUD: As well as can be expected, Miss Lyd.

LYD: One of the loveliest dancers that I ever saw. I tell you when you and Jack waltzed across that floor, people just sat down to watch. How long since we've seen each other, Maud?

MAUD: Almost four months.

LYD: Is it? You don't change, Maudie, I declare, you don't change.

MAUD: You look fine, too, Miss Lyd.

LYD: Oh, I change, honey, I know that. I change and the world changes, but you don't, Maud. You look as pretty and sweet as you ever did.

MAUD: Thank you.

LYD: I often think of the good times we had when you were young and I was young. Do people have such good times now, Maud? No cares. No cares in the world. I can see you now. You and Jack dancing waltzing, proud and graceful...

MAUD: Miss Lyd...

LYD: I can see you. I can see you. And the day he asked you to marry him. You couldn't decide. There was Jack and the Morris boy from Wharton, and the Reeves boy who had the sugar plantation. Jack came to me and said, speak to her. If she doesn't marry me, I'm lost. And I spoke to you and you married him. I told you Maudie, he'd be loyal and faithful and kind and loving. And hasn't he been? Hasn't he always been loyal and kind and faithful and loving?

MAUD: Yes. Miss Lyd...

LYD: Through good times and bad.

MAUD: Yes. I have to talk to you...

LYD: And what more can one ask in a husband?

(While Maud has been in the room, she has been looking out the window. She gets up from her chair.)

MAUD: Is that car stopping here?

LYD: It's Lee.

MAUD: I'd better go.

LYD: Why, the very idea. Lee would be insulted. He'll be so happy to see you. He loves you and Jack.

MAUD: I'll be back later. I wanted to talk to you alone, Miss Lyd.

LYD: You can talk to me alone. We can go in my bedroom. It's small and dark and it's making a nervous wreck of me, but no one will bother us there.

MAUD: No, really. I'll come back some other time. I don't want to see anyone else...

(Lee comes in the screen door.)

LYD: Daddy, here's Maud.

LEE: Hello, Maud.

(She doesn't look at him. She starts out.)

MAUD: I'll go on.

LYD: Why, no. Maud, what is this? We can talk in front of Lee. I don't have any secrets from him.

LEE: I'd like to hear anything you have to say, Maud.

MAUD: I'd better go.

LEE: Lyd, you go in the bedroom. I'll talk to Maud.

(Lyd looks puzzled, but starts out of the room.)

MAUD: No, I want her to stay.

LEE: Maud, please...

MAUD: *(To Lyd.)* I want you to hear about your precious husband...

LYD: What in the world is this all about?

MAUD: Let him tell you. Let him tell you what he's done to my husband.

LEE: Maud, Jack has owed me that money for ten years.

MAUD: Why did you wait for the last minute before the note was due to tell him this time you weren't going to renew it and would insist on collection. Why?

LEE: Because I just made up my mind yesterday.

MAUD: I don't believe you. Do you hear that? I don't believe you. Now he has no other chance to get the money, you and your son-in-law made it impossible for him to pay you.

LEE: I know it's hard, Maud.

MAUD: I'm begging you not to do it. I wanted him to come here, but he's too proud to beg. He'd die if he knew I was here. I've lost my pride. I've had to lose my pride, because I know if you do this thing he can't stand it. He's been trying all afternoon to get you your money, and the only way he can raise it is to sell our house.

LYD: Sell your house, Maud? Sell your house?

MAUD: Even then he won't have enough.

LYD: Oh my, father. Don't sell your house, Maud. Lee, they can't sell their house. What in the name of heaven is this all about?

LEE: Maud, don't burden Lyd with this. My wife isn't well. Lyd, you go in your room and I'll talk here to Maud...

MAUD: And what about my husband? Why do you think I'm here begging? If he loses this, he's threatening all kinds of things to harm himself.

LYD: Maud, what on earth has happened?

LEE: Lyd, I don't want you here. Go in the other room. I beg you.

LYD: I want to hear, Lee. I want to hear. What is it, Maudie? After all these years, there mustn't be bad feelings between us.

MAUD: We've owed Mr. Lee some money for ten years. He has a mortgage on our land. Jack's been having worse and worse luck with his cotton. All he's been able to pay is the interest. Mr. Lee has kindly renewed the note for us each year. It's due again in two days and this morning, that arrogant husband of Emily's came marching into our house, demanding we pay in full. He threatened to ruin Jack and take his land if he didn't. Jack went all to pieces. He can't take much more.

LEE: Is it my fault, Maud? Jack hasn't been a success as a farmer. Other people have made a living at it. Jack is stubborn. Many times I've begged him to get out of it. But he's gone on year after year, getting in deeper and deeper...

MAUD: I don't know whose fault it is. But it's not his. He works from early morning until late at night. This will kill him, Mr. Lee...I know it will kill him, the same as if you took a pistol and shot him, if you take his land...

LYD: Oh, no, Maudie.

MAUD: And if any harm comes to my husband, I'll blame you. I'll never let you forget it. I'll scream after you in the streets, what you've done. I won't let you forget it. My curse will follow you into the grave, so you can't forget it.

(She goes to the screen door. Lee goes to a chair. He seems very tired. There is silence for a moment.)

LYD: Lee...

LEE: Yes, Belle?

LYD: Don't do it. Not if it means you have to take their land, or they have to sell their house. I remember Papa had to mortgage this very house to get the money to send Lottie away for her health. Mama cried for three months for fear we would lose it. I remember Mama crying. I remember the day the note came due, and we didn't have the money for the payment. Papa was too proud to ask for an extension and Mama went without his knowing it to Mr. Marcus Weems and got it extended. We've got enough without taking anybody's home...

LEE: I'm not taking their home.

LYD: But if they have to sell it to get money to pay you, it's the same thing.

LEE: I've talked to some of the fairest men in this town and they all tell me I have the right to my money.

LYD: But two days, Daddy, that's no warning. Maud is right. That's not time at all.

LEE: I only made up my mind yesterday. We promised Richard. They've had ten years. I need the money at this time very badly.

LYD: Don't we have enough? What do we lack? Nothing. We're blessed. We've always been blessed.

LEE: I've sold the farms, Belle. We've living off that money now. I won't be making anything else for a while, and there are four of us to consider.

LYD: Just give them some time, Daddy...

LEE: It would be the same thing if I'd given them six months. Jack is just not a farmer. Other men have made money these last years. I know it's not his fault, but it's not mine either.

LYD: What if anything happened to Jack? What if he did something to himself because of this? How would you feel? I know how I would feel. I'd never be able to hold up my head again.

LEE: Don't ask me, Belle. Don't keep at me. I've made up my mind what I have to do.

LYD: Daddy, you can't refuse me this. Please, don't refuse me this. I couldn't stand it if anything happened to Jack. She said you gave him no warning. You carried him all these years and you should have given him warning. She said if you did this thing, and anything happens to Jack, her curses would follow you to your grave. I can't stand it, Daddy. I can't stand it. I won't sleep a wink ever again worrying over what might happen. You have to think of me, too. I'm too nervous to stand this. *(She is crying.)*

LEE: All right, Belle. Don't cry. I'll go over and tell him to forget it for another year.

LYD: I'm only thinking of you.

LEE: I'll do anything you want, if you just won't cry.

LYD: I don't want you to have something like Jack's death on your conscience.

LEE: *(Speaking sharply.)* All right, Belle. I told you I would go over and straighten it out. I'll give him six months more. But you've got to understand that I'm trying always to do the right thing for you and the children.

LYD: I know that.

LEE: And I'm tired, too. I'm tired. I've worked hard all my life and I've tried to do everything in my power to please you and Emily, and I've got to have some peace soon.
(He goes out the screen door. She picks up the banjo. She starts to pick at it. She plays "The Old Gray Mare." She puts it down halfway through and returns to looking out the window. Emily comes in.)

LYD: Emily, a terrible thing happened.

EMILY: All right, Mother. You can tell me later.

LYD: Emily, you don't know what it's done to me.

EMILY: All right. I'm sorry. Whatever it is, I'm sorry. I've got my troubles, too. Was Richard back here?

LYD: No. Emily, are you upset by that letter? I wouldn't let some cat upset me…

EMILY: Mother, did you read my letter?

LYD: It was wadded up on the floor. I had to read it to see what it was.

EMILY: Give it to me.

LYD: I haven't got it. I put it back on the desk.
(Emily gets the letter and tears it up.)
Your trouble always has been that you're too sensitive for your own good. You are very sweet looking when you fix yourself up. Of course, you can't go around looking any old way. Nobody can. I was never a beauty, but I was always the most popular girl in this town. There's no reason why you can't be. You're a lovely dancer. You're the picture of grace. You have

a sweet singing voice, when you sing. What's come over you, Emily? Has Richard left you? Is that it? Well, now, don't worry. I'll get Daddy to talk to him as soon as he puts his foot in the house. Now, don't cry, Emily. You're getting me all nervous. You know Daddy was always able to talk to Ben and it did some good. Ben always stopped drinking for a while afterward. Daddy will get Richard to come home to our baby girl. I promise you. I swear.

(Richard comes in the screen door.)

LYD: Emily. Emily. Dry your eyes and look who's here. *(Lyd goes into the bedroom and closes the door after her.)*

(Richard stands by the screen door, looking at Emily.)

RICHARD: Am I forgiven?

EMILY: Yes.

(She goes to him. He takes her in his arms.)

Thank God you've come back to me. Where were you? I went all over town looking for you, and I couldn't find you anywhere.

RICHARD: I was very upset. Oh, I went out in the car by the old River Road.

EMILY: I was so scared. I thought you had left me. I need you. I need you.

(He holds her close to him.)

Richard, I don't like quarreling. I'm not used to it. Mother and Daddy never quarreled. *(A pause.)* The room looks naked without Mother's pictures, doesn't it? *(A pause.)* Richard, one night, after I was divorced from Ben, and I was living alone in Houston, I got so lonesome I thought I was losing my mind, and I got in my car and rode out by Rice Institute. It was around ten at night, and I saw a nice-looking soldier standing on the street curb, and I stopped my car and asked if he would like a ride to the end of Main. He said he would and he got into the car, and we talked as we rode and he seemed so nice that I asked if I could drive him to where he lived, and he said he wasn't in a hurry to get home, unless I had some place to go, and so we rode around for awhile, and then I asked him if he'd like to stop at a drive-in and we had something to eat and drink. I asked him if he'd like to drive for awhile, and he took the wheel and we drove a block or two, and then he turned off Main and started driving into Herman Park, and I said, I don't think we should leave Main, and he said he knew all about that, and about lonely women that pick up soldiers on street corners, and he stopped the car and tried to kiss me, and I fought him, and he beat me and pushed me out of my own car, and he left me in the middle of those dark, piney woods. I had no money. I had no one to call for help. I had to go to the police alone and try to explain what had happened so they could get my car back. I was ashamed and humiliated...

RICHARD: Why are you telling me this, Emily?

EMILY: I don't know. I just felt I wanted to tell you. I needed to tell someone. I've never been able to tell anyone before. You told me about borrowing money from Lucy Douglas, and I want to tell you about this. I don't want any secrets between us. I don't want you to think, Richard, that just because Mother and Daddy have always been able to take care of me, that my life has been so easy. I've had my problems, too.

RICHARD: I know you have.

EMILY: Take care of me, Richard. I need somebody to take care of me, like Daddy has taken care of Mother. I'm so tired of being alone. I can't ever be alone again.

(He kisses her. He holds her in his arms for a moment, comforting her.)

RICHARD: Emily, I was awfully wrong, acting so ugly about your Daddy.

EMILY: You were upset and disappointed. I understand.

RICHARD: I was very wrong. I've been thinking about it, and do you know what I think would be fair?

EMILY: What?

RICHARD: If I asked your Dad to let me invest only what I collect from Jack Barker. That's money he never would have gotten himself, anyway. If I only get a thousand, I invest a thousand. If it's fifteen thousand, I invest fifteen thousand. So you think that's fair?

EMILY: Yes. I think that's very fair.

RICHARD: I just can't miss out on this now, Emily. I know I've been cross and irritable, but I've been very worried. *(A pause.)* You see, it's been a very puzzling thing about my life. I get so close to something big and important, something that will make me respected and give me security for the rest of my life, and then just as I'm about to reach out and get it, something unforeseen will happen and the whole thing blows up right in my face. It's a very frightening thing to me, Emily. I get desperate sometimes when I think about it. A man doesn't have the respect of anyone unless he has money and position. And those things were almost mine many times, and then at the last minute something always went wrong, and it didn't work out. Sometimes I think if I miss another opportunity, I'll go crazy. I'm a nice-looking man, I've worked hard. I'm smart. I didn't let not having an education get me down. I studied on my own to make up for that. I read. I worked all night some nights studying and reading and learning. Now all I need is just a little more luck. And where do you get that from? I feel though luck is finally with me. And all any man needs is one break. Do you know the lives that have been changed over night because of that? *(A pause.)* And now is my turn to get that break. I know it. I feel it.

EMILY: I know it, too.

RICHARD: And honey, I wish you'd have a talk with your dad and try to find out why he's changing toward me.

EMILY: I know that's just your imagination. Daddy hasn't changed toward you. He's conservative and he's been worried about what to do, that's all. I know when you tell him your plan about only using the Jack Barker money that you'll see he'll be very happy again.

RICHARD: No. I think it's more than that. I think he's changed his feeling toward me, some way. I can't figure out why. Before we were married, we used to have long talks together. I felt then he was crazy about me. I'm fond of him, and I always want him to like me...

EMILY: He likes you. I know he does. But I'll talk to him...

(Lyd comes in from the bedroom.)

LYD: Look at the love birds. Well, that's how it should be. Lee and I never had a cross word in our lives. Not in our whole lives.

(Richard goes to the desk.)

RICHARD: What happened to your pictures?

LYD: I put them away for a little while until we have all got over our nervousness. Soon as Addie comes, I'll have her put them back up.

(Richard picks up some papers at this desk.)

You too missed all the excitement. Maud Bakker came over here and told Daddy and me if he foreclosed on Jack, he would kill himself, and her curses would follow Daddy to his grave. It made me so nervous I almost died.

RICHARD: I wish she'd told me that.

LYD: It was just heartbreaking to hear the poor thing.

EMILY: Did it upset Daddy?

LYD: Of course it did. He's not made of stone. He went over right away to tell Jack he's going to give him another six months.

EMILY: Mother!

(Richard looks at Emily. He gets up and goes to the window and stands there.)
Richard, I'm going to find Daddy. I'll be right back.

(She goes out the screen door. Lyd hasn't understood what she has done or what they are upset about. She watches Richard for a moment. His silence makes her nervous.)

LYD: Why don't you go with her? She runs around in this heat like it was the middle of January.

(He ignores her.)

Son, do you and Emily ever play honeymoon bridge? Lee and I used to play by the hour.

(He doesn't answer, goes to a chair, and sits.)

I love games. There's an old mah-jongg set around here some place. Maybe we could all four play some night.

(Richard is staring at her with complete contempt. He is making her nervous and self-conscious.)

Bridge is my game, though. I used to rather play bridge than eat. No more. Too many cats at the bridge tables these days. I declare, so many strangers in this town and they're all cats. Well, one of them catty strangers met me at a bridge party and I was introduced to her as Mrs. Davis. She looked at me and said, "Mrs. Davis? Oh. Lee Davis' mother." Well, I forgot what I was talking to one of those strangers at a bridge party, and they told me her name, but I can't keep names in my head, and I was telling her about the catty thing that said I looked like Lee's mother, and Alma was standing beside me and punching at me until I thought I'd be black and blue, and I told her to stop. You know Alma, she never wants you to say anything, and I went right on talking and I noticed the strange lady turned twenty colors and excused herself, and after she had gone, Alma told me it was the same woman.

(She chuckles to herself. Richard continues staring at her. She picks up the banjo from the floor and puts it in her lap.)

Where did Emily say she was going?

RICHARD: You heard her.

LYD: No, I didn't.

RICHARD: She's going to keep Mr. Lee from signing the Barker note. To keep him from letting you make a damn fool of him.

LYD: My husband adores me. He idolizes me, and I idolize him. Every day of my life, he has brought a tray to my bed with little red roses on it and two slices of bacon and a poached egg and toast and coffee and kissed me and said eat your breakfast. Can you tell me of a better husband than that? *(She plunks the banjo.)*

RICHARD: Put that down. It makes me nervous.

(She holds it quietly in her lap for a moment. Richard looks at her with complete contempt.)

RICHARD: I wonder if you know what you're doing, or do you care? Go in your room, you crazy old woman.

(Lyd pays not the slightest attention.)

Go in your room, I said. I might tell you a few things I'd be sorry for.

(Lyd continues to ignore him.)

Did you hear me? I said get in your room.

LYD: I heard you, but I'm not going. I don't want to go in my room. My pictures are hid, and you'll never find them. From now on, you and Emily can't scare me about burning them. So I'll just sit here as much as I please.

(Richard glares at her.)

What are you looking at? What does Emily think she's going to do with Lee? Lee promised me he's going to sign that note, and nothing on God's green earth can make him change a promise he's made to me.

RICHARD: What do you want to do? Kill your husband? Don't you ever want him to have anything? Sure, he'll do what you say, because if he didn't, you'd nag him to death.

LYD: Is that so?

RICHARD: It certainly is. If you don't stop nagging him, he won't be here very long to nag.

LYD: I hope God strikes me dead if I ever nagged him in my life. How do I nag him?

RICHARD: How do you nag him? Oh, my God. Daddy, shut the window. Daddy, I don't feel well. Daddy, get me this. Daddy, get me that. A woman making her husband get up at the crack of dawn and bring her breakfast to the bed and is so silly she has the town laughing behind her back because she is so bragging about it. Why don't you get out of here? You make me sick just to look at you.

LYD: Sticks and stones may break my bones, but words can never harm me.

(Again she plunks the banjo.)

RICHARD: Put that down.

(She plunks it again.)

I said put that down. I've got a splitting headache.

(There is a pause. She slyly plunks it again.)

Give it to me. *(Richard grabs it out of her hand.)*

LYD: Don't you dare harm that. That banjo belonged to my sister Mame. We were a family of musicians. Mama played the piano, Teenie the guitar, Sissie the violin, and Mame the banjo. I could play them all. I never saw the instrument I couldn't play by ear. The times we used to have, right here in that front parlor. Mame died a very young girl. She's bound to come calling on you one of these nights. You didn't know we had a ghost here, did you? It's Mame. She visited Ben. He laughed at me, when I warned him, but one night she came calling. She comes all dressed in a gray, long flowing gown, and her long blonde hair flying behind her. We call her the lady in gray. I tried to call out to her one night, but when you speak to her she just floats away. Everybody sleeps in here is bound to see her sooner or later. I've seen her three times. Once in the daytime, twice at night. First time I saw her, I fainted dead away. A fortune teller told me once there was gold or oil under the house and Mame was trying to tell us about it. But we never found out, because when you speak to her she just fades away. Addie says if you pinned a verse of the Bible in the room some place, she'd stop coming, but I don't mind her visits. Of all my sisters, I was closest to Mame.

(Richard looks at Lyd and doesn't answer.)

What are you staring at? Don't you believe me?

RICHARD: Why don't you die? Why don't you go to the river and finish the job? You crazy old thing, messing up everybody's life, making them hold on to this moldy old house and now nagging him until he's about to give that broken-down red neck his land back.

(Lyd gets up and starts out of the room.)

Come back here.

(She continues on.)

Come back here and sit down.

(She goes on.)

God damn it. I said come back here.

(Lyd turns toward him.)

LYD: I don't like you. I never liked you. I liked Ben in spite of his drinking, but you're the first person in my life I never liked. Give me my banjo.

RICHARD: I think I'll break it. I bet that would stop Mame coming back.

LYD: Give me my banjo, Richard.

RICHARD: Take the God-damned thing. *(He slings it across the room.)*

LYD: Why did you have to do that? You're mean. Mame gave me that when she was dying. I've taken care of it for more than forty years. *(She picks it up.)* You didn't hurt it. It's a good thing for you, you didn't hurt it. Let me tell you about my husband, young man. He seems like the sweetest, mildest man in the world, and he is. Until he's roused. I never saw it but once. The day he told Ben to leave. I never hope to see it again. If I didn't love peace, and you weren't Emily's husband, I would tell him what you did and I might see that temper again.

(She walks out and goes to her bedroom. Richard is very restless and paces around the room. Emily comes in the screen door.)

RICHARD: Did you get to him in time?

EMILY: No.

(Richard turns and goes back to the window.)

RICHARD: God damn it. God damn it to hell.

EMILY: I'm sorry, D. I did what I could.

RICHARD: What good does that do for me, I'd like to know?

EMILY: *(Calling.)* Mother!

(Lyd answers from left room.)

LYD: What?

EMILY: Come here. I want to talk to you.

LYD: I don't want to. You come here.

EMILY: Mother, I want to see you right this minute. In front of Richard. Do you hear me?

LYD: Yes. *(She comes out.)*

EMILY: I'm sick of this, Mother. I've told Daddy so. You both do everything in your power to get Richard to stay here and take responsibility and then you do everything you can to make it hard for him.

LYD: I'm sure I don't know what you're talking about.

EMILY: Oh yes, you know what I'm talking about. And it's going to stop. I've warned Daddy and I've warned you for the last time. This isn't seven years ago and Richard isn't Ben. He's no child. He's stayed here to do you a favor, not for himself. He can make me a living. A good living. If he stays on here, he takes responsibility and when he's done a thing you and Daddy have to let it alone. It's done. If you don't like what he's doing, or what he's done, or what he wants to do, than tell us now. We'll leave, and if we leave you'll never see us again. Or hear from us again. I mean that.

LYD: I don't want you to leave. Who said anything about leaving?

EMILY: All right. Make up your mind. I've told Daddy that if we stay, we're going to sell this house to make up for what we lost to Jack Bakker.

LYD: You're not going to sell my house. Nobody is going to sell my house.

EMILY: That's up to you and Daddy.

LYD: Daddy won't do it. He won't let anybody sell this house.

RICHARD: No. Daddy won't do it. Because you'd nag him to death until he didn't. Why do you think I came here in the first place? Did you know

I came here because your husband has had two heart attacks and can't work and may drop over dead at any time?

EMILY: Richard, please...

RICHARD: Do you know that I wanted the Jack Barker money to invest so he could do nothing in peace the rest of his life? No, you didn't know. You're too selfish to have another thought except for yourself and your house. Well, I don't want your house. I don't have to beg you for anything, old woman. I never will. I wouldn't stay here now with you if you gave me ten houses. I'm sick of you and your husband. He can drop dead, and you can go to the river, and I wouldn't lift a finger to help either of you. But I have done plenty already. Whether you know it or not, or appreciate it, I don't care, but I know what I've done, what would have been done if you'd stayed out of it. But you didn't. And that's fine. But you're not cheating me out of what is mine, and he's not. Not if I have to take it out of somebody's hide. So you can tell him that when you're begging him not to sell your old house. And maybe by then you'll have figured out how he can pay me if he doesn't.

EMILY: Richard...

RICHARD: I'm through, Emily. I'm fed up with them. I don't care what they do. I want what's coming to me and I'm clearing out.

(He goes. Emily runs to the screen door.)

EMILY: (Calling.) Richard! Richard!

(He doesn't answer. She goes to her mother.)

My God, Mama, don't do this to me. You and Daddy. Why did you bring him here if this is how you're gonna act. What do you want of me? I know you love me, but what is this war between us?

LYD: Emily...

EMILY: Whatever it is, I give up. I surrender. I gladly lose. You know I haven't asked much of you and Daddy these last years, Mama, but help me to keep this marriage together.

LYD: Emily...

EMILY: Because I want him and need him and love him.

LYD: Emily, I love you...

EMILY: You don't love me. That's what you love. *(She points toward the wall.)* That little girl you could dress up and show off. You don't love me. You've never loved me. Can't you see what you've done? Don't you understand you've ruined my life always with your interfering. *(A pause.)* Mama. I didn't mean that. What I meant was... *(A pause. She kisses her.)* It's all right, Mama. It's gonna be all right. You'll see. Mama don't look at me that way. It's my fault. We should have never come here. I blame myself for that. Nobody else. But we'll leave now. I swear to you. Don't worry. Everything will be all right. *(She goes.)*

(A child is heard practicing again on the piano in the distance. Twilight is beginning. Lyd goes to the window. She seems very weak and tired. She turns and sees an imaginary person come in the screen door.)

LYD: Why come in, Lillie. I'm so relieved to see you. They told me there was a terrible automobile accident and you were killed. Thrown right out of the car onto Miss Lizzie Thomas' front yard. Mama will be relieved. So relieved. *(She picks up the banjo.)* Yes'm. We're a family of musicians. *(She strums a few chords. She stops. She points to the wall. She laughs.)* That's Emily when she was a toe dancer. She was grace itself. She weaved back and forth like a pretty flower. My daughter Emily. Certainly you passed her on the way out. She's married to a man that adores her. Emily was always so popular. Her popularity with men she gets from me. I could have married Les Benton or Douglas Lee or Stanley Nation, but they had outside children and Papa felt it was his duty to tell me. I wouldn't have had them, diamonds dripping all over them after that. And I waited. And I was glad I waited, because then Mr. Lee came along. Mama, Papa, Mama…Emily has married a man that's very sarcastic and despises me and they want to take my house. I'll tell Sadie. I'll tell Brother Davis. He's dead. They won't take my house. They certainly never will while I live take this house.

(She is frightened. The twilight has turned to semi-darkness. The child continues practicing. She goes out the screen door. Addie comes in from the kitchen and turns on the light in the large room.)

ADDIE: Miss Lyd. Miss Lyd. *(Goes to the inner room.)* Are you back in that dark room with all the lights off? Are you tryin' to dig yo' grave? Come on out here in the light. *(She turns and goes back.)* You told me you wouldn't move from that chair. Well, I did it. This certainly proves I love Miss Lyd Davis. Everybody hollerin' at me. They say if you're gonna steal why don't you steal something you can use. Everybody stopping to stare. White and black. Me going down the road with Miss Lyd Davis' pictures under my arms. What do you want for supper? *(A pause.)* You hear me. Stop playing possum and trying to scare me. What do you want for supper, Miss Lyd? Miss Lyd… *(She opens the door. She turns on the lights in the small room. She sees no one is inside. She calls only once more.)* Miss Lyd. Miss Lyd…

(Lee runs in the screen door. She runs to him.)

Mr. Lee, I just got here. Miss Lyd promised me she wouldn't leave this chair and now I can't find her... *(She goes out of the room into the other part of the house calling.)* Miss Lyd. *(She comes back to Lee.)* She's not in the front room. Mr. Lee, you hear me? She's not in the living room.

LEE: You better go down to the river and get her, Addie.

ADDIE: Let me call over to Miss Alma's first. She might be there.

LEE: Go on, Addie...

ADDIE: Or maybe Miss Emily or Mr. Richard took her...

LEE: I passed them in their car. She wasn't with them. Go on, Addie. What's the sense of wasting time? She never visits anywhere by herself. You know and I know where she has gone. Go on down to the river bank and get her.

ADDIE: I can't. I can't. I'm scared to go. You go this time, Mr. Lee. Don't make me go any more. It just breaks my heart when I see her down there. Her eyes all glassy and staring, her heart beating like a little bird's, standin' there, starin' at the water, sayin' I don't mean to do it. I don't mean to do anythin'. I swear...I swear. I just gets nervous. She don't want me down there. It's you she wants. You go, Mr. Lee. I can't. I can't.

LEE: All right, Addie. All right. But I'm tired. I've got to get some rest sometime. You hear me, Addie? I've got to get some rest soon.

ADDIE: Yes sir. Yes sir.

(He goes. Addie is crying.)

I can't. I can't any more. It just breaks my heart. It just breaks it.

(She continues crying as the curtain falls.)

ACT III

It is two hours later. Lyd is in the bedroom asleep. Lee is sitting by the side of her bed. Alma is in the room. Addie comes out from the kitchen.

ADDIE: How is she?

ALMA: She's fine. The doctor just left. He gave her something to make her sleep.

(Addie goes to the door of the small room. She stands listening. She comes back to Alma.)

ADDIE: I tell you Miss Alma, if anything had happened to her, I would never in this world have forgiven myself. I promised Mr. Lee I would never leave her side, but she just begged me so...

ALMA: Now, Addie, it's done. You've nothing to reproach yourself for.

ADDIE: Mr. Lee hardly speaks to me. He's mad at me.

ALMA: No, he's not, Addie. He's just worried to death. I tell you that poor man is being pulled in a thousand different directions. He's trying to please everybody. That's how he's spent his life.

ADDIE: Yes'm.

ALMA: Did you hear I'd sold my house?

ADDIE: No, Ma'am.

ALMA: Sold it this morning. I have to be out in a month. They're going to put a filling station up there. This will be the last house left on the highway.

ADDIE: Miss Lyd says it was the first.

ALMA: Yes, it was. I never felt about my house like Cousin Lyd did hers. Not about the house or the family. I can hardly keep them all straight. Lyd knows every fifth and sixth cousin.

(Emily comes in the screen door.)

EMILY: How is Mother?

ALMA: She's all right now, Emily. She's in bed resting.

EMILY: Did Daddy have the doctor?

ALMA: Yes, he's given her something to make her rest.

ADDIE: It was my fault, Miss Emily. I shouldn't have left her alone, but she asked me to take her pictures and hide them. She had taken it into her head that they were going to be burned or something.

EMILY: It's nobody fault, Addie. It's just nobody's fault. How's Daddy?

ALMA: He seems very sad to me, Emily. He's very troubled. Where's Richard?

EMILY: He's not coming back tonight.

ALMA: Will you be here the rest of the night?

EMILY: No. But I'll get Addie to stay.

ALMA: Then I'll go on. I'll be back in the morning.

EMILY: All right. Thank you, Cousin.

ALMA: That's all right, Emily. Where are you and Richard staying?

EMILY: I don't know.

ALMA: You're welcome at my house.

EMILY: Thank you.

ALMA: Good night.

EMILY: Good night.

> *(Alma goes out the screen door. Emily goes over to Addie.)*
> Where was Mother when they found her?

ADDIE: She had gotten as far as the old train bridge. She had fallen and was lying on the ground crying.

EMILY: I think I'd better go in and speak to Daddy. *(She quietly opens the door to the small room. She goes over to her father and whispers.)* Daddy. I'm here. Alma just got word to me. I'm sorry I was so hard to find.

LEE: That's all right, Emily.

EMILY: How's Mother?

LEE: She gave me an awful scare, Emily. She's going to be all right, but she gave me an awful scare.

> *(Lyd opens her eyes.)*

LYD: Who's there, Daddy?

> *(Emily goes over to her Mother's bed.)*

EMILY: Emily, Mother.

LYD: Who?

EMILY: Emily, Mother.

LYD: Who?

> *(Lee comes over to the side of the bed.)*

LEE: It's Emily, Belle. You know her.

LYD: No, that's not Emily.

LEE: Yes it is, Belle.

LYD: No. That's not Emily.

EMILY: Who am I then, Mother?

LYD: I don't know. But you aren't Emily. Daddy. Where's Emily? I want to see Emily.

> *(Richard comes into the screen door. Addie goes up to him.)*

ADDIE: Miss Emily's in with her Mother.

RICHARD: How is she?

ADDIE: All right.

(He crosses over to the window, and Addie goes out of the room.)

LYD: Daddy. I want Emily.

LEE: All right, Belle. She'll be along in a little.

(She closes her eyes and rests her head back on the pillow. He motions Emily away from the bed and whispers.)

We'd better let her get some more sleep.

EMILY: I'll wait for you in the next room. *(She goes out the door. She sees Richard.)* I thought you weren't coming back here, D.

RICHARD: I changed my mind. I want to be here when you talk to your father.

EMILY: Daddy will be out in a little.

RICHARD: All right.

EMILY: I haven't gotten a chance to discuss anything at all with him.

RICHARD: All right.

EMILY: I think I'll get our things packed. I'll just take what we need. Addie can send the rest on when we know where we're going.

(She goes out. Lyd opens her eyes.)

LYD: Lee...

LEE: Yes, Belle.

LYD: I hear Emily crying.

LEE: No, she's not, Lyd.

LYD: She is. I hear her crying. She's cried so much in her life, Lee. I used to wake up in the night when she was married to Ben and hear her crying and when she was just a girl and she'd come home from a dance and she should have been laughing and happy, she wasn't. I'd wake in the night and hear her crying then. And I'd get out of bed and go to her and say, honey, what's the matter? She'd say, Mama, the boys don't like me, and I'd say, why? You're very sweet looking. And the next day I'd dress her up and tell her to sit on the front gallery and some day a handsome young man would come along and fall in love with her and they have, Lee. Two handsome young men. Two of the handsomest young men God ever gave the breath of life to. Ben, and now Richard. Go tell her not to cry, Lee. Tell her everything's going to be all right, tell her her mother says so. *(A pause.)* I hear so many things sitting in my room here. Crying and laughing and once in a while, far away, the sound of Indians. I'm from a long line of Indian fighters. Once my grandmother...my grandfather... *(A pause.)* One day I came home from town and there was Emily sitting on the gallery, all dressed up and she looked as pretty as a picture and I said: "What are you doing out here all dressed up? Waiting for your sweetheart?" And she broke out crying and ran into the house.

(She lays her head back on the pillows and again closes her eyes. Emily comes into the sitting room with a small suitcase.)

EMILY: Richard, I've put all my things in the suitcase. What do you want me to pack of yours?

(Richard lies down on the couch.)

RICHARD: I don't want you to pack for me. I'll do it.

EMILY: I don't mind. Just tell me what you want.

RICHARD: I'll do it myself.

EMILY: All right.

(A pause. Richard turns away from her.)

Mother didn't recognize me. She kept saying who are you. Daddy said this is Emily and she said no it's not. And I said who am I if I'm not Emily, and she said I don't know. Who are you? *(A pause. She looks around the room.)* So much of my life has been spent here, in this room, going in and out of that screen door. I must have gone out into the world for the first time through that door. I used to sit here and think about the past and the girls that were me coming in and out and try to remember what those girls were like, and what they wanted, and I look out the window and see how this street has changed during my life time, how the grass and the trees have become concrete and filling stations, and where maybe three cars passed an afternoon, now, the cotton trucks and the cars and the beer trucks never stop day or night. *(A pause.)* Who am I? That's a good question. *(She goes to Richard.)* Honey, I think the sensible thing would be for us to go over to Alma's tonight and then tomorrow we can have a long talk with Daddy.

RICHARD: No. I want to get everything settled tonight.

EMILY: But Daddy is so tired, Richard. He's been very upset.

RICHARD: You can go, if you want to. I'm getting everything settled tonight.

EMILY: All right. I just hope we can all be reasonable and calm, that's all. I know it's all been very disappointing for you. I can't tell you how sorry I am that it's turned out this way.

(Richard doesn't answer her.)

Don't be mad at me, honey. I've done everything I can.

RICHARD: I'm not mad at you.

EMILY: Then what is the matter with you, Richard?

RICHARD: There's nothing the matter with me.

EMILY: You've been so strange all evening.

(A pause. He doesn't answer.)

Can I get you anything?

RICHARD: No.

(Lee comes out of the small room.)

EMILY: Is Mother asleep?

LEE: Yes.

EMILY: When you feel like it, Richard and I thought it would be wise to have a good long talk. We…

LEE: What happened here this afternoon, Emily?

EMILY: Daddy, we just all got excited. Very excited. I did. Richard did. Mother did.

LEE: She was very upset, Emily. I've never seen her so upset.

EMILY: So was I. So was Richard.

LEE: It's very unfortunate. I was hoping we could all get along. I'm afraid it's impossible now.

(A pause. No one says anything. Emily goes over to Richard. She puts her arms on his shoulders.)

I want to pay Richard what he thinks fair for the work he's done here. You two will have to find a home some place else. Naturally, I'll take care of your expenses until Richard can get another job. I'm sorry, Richard, you gave up your job for my sake, but I assured you I'll stand behind you until you get located again.

EMILY: All right, Daddy. All right. Now Richard and I will go to Cousin Alma's tonight…

RICHARD: That's not all right with me. *(He pulls himself free of Emily and crosses to Lee.)* You made some promises to me that I'm not forgetting about.

LEE: What do you mean?

RICHARD: What do you think I mean? What do you think I am, Ben Lacque? You're not going to ship me off without any job and think you can settle with me for a month's salary and fifteen dollars a week spending money while I find one.

LEE: I guess I didn't make myself clear. After today, it's impossible for you to continue living here.

RICHARD: And I guess I didn't make myself very clear.

EMILY: Richard…

RICHARD: I'm not Ben Lacque. You're not settling with me for a month's salary and fifteen dollars a week spending money.

LEE: What do you mean settling with you?

RICHARD: I'll tell you. I'll tell you exactly what I mean.

EMILY: Richard, please…

RICHARD: When I first came to this house you took me aside and told me how tired you were and how you'd like to retire if you only had a son. Then, when you saw Emily was serious about me and I kept coming around, you began to confide in me about your finances and who owed you money and how you'd like to sell your land and retire if you only had a son to manage things for you. And I bit. I got interested. I got very interested. I asked your daughter to marry me and she agreed and I got her to come here and live. I got you to let me sell your land for you and try and let me collect Jack Barker's debt and you wanted me to go into the insurance business and I wanted to invest in oil wells and I said I would think about your proposition if first you'd come and talk to Tom Carter with me about mine, and you said you would. Isn't that true?

LEE: Yes.

RICHARD: All right. After I marry your daughter and you go with me to see Tom Carter, and ask for time to think over his deal, and then you ask me to go and see him again, and I take you, and then again you want more time to think about it, and after waiting for two weeks you finally tell me your friends are finally advising you against investing in oil. Then when I have everything ready to settle with Jack Barker, you let your wife talk you into calling that off...

LEE: My wife was very upset. I had to call it off.

RICHARD: I don't care how it happened. You called it off. *(A pause.)* Well, didn't you?

LEE: Yes.

RICHARD: All right. Then Emily comes home and tells me you feel badly about having to do it, and that to make up for it, you'd think about selling the house.

LEE: I told her I felt badly about going back on my word to you and that I'd do all in my power to get Lyd to sell the house.

RICHARD: What have you done about it?

LEE: Nothing.

RICHARD: You haven't mentioned it to your wife?

LEE: She's been in no condition to discuss it.

RICHARD: What are you going to do about it?

LEE: Nothing. If it had been handled wisely, perhaps something could have been done about it, but now it's impossible. I'm doing the best I can under the circumstances. I'm very tired, Richard, so I'd like to end this as quickly as possible. I want to pay you fairly for the months you've worked here for me and settle on expense money until you find another job.

RICHARD: I said—no, thank you.

EMILY: Honey, let's don't argue about it tonight. Let's just go now. We'll talk about it in the morning. What good is it going to do...

RICHARD: I told you I'm not Ben Lacque.

(She takes Richard's arm.)

EMILY: Daddy, we're going. We'll call tomorrow...

LEE: What do you mean, you're not Ben Lacque? Why do you keep mentioning his name? I don't see what he has to do with anything concerning us.

(Richard yanks his arms free from Emily.)

RICHARD: I'll tell you what I mean. He's a spineless weak sonofabitch that you can see drunk any day of your life walking down West Milam Street in Houston, going into the pool halls. I've known Ben Lacque for a long time. Longer than you have. He's no good now and he never was any good. About eight or nine years ago, he began to come into the pool halls and blow off his top about how he was going to marry some rich old man's daughter in Harrison and how this man, out of gratefulness, was going to buy him the moon.

EMILY: Richard, please...

RICHARD: I'm sorry. It's the truth. And by God, he's going to hear the truth.

LEE: Emily, I want you to leave. I don't want you to listen to this.

EMILY: No, Daddy...I...

LEE: I insist you go this instant, Emily.

EMILY: No.

LEE: Then I'll go. I won't have this continued in front of you. *(He starts out of the room.)*

RICHARD: Come back here.

(Lee continues leaving.)

I said come back here.

(Lee is at the screen door.)

All right. Go ahead. If you want your daughter to hear it by herself.

(Lee pauses. He turns and comes back into the room.)

Are you ready to listen?

LEE: Yes.

RICHARD: All right. He used to slip into Houston on drunks every now and again after he was married, and he was full of how easy he had it, and of all the things you were going to do for him. Then one day, he turned up in town again, for good. He didn't have a job and he had very little money. What he had was all gone after one good drunk. He said you had kicked both of them out and were paying their expenses and giving them fifteen dollars a week spending money until he got a job.

LEE: I couldn't do anything else. He was a drunk. A worthless drunk. Emily can tell you...

RICHARD: You knew he was a drunk before he married your daughter, didn't you?

LEE: I hoped I could help him. I hoped when he saw all the opportunities there could be here for him, he would straighten himself out. You just couldn't help Ben Lacque. I tried everything. Emily knows I tried everything and in every way to help him.

RICHARD: That may be.

LEE: But he was drunk. Irresponsible. Worthless. I had to throw him out of my house.

RICHARD: You knew why Ben married your daughter, didn't you?

LEE: No.

RICHARD: Then I'll tell you. He married her because of all the promises you made to him. If you hadn't flattered him and encouraged him and led him to believe all kinds of things that you were going to do for him and with him, he would never have married her.

(Lee again tries to leave the room.)

I'm not through.

LEE: My wife is not well. I'm not well. We can continue this in the morning.

RICHARD: You know why I married your daughter, don't you?

LEE: Emily, I ask you to leave, I beg you to leave.

(Emily has gone to the window. She has her back to both of them.)

RICHARD: You know why I married your daughter?

LEE: No.

RICHARD: Don't lie.

LEE: I don't know. I don't know.

RICHARD: Because you flattered me and encouraged me. Because of all you implied that you'd let me do, because of all I thought would be done. I was willing to live up to my part of the bargain. I married your daughter. Now I ask you why you won't live up to yours.

LEE: I made no bargain with you.

RICHARD: Yes, you did.

LEE: I made no bargain with you. I made no bargain with you.

RICHARD: Yes, you did. The same kind of bargain you made with Ben Lacque.

LEE: You're lying. I don't know what you're talking about. Emily, don't stand here and listen to his lies. I never bargained with either of them to marry you.

RICHARD: Yes, you did.

LEE: You lie. You lie.

RICHARD: Oh, we didn't talk about it in those terms. No. You're too much of a gentleman to do that. But we talked about it just the same. Son, I'm old. I need a son to help me manage things. All that I have will belong to Emily and her husband some day. I'm tired. I'm tired. I'm tired.

LEE: And I think you're crazy. I think you're crazy. That's what I think.

RICHARD: Don't lie to me. Look at me.

LEE: I don't want you here. I want you to get out of here and leave us alone.

RICHARD: I said look at me. *(He grabs Lee.)* Do you think Ben would have married Emily if you hadn't made your assertions and your promises? Do you think I would have?

LEE: I threw Ben out of here. If I had the strength left, I would take my hands and throw you out. I would kill you.

RICHARD: I asked you a question. I want an answer.

LEE: I heard your question. I gave you an answer.

RICHARD: No, you didn't. That's not an answer to my question. I asked you if you thought I would have married your daughter if you hadn't come sucking around me making your assertions and your promises? Well, do you? Do you?

LEE: No. No. No. *(He turns away from Richard.)* Now will you go and leave us alone. Now will you please go and leave us alone? *(A pause.)* Blame me, Emily. Don't reproach yourself. I should have known, but I kept telling myself he has no bad habits. What if he's ambitious? It's good for a man to be ambitious. I was proud of him. Then I got scared of his ambition. Money goes so fast. I'd worked hard all my life, and I was scared. I was terrified of his ambition. Emily, honey. Don't stay here. Go in with your Mother. I'll be there before long. Emily…

(She doesn't answer. Lee waits for a moment, and then understanding that she won't leave or answer him, he turns to Richard.)

I'll deposit the money you want in your account at the bank tomorrow. *(Richard goes out upstage right center. Lee stands looking down at the floor. After a moment he turns and looks at Emily. He reaches out to her, tentatively, but finally lets his arm fall to his side.)*

If I had the strength left, I would have thrown him out. I would have killed him. *(He again goes toward his daughter.)* Emily. Emily. Don't grieve. Try not to grieve. He wasn't worthy of my girl. I know you'll be better off without him. You'll find another husband, one that will love you and take care of you, and bring you the kind of happiness you deserve. The kind your Mother and I always wanted you to have. Emily, do you hear me? Do you?

(A pause. She doesn't answer.)

I'm old, and I'm tired, and if I've done anything to harm you, I'm sorry. I'm deeply sorry.

(Emily goes to the window and looks out.)

EMILY: It's light enough out to be morning. The stars and the moon seem so close. *(A pause.)* I just think I'll take my car, Daddy, and ride into Houston tonight.

LEE: All right.

EMILY: I don't want to go back to the boardinghouse. If it's all right with you, I want to sell my car when I get there. I want to find an inexpensive apartment for myself. I'll use the money from the car to buy some furniture and keep myself going until I find a job.

LEE: I don't want you working, Emily. There's no need for that. We'll make out.

EMILY: But I want to. And you have to be sensible now and let me. The money you have can go so fast, if you aren't careful. *(She goes toward the suitcase.)* I'll go to the hotel tonight, and when I have my apartment, I'll have Addie send on my clothes.

(A door slams in the front of the house.)

He's gone. *(A pause.)* Next door to the boardinghouse in Houston was a man, a widower with two children. He was very nice, steady and reliable, and the floor manager at Leon's Department Store. We sometimes took the same bus in town. Twice he asked me out, and once he invited me over to meet his children, but I stopped going out with him when Richard came to call. I thought he was nice, but not handsome. I always felt I had to have someone handsome. *(A pause.)* I wonder, Daddy, why a girl who has never really considered herself very attractive always felt she had to have a handsome husband… *(A pause. She cries.)* Don't give Richard anything. He lied. He lied. He lied. *(A pause.)* But I guess we lied, too. I guess we all lied to ourselves and to each other. *(She starts for the suitcase.)*

LEE: Please don't leave us. Don't leave us. *(A pause. He turns away.)* I don't blame you. I want you to go. We weren't good for you. We loved another world, a world that was gone and we didn't know was gone. They changed the world, and we had nothing to say about it. Nothing…

(He cries. She goes to him and puts her arms around him.)

EMILY: Don't cry. It's going to be all right again. You did what you thought was best. It'll all come out all right, Daddy. *(A pause.)* Do you remember when I was a little girl and you used to lie awake at nights and worry what would happen to people here when the mechanical cotton picker came along? We'll all be ruined, you used to say. I'd lie awake myself after hearing you and cry and cry and cry for all the tenant farmers and the sharecroppers and their jobs, that would be taken away from them. What will people do, you used to say. What will they do? Well, they got along. The cotton pickers came, and people went on and the world didn't stop. And I'm going to get along, Daddy. And you will. And Mama.

(Lyd calls from the next room.)

LYD: Emily. Emily.

(Emily goes into her Mother's room.)

Emily. Emily.

EMILY: Yes, Mother.

LYD: I thought I heard you. Where is Lee?

EMILY: He's out here, Mother.

LYD: I was asking for you before. Did Lee tell you? There was this girl standing here and she kept saying, I'm Emily, but I knew…who was that girl, Emily…

EMILY: That was me, Mother.

LYD: You?

EMILY: Yes. Me.

LYD: But you were so changed.

EMILY: I was frightened and unhappy…

LYD: And you're not unhappy now.

EMILY: Yes, Mother. I'm still unhappy…

LYD: Because you quarreled with Richard?

EMILY: No, Mother.

LYD: Why?

EMILY: I can't tell you that, Mother.

LYD: Are you afraid?

EMILY: No, Mother. I'm not afraid.

LYD: That's good. You said today I'd always ruined your life, Emily. I'm sorry if you think that. I didn't mean to do that…

EMILY: I didn't mean that, Mother.

LYD: Didn't you?

EMILY: No. I was angry and I wanted to hurt you. I hope you'll forgive me.

LYD: Of course, I forgive you. You're my baby. You're the only baby I have. Lee and I wanted a child so. I don't think there was a child born in this world more wanted than you were, Emily.

EMILY: I know, Mother. You go back to sleep now.

LYD: All right, honey. And let's be happy. Let's everybody try and be happy.

EMILY: All right, Mother.

(She kisses her mother goodbye and goes out. Lyd closes her eyes for a moment. Emily goes out to her father.)

I'm going, Daddy, and I want you to promise me that you'll have Addie stay here with you all the time now. I want her to come here and live. Will you promise me that?

LEE: We'll see.

EMILY: No. I want you to promise me this one thing before I go. I wouldn't feel at peace ever knowing that you were alone.

LEE: I promise.

EMILY: I'll call tomorrow and let you know where I'll be. After I'm settled in a week or two, you and Mother can come and visit me in my apartment. And I can ride over on the bus weekends and see you. And tell Mama I said I want the pictures all up when I come back. I've seen the room without them, and I don't like it. I don't like it at all.

LEE: All right, Emily. Take care of yourself.

EMILY: I will. You take care of yourself.

(She kisses him. She goes out the screen door with her suitcase. He stands at the door watching her go. He turns back into the room. He goes to the door, and calls: "Addie. Addie." Addie comes in with Lyd's pictures.)

ADDIE: I went over to my house to get these. I figured Miss Lyd would be asking for them.

LEE: Thank you, Addie. *(He puts them down on the dresser.)*

ADDIE: Want me to put them back up now?

LEE: No, you can put them up tomorrow.

ADDIE: Yessir. *(She opens the door to Lyd's room and looks at her. She closes the door.)* She's sleeping sound.

LEE: That's good.

ADDIE: Mr. Lee, do you feel all right?

LEE: Yes. I'm just awfully tired.

ADDIE: Where's Miss Emily?

LEE: She's gone on, Addie. She and Mr. Richard are separating.

ADDIE: I'm sorry to hear that.

LEE: You can go home now, Addie. There's no sense in both of us staying up tonight. I'll just rest here on the bed and if Lyd needs anything I can get it for her.

ADDIE: I don't want to leave you alone, Mr. Lee. I don't mind staying.

LEE: I don't want you to stay, Addie. There's nothing for you to do.

ADDIE: Yessir. *(A pause.)* You're mad at me, aren't you, Mr. Lee. I swear to you…

LEE: I'm not mad at you, Addie. I'm certainly not mad at you.

ADDIE: Yessir. I hope not. You and Miss Lyd mean more to me than anything in this world.

LEE: I know that, Addie. You go on now.

ADDIE: Yessir. You sleep so sound, you sure you'll hear Miss Lyd if she calls you?

LEE: Yes, I will.

ADDIE: All right. Good night. I'll see you in the morning.

LEE: Good night.

(She goes out the door into the house. Lee goes once more to the window. He stands there for a moment and goes to the dresser. He takes the pictures Addie has brought and looks through them. He puts one or two back on the walls. He suddenly seems very tired. He goes over to the light switch and turns off all the lights, except for a table lamp. He goes to the door of his wife's bedroom. He opens it and he stands looking in at her for a moment. Then he calls to her softly.)

Lyd. Lyd.

(She opens her eyes.)

LYD: Yes, Lee?

LEE: Lyd, I'm lonely. I'm so lonely.

LYD: Are you, Lee? Come here to me.

(He goes to her. She takes him in her arms. She holds him close.)

LEE: Emily's gone.

LYD: Has she, Lee?

LEE: I sent her away. It was for her good, Lyd. We've never made her happy.

LYD: Maybe she'll come back.

LEE: She'll never come back. I wouldn't want her to come back. I want her to find her own home. I pray she does. This can't be her home.

LYD: Why, Lee?

LEE: I don't know. It just can't be.

LYD: Then it can't be.

(He lies down beside her on the bed. He puts his head on the pillow. He is soon asleep. Lyd carefully gets off the bed and pulls the windows down. She

gets a sweater and puts it on, goes outside the door for a moment, and comes back with the gas stove. She plugs it in the wall and turns it on, but forgets to light it. She sees her pictures that Addie has brought and gets them, and starts to put them on the wall. She sees one of Emily, and goes over to the light with it. She holds it up to the light.)

What's to happen to my house, Emily, when I'm gone, if you're not here to live in it? What'll happen, Emily? *(She puts the picture up on the wall. She goes to the chair by the window and sits down looking out of the window. She puts her head back against the chair with great weariness. She talks to Lee as if he were right beside her.)* What's to happen to my house, Lee? This house was build to last forever. My great grandfather built this house and he got the best bricks and lumber for miles around to put in here, because he said this was to last forever. His name was Robedaux and he was in some kind of terrible trouble back in Virginia and he had to take his slaves and his wife and his children, and all he had, he had to sell, and move here. And when he came, he looked around and he was very satisfied and he said, we're home, we can rest now. This is to be our home forever, and our children's home, and their children's. Our wanderings are over. But he was so wrong, Lee. This was a place of rest to you and me. But Emily's wanderings are just beginning...

(She closes her eyes. She is asleep.)
(The curtain falls.)

END OF PLAY

TOMORROW

Adapted from a Story by William Faulkner

ORIGINAL PRODUCTION

Tomorrow was originally presented at The HB Playwrights Foundation, April–May, 1968. Herbert Berghof Director, Philip Lerman Design, Sherry Amott and Whitney Blausen Costumes, and Anthony Quintavalla Lighting, with the following cast, in order of appearance:

THORNTON DOUGLAS . . . . Edward Anthony, Kenneth Bridges,
Romulus Linney

PAPA FENTRY . . . . Oliver Berg, Brooks Rogers

MRS. PRUITT . . . . Leigh Burch, Naomi Riordan

JACKSON FENTRY . . . . Robert Duvall, Michael Holmes

ISHAM QUICK . . . . Richard Frey, Richard McConnell

SARAH EUBANKS . . . . Olga Bellin, Marlene Mancini

WALTER . . . . Richard Frey, Andre Sedriks

MRS. HULIE. . . . . Dorothy Farrell, Jean Francis

THE PREACHER . . . . Oliver Berg, Brooks Rogers

LES THORPE . . . . Edward Anthony, Thomas McCready

DAVE THORPE. . . . . Richard Frey, Andre Sedriks

JACKSON AND LONGSTREET

BUCK THORPE . . . . Franc Geraci, Richard McConnell

MAYBELL BOOKWRIGHT. . . . . Susan Kornzweig, Carol Pearce

ACT I

At rise the stage is in darkness. A spotlight appears stage right and we see Thornton Douglas, attorney, standing in the spotlight. He begins addressing the audience as if it were a jury.

THORNTON DOUGLAS: *(Addressing the audience as if they were a jury.)* All of us in the country, the South, have been taught from birth a few things which we hold to above all else. One of the first of these—and not the best, just one of the first—is that only a life can pay for the life it takes; that the one death is only half complete. And that's what I am talking about—about us who are not dead and "what we don't know"—about all of us, human beings who at bottom want to do "right," want not to harm others; human beings with all the complexity of human passions and feelings and beliefs. Let us now together reconsider this case. Gentleman of the jury, I hope in this spring term you will acquit H.T. Bookwright of Frenchman's Bend who shot Buck Thorpe, a brawler, gambler, distiller of illicit whiskey, a cattle thief. Buck Thorpe abducted Maybell, Bookwright's seventeen-year-old daughter. Bookwright went after him and Bookwright had to kill Buck Thorpe "in self-defense." Thorpe had a pistol in his hand when they found him. From all accounts, he not only was no good, but dangerous, and if it hadn't been Bookwright, sooner or later somebody else would have had to shoot him. Nobody thought a jury in this county would convict Bookwright. Well, the jury in the fall term didn't convict Bookwright, but they didn't free him either. One man voted against freeing him and he hung that jury—eleven to one for acquittal. That man was born and raised and lived all his life out there at the very other end of the county thirty miles from Frenchman's Bend where the killing took place. He said under oath that he had never even seen Bookwright before; I doubt if he ever heard his name. And so I tried to find out why that twelfth man, hill farmer, Stonewall Jackson Fentry, wasn't going to vote Bookwright free. I couldn't figure out any reason for it. I drove out of the rich flat land into the hills, among the pine and bracken, the poor soil, the little tilted and barren patches of gaunt corn and cotton which "somehow endured," and the people they clothed and fed somehow endured…right up to his papa's mailbox, G.A. Fentry.

PAPA FENTRY: *(Offstage, back of audience, holding shot gun across his middle.)* Stop! Stop where you are!

THORNTON DOUGLAS: Mr. Fentry. Can I talk to your son?

PAPA FENTRY: You've badgered him and hurried him enough. Get out of here! Get off my land! *(Shot.)* Go!

THORNTON DOUGLAS: Yes sir! That brought me to the next mailbox within the mile—the Pruitts.

(Mrs. Pruitt seated in the audience calls to him.)

MRS. PRUITT: Howdy, Mr. Douglas.

THORNTON DOUGLAS: Howdy, Mrs. Pruitt.

MRS. PRUITT: So Jackson Fentry hung your jury for you.

THORNTON DOUGLAS: It looks like he did. You see this was my first case and it's important to me to try and find out just why I lost it. If I did something wrong in my presenting it, or if no matter what I had done, good or bad, Jackson Fentry would have still voted to convict Bookwright. Tell me… *(A pause. Again he turns to the audience.)* And Mrs. Pruitt told me how Fentry's pa and his grandpa worked the place I just saw—made a living for themselves, raised a family, paid their taxes, and owed no man. And how Jackson was helping from the time he got big enough to reach up to the plow handles. Until he was twenty-five and already looking forty, asking no odds of nobody, not married and not nothing, him and his pa living alone and doing their own washing and cooking because how can a man afford to marry when him and his pa have just one pair of shoes between them…until one night about twenty-two or twenty-three years ago…in the summer of nineteen two as near as she could remember, Jackson Fentry came to see Mrs. Pruitt.

(Mrs. Pruitt seated in the audience. Fentry comes to her.)

FENTRY: Pruitt. Pruitt.

MRS. PRUITT: Hello, Fentry.

FENTRY: Hello, Mrs. Pruitt. Is your son here?

MRS. PRUITT: No, he's gone into town. What do you want him for?

FENTRY: I got me a job working in a sawmill over to Frenchman's Bend. I traded with a man to help out my Pa at the farm while I'm gone. I wonder if you and Pruitt would be kind enough to go up there every now and again to look in on my Pa and see if he's all right.

MRS. PRUITT: I sure will.

FENTRY: Thank you.

MRS. PRUITT: How long are you going to be gone?

FENTRY: I don't know. *(Fentry leaves.)*

MRS. PRUITT: *(Calling after him.)* Good luck to you.

THORNTON DOUGLAS: The man who later hung my jury, Jackson Fentry, stayed at the sawmill two years. He came home the first Christmas, visited his Pa, and the next day got up before daylight and walked back to that sawmill. When the next Christmas came, they were expecting him home again.

(The lights are brought upstage center on the sawmill. Fentry enters. There is a small room with a bed, two chairs, and a table. There is a stove in one corner of the room for cooking. This is where Fentry lives. It is just before Christmas of his second year at the sawmill. He is at the stove finishing cooking his meal. Isham Quick, twenty, the young son of the sawmill owner, comes into the boiler room.)

ISHAM: Merry Christmas, Fentry.

FENTRY: Merry Christmas, Isham.

ISHAM: Pa wanted to know if you were going home for Christmas again this year?

FENTRY: I am. I'm leaving soon as I can eat this.

ISHAM: How far is your farm?

FENTRY: Thirty miles.

ISHAM: How you get there?

FENTRY: I walk it. I'll be home before midnight tonight.

ISHAM: When will you be back?

FENTRY: Day after Christmas same as last year.

ISHAM: Don't you get lonesome by yourself out here this way?

FENTRY: Nope.

ISHAM: Do you ever go hunting?

FENTRY: I hunt some.

ISHAM: Maybe when you come back we can go hunting together sometimes.

FENTRY: All right.

(Isham stands for a moment watching him eat. He can think of nothing else to say and starts out the door.)

ISHAM: So long.

FENTRY: So long.

(Isham goes out the door and exits left. A young woman, poorly dressed, thin, gaunt, almost emaciated comes in right. She is pregnant. Her clothes are patched and worn and no protection at all against the cold. If she were not so ill and starved-looking she might be pretty. Even so there are pride and dignity in her face. She goes toward the boiler room and faints. Fentry has finished the little food he prepared for himself and scrapes the dish and then starts outside to wash the dishes. He hears the woman moan in pain. He stands listening for a moment, and the sound comes again. He goes outside.)

He sees her. He goes to her and gently rolls her over on her back. He sees how cold her thin arms and legs are and takes his coat off and puts it over her. It is difficult to tell at first if she is alive or dead, and he stands for a moment looking at the careworn, hurt face. He feels her pulse and knows then that she is living. He watches her for a moment longer, and then shaking her gently, he tries to rouse her.)

FENTRY: Lady. Lady.

(She opens her eyes.)

SARAH: Where am I?

FENTRY: You're at Ben Quick's sawmill over at Frenchman's Bend. *(He looks down at the thin, emaciated face.)* I'm Jackson Fentry. I'm the watchman out here in the winter time when the mill is shut down. You sounded to me like you was in pain. Are you in pain?

(The woman shakes her head weakly, no. She shivers, and he puts his coat more securely around her.)

How long have you been here?

SARAH: I don't know. I remember walking down the road back yonder. I don't remember passing the sawmill. I knowed I was feeling dizzy and I said to myself I hope I ain't going to faint, but I guess I did. Though when I did, and how I got here, I don't exactly remember. *(She rests her head back on the ground.)* What day is it?

FENTRY: Christmas Eve.

SARAH: Is it the morning or the afternoon?

FENTRY: It's the late morning.

SARAH: Then I haven't been here too long. It was early in the morning on Christmas Eve when I started this way. *(She tries to get up.)*

FENTRY: Let me help you.

SARAH: Thank you. I think I'd better be getting on now.

(He gets her up, but she is still very weak and has to lean against Fentry.)

I'm sorry. I guess I will have to rest awhile longer. I haven't quite gotten my strength back.

FENTRY: Let me help you in here so you can rest by my fire. It's so raw and cold out here.

SARAH: Thank you. It has been a cold winter, hasn't it?

FENTRY: Yes'm.

SARAH: There was ice this morning early when I left the house. I seen it on the ditches as I passed.

FENTRY: Yes'm.

SARAH: I said to myself Jack Frost has been here.

FENTRY: He sure had.

(She is gasping for breath and holds on to him. They pause for a moment.)

SARAH: How far we got to go?

FENTRY: Just in this door here. Can you make it?

SARAH: Yes, sir. I can make that.

(They start on again slowly. They reach the doorway. She rests again by the doorway for a moment.)

Thank you. You say it's warm in here?

FENTRY: Oh, yes, ma'm.

(He helps her inside the door and to the chair. She sits slowly down and rests her head back against it as if this little exertion was made at great cost.)

You set here, Mrs.

SARAH: Thank you. *(She looks around.)* It is nice and warm in here. I love a good fire in the stove.

FENTRY: I could get it warmer. I was letting it die out because I was about to leave for my papa's farm for Christmas. *(He goes to the stove and starts to feed it wood.)*

SARAH: Don't go to no trouble for me. I can't stay more than a minute to get my strength back and to get some of the coldness out of my bones.

(A pause. She leans her head back against the chair again and closes her eyes. Jackson Fentry looks at her.)

FENTRY: Can I get you anything to eat?

SARAH: No, thank you. You'd think I'd be hungry, wouldn't you, thin as I am, and carrying a baby and all, but I don't have no appetite. I lost my appetite about three months ago and I can't ever seem to git it back again. I did used to love to eat, too. My, that fire feels good. *(She looks around.)* This where you live?

FENTRY: Yes, ma'm. Mr. Ben Quick is going to build me a house next spring to live in, but he told me to stay on out here for the time being. It's warm and dry and does for me.

SARAH: I think it's just fine. Have you been here long?

FENTRY: Over a year. Be two years this spring.

SARAH: Is your home near here?

FENTRY: No. I was raised thirty miles from here on a cotton farm I worked with my daddy. My mama is dead, my daddy is on the farm all alone now. You from around here?

SARAH: Sort of. Off an' on, that is. My husband never cared for this county and he was always trying to find work away from here. But he always had to come back.

FENTRY: Are you on your way home now?

SARAH: No, sir.

FENTRY: Were you going to the store at Frenchman's Bend? If you were, you sit right here and I'll go and get whatever it was you wanted.

SARAH: I wasn't going to the store.

FENTRY: Were you going into Jefferson?

SARAH: No, sir. I wasn't going no place. I was just going.

FENTRY: Just going? *(A pause.)* Is your husband dead?

SARAH: No, sir. He just disappeared three months ago when he heard about the baby coming. I stayed on with the people we were living with at the time as long as I could, but the last week two of their children got taken sick, and the husband was out of work, and they just couldn't do for me anymore. They didn't ask me to leave, but I just figured it would be easier on them if I did, so I got up this morning while they was still asleep and started out.

FENTRY: Don't you have any people?

SARAH: I have a Papa and three brothers.

FENTRY: Can't you go home to them?

SARAH: No, sir. They asked me to leave and never come back when I married my husband, and I don't ever intend to go back.

FENTRY: But when they know...

SARAH: I don't intend to ever go back. Not if they all got on their knees and begged me. Papa has his pride; and I've got mine. You live here all by yourself?

FENTRY: Yes, ma'm.

SARAH: You're not a married man?

FENTRY: No, ma'm.

SARAH: I get sick every winter time, it seems like to me. A woman come over to where I was staying and said, you look poorly. You ought to get a doctor. Nothing wrong with me that sunshine couldn't fix, I said. I don't care a whole lot for the winter time, do you?

FENTRY: No, ma'm. Do you want some more wood on the fire?

SARAH: No, it's just fine. *(She rubs her hands together.)* I love sunshine. When I started out this morning, I said to myself, I'm going, if my strength holds out, till I come to where it's warm and the sun is shining. *(A pause.)* Well, my strength didn't hold out very long.

(The wind whistles around the corners of the boiler room.)

Listen to that wind. I love to hear it when I'm inside like this and warm. Oh, but that wind was cold walking right into it, like I had to. It just cut through you like a knife. It knew no mercy. It... *(She begins to tremble.)* Lord, what's the matter with me? Look at me tremble, will you? Just the thought of that cold wind and I begin to shake and tremble... *(She closes her eyes.)*

FENTRY: Why don't you rest over here on the bed? You can't rest good in that chair.

SARAH: No. No. I can't stay.

FENTRY: Just for a minute.

SARAH: Well, all right, then. Just for a minute. *(She gets up slowly. She goes to the bed and lies down.)* This does feel good, Mr....

FENTRY: Fentry. Jackson Fentry. And you're Mrs....

SARAH: Eubanks. Sarah Eubanks. I was a Thorpe, but I married a Eubanks. If I have a girl, I'm going to name her Vesta after my mama. If I have a boy, I want him named... *(A pause.)* I don't know now. I was going to name him after my husband. I don't know now...

(The wind again howls around the boiler shed.)

Listen to that wind whipping around outside again. It sounds right friendly, don't it, when you're inside and warm this way listening to it. When I was a little girl of ten, my Mama died, and they say I got everything mixed up that winter, because I grieved so, and that I would wake all winter long, and when the wind would blow around my house, I would think it was my Mama calling me, and I would answer and call back to her and ask her where she was hiding. *(A pause.)* I never grieved no more after that. When I got over that, I vowed to myself nothing would break my heart ever again and it didn't for the longest kind of time.

(Fentry covers her with a screen he gets from outside that was protecting a tree. She has closed her eyes. She is soon asleep. Fentry stands watching over her as the lights are brought down. The lights are brought up downstage right. Walter, forty, stands behind a section of a store counter. Fentry comes into the store.)

WALTER: Hello, Fentry.

FENTRY: Hello.

WALTER: I thought you was going to your farm for Christmas.

FENTRY: I changed my mind.

WALTER: Where are you going?

FENTRY: No place.

WALTER: Are you spending it alone?

FENTRY: I reckon so. *(Fentry points to some candy.)* How much is that hard candy?

WALTER: Depends on how much you want to buy.

FENTRY: How much would four cents get me?

(Walter dips into the candy. He comes up with four cents worth.)

WALTER: I'd say this would do it.

FENTRY: Give me four cents worth.

(Walter takes the candy and puts it in a sack. Fentry gets four cents and hands it to him.)

WALTER: Thank you.

(Fentry goes out as the lights are brought down. The lights are brought up center on the boiler room. It is now dark. Sarah is still asleep in the bed. Fentry comes in and lights the kerosene lamp. He puts more wood in the stove. She wakes up as he is doing this.)

SARAH: Mr. Fentry?

(He turns around.)

FENTRY: Yes, ma'm.

SARAH: How long have I been asleep?

FENTRY: About ten hours.

SARAH: Ten hours?

FENTRY: Yes'm.

SARAH: Why didn't you wake me?

FENTRY: I figured the sleep would be good for you.

SARAH: My heavens.

FENTRY: You feel better?

SARAH: Yes, but I'm ashamed and mortified. I'm so sorry. You should have waked me, or gone on off…

FENTRY: I have no place to go.

SARAH: Aren't you going to your farm for Christmas?

FENTRY: No'm.

SARAH: I thought you said…

FENTRY: I changed my mind.

SARAH: What made you do that?

FENTRY: I just changed it.

(He goes back to put the wood in the fire. She watches him.)

SARAH: Is it still cold out yonder?

FENTRY: Yes, it is. Why don't you stay on here the rest of the night?

SARAH: Well…

FENTRY: I can make me a pallet on the floor here by the fire.

SARAH: Thank you, but I wouldn't care to put you out any.

FENTRY: You won't be putting me out.

SARAH: Have you had your supper yet?

FENTRY: No'm.

SARAH: Can I get it for you?

FENTRY: No'm, you stay on in bed. I can get it.

SARAH: I want to do something.

FENTRY: You can help me when you're stronger. *(He hands her the sack of hard candy.)* I went to the store and brought you this. I thought you might like it.

SARAH: I sure thank you. *(She opens it.)* It's hard candy. Well, I declare.

FENTRY: Merry Christmas.

SARAH: Thank you. Merry Christmas to you, too.

FENTRY: If I fixed you something to eat now, would you eat it?

SARAH: No, I'm still not hungry. I'll just have a taste of my Christmas candy. *(She cries.)*

FENTRY: What are you crying for, lady?

SARAH: I don't know. I'm just tired and nervous, I guess. I've been crying a lot lately. It don't mean anything; I quit as soon as I start. *(She wipes her eyes.)* See. I never used to cry before. When I was a girl, people used to accuse me of being hard hearted because nothing could get me to cry. When my papa told me I had to leave home after I married my husband, I didn't shed a tear. I said if that's how it has to be, that's how it has to be...but lately that's all changed. Somebody'd walk up to me and say good morning or good evening and I'll cry, or ask me what time is it, and I'll cry. Did you ever hear of anything like that? I didn't used to talk this way, either. I used to go a whole day without saying a word. And now I can't stand it silent or quiet. You know what worries me most about death?

FENTRY: No, ma'm.

SARAH: That it's silent in the grave. Nobody to talk to or to talk to you. *(She opens the candy and takes a piece.)* Oh, it's so good. *(She hands the sack to him.)* Will you have some?

FENTRY: No, thank you.

SARAH: Is it going to be a clear night?

FENTRY: Yes'm.

SARAH: Stars?

FENTRY: Yes'm.

SARAH: Who do you talk to out here when you get lonesome?

FENTRY: Nobody. There's no one out here in the winter time but me.

SARAH: Don't you miss having somebody to talk to?

FENTRY: Sometimes. *(A pause.)* Why don't you stay on out here until after your baby is born? I have enough to eat for us both. It's warm and dry here.

SARAH: Mr. Fentry...I...

FENTRY: Don't answer me now. You just think it over. I have to go and get us some more wood. You can tell me your answer when I come back.

SARAH: Yes sir.

(He goes on out. She sits up in bed eating a piece of candy. She looks around the boiler room. She seems resolved to go. She gets up out of the bed and starts weakly across the room. She opens the door. The wind comes whipping in. We can hear it roaring outside. She quickly shuts the door. She stands against the chair, panting and exhausted. Fentry comes in with the wood. He puts it down.)

FENTRY: It's even getting colder out there now. *(He goes to the stove to warm his hands.)*

SARAH: Did you mean what you said about my staying on here?

FENTRY: Yes'm.

SARAH: Then I'll stay. For to tell you the truth, I don't have the strength to go.

(She starts back across the room for the bed, as the lights are brought half down. The lights are brought up center. It is a month later. Fentry is outside chopping wood. Sarah comes outside the door.)

FENTRY: What are you doing out of bed?

SARAH: I feel better today. *(She stands in the doorway.)* It's warmer today.

FENTRY: Yes, it is.

(She comes out into the yard.)

SARAH: Do you know I've been here for a month?

FENTRY: A month and three days. *(He puts his ax down. He goes to her.)* You better go back inside. It's still raw and cold out here.

SARAH: All right.

(She goes inside the boiler room. He follows after her. She sits on the chair. He brings in an armful of wood. He puts it in the stove. He goes over to the chair.)

FENTRY: Marry me, Sarah?

SARAH: I can't marry you. I've told you that. I have a husband somewhere.

FENTRY: He's deserted you.

SARAH: I can't help it. We're married in the sight of the law.

(Isham Quick comes into the boiler room. He sees Sarah sitting there. He seems embarrassed and surprised.)

ISHAM: I'm sorry, Fentry. I didn't know you had company.

(He goes back outside. Fentry follows him out the door.)

Who is that?

FENTRY: My wife.

ISHAM: Since when? You didn't have her Christmas Eve when I was out here. You didn't…

FENTRY: She's my wife. Do you want us to leave?

ISHAM: What do I want you to leave for? I don't care what you do out here. I didn't come here to spy. You can have twenty wives out here for all I care. I just came to get you to go hunting.

FENTRY: Some other time.

ISHAM: All right. Papa said to tell you to pick out the site of where you want your house. And you and me can start building it this spring.

FENTRY: I know where I want it to be.

ISHAM: Show me where it is while I'm out here. Maybe if we have a warm day any time soon I'll get Papa out to look it over.

FENTRY: All right.

(They go. When they are out of sight, Sarah comes back to the door. She is looking for Fentry. She doesn't see him and starts back inside, toward the bed. On her way she has a quick seizure of pain. She winces, pauses, and then goes on to the bed. Fentry comes into the room.)

SARAH: It's time. You'd better get Mrs. Hulie here.

FENTRY: I will.

(He hurries out the door. Isham is still in the yard.)

FENTRY: Will you do me a favor, Isham?

ISHAM: Sure.

FENTRY: Will you ride over to Mrs. Hulie's, the midwife, and tell her to come out here right away?

ISHAM: I'll be glad to.

(He hurries off, Fentry goes back into the house. Sarah is on the bed.)

FENTRY: I got Isham to go for me.

SARAH: Who's he?

FENTRY: The man that came up just now. His pa owns the sawmill.

SARAH: Was he surprised to see me out there?

FENTRY: I reckon.

SARAH: Did he ask who I was?

FENTRY: Yes, ma'm.

SARAH; What did you tell him?

FENTRY: I said you were my wife.

(She shivers.)

Are you cold again?

SARAH: Yes, all of a sudden. Is there wood in the fire?

FENTRY: Yes, there is. Want me to put some more in?

SARAH: If you don't mind.

(He goes to the stove and puts the wood in.)

FENTRY: It's red hot now. It'll have this room like an oven before too long. *(He goes over to her.)* Isham and his papa wanted me to decide where I'd like my house built. I showed him. I think I have a nice place picked out. When you're stronger, I'll show you.

SARAH: I'd like to see. *(She has a sudden spasm of pain. She grabs his arm.)* I'm afraid.

FENTRY: What of?

SARAH: I'm afraid I'm gonna die. I don't want to die…

FENTRY: From childbirth? You won't die from that. You'll get up from here feeling just fine. Lots of women…

SARAH: No, I'm not afraid of childbirth…

FENTRY: Of what, then?

SARAH: I don't know. I'm tired and worn out, and my spirits are low…

FENTRY: You'll feel better afterwards, you'll see. Carrying the baby has worn you out.

(She has another seizure of pain.)

SARAH: Fentry. Fentry.

(He holds her.)

I ain't had much in my life, and that's the truth. Work and hunger and pain. I'm afraid. I'm afraid. I don't want to die.

FENTRY: You're not going to die. You hear me. You are not going to die. I won't let you. I promise you.

(She relaxes and lies back on the bed.)

You hear me?

(She closes her eyes.)

Are you warmer now?

SARAH: Yes, thank you.

FENTRY: Try and sleep now until Mrs. Hulie gets here. Try and rest.

SARAH: All right. Don't leave me if I sleep.

FENTRY: I won't.

SARAH: In the summer time it's warm in the day and in the night. In the summer the sun burns and cooks the coldness and tiredness out of you. *(She holds her hand out to him.)* Don't leave me.

FENTRY: I won't. I ain't going to never leave you, unless you ask me to. Never. Never.

(She closes her eyes. He watches for a moment. He goes back outside and starts to chop the wood. Sarah wakes up and sees he's not there.)

SARAH: *(Screaming.)* Fentry! Fentry!

(He comes running in to her.)

FENTRY: What's the matter?

SARAH: Don't leave me. Please, please don't leave me.

FENTRY: I won't. I won't. I was just out there chopping wood. We'll need it for the fire.

SARAH: All right. I'm sorry. I'll be all right.

(She closes her eyes. She has another little spasm of pain but doesn't call for him this time. She manages to survive it by herself. She falls back on the bed again and is soon half asleep. Fentry comes in and puts the screen in front of her and sits at table right. Mrs. Hulie, the midwife, a large, buxom woman, fifty, comes from behind the screen.)

MRS. HULIE: The baby's here. A fine boy.

FENTRY: Thank you.

MRS. HULIE: I'm worried about the Mama. She's not doing too well. I ain't going to lie to you, Mr. Fentry. I think she is in a serious condition. She asked me straight out how she was, and I told her I didn't think she was too well, and she asked me to tell you that.

FENTRY: Yes, ma'm.

MRS. HULIE: She says she's afraid she's going to die and that she will never get up off that bed in there. And I hate to tell you this, but I don't think she will either.

FENTRY: What is it? Was it having the baby?

MRS. HULIE: No. She was sick long before the baby. She's just played out it seems to me.

FENTRY: Yes, ma'm. I'll make her rest. I'll take care of her. I'll nurse her.

MRS. HULIE: She wants to see you now.

(Mrs. Hulie removes the screen and goes outside. The woman seems exhausted and completely spent, as if the childbirth had taken her last bit of energy. He goes over to her on the bed. He looks down at her. She has the baby beside her.)

SARAH: Ain't it small?

FENTRY: Yes, it is.

SARAH: Not a bit pretty, is it?

FENTRY: New babies never are, they tell me.

SARAH: How many new babies you seen in your life?

FENTRY: Not too many.

SARAH: It's a boy.

FENTRY: That's what Mrs. Hulie said.

SARAH: So I don't guess it matters if he's pretty or not. He's light complected, like me.

FENTRY: It's a fine-looking baby. *(He puts his hand down and takes hold of the baby's hand.)* Hello, son. Welcome. *(He looks over at Sarah.)* Can I git you something to eat?

SARAH: No.

FENTRY: You got to eat. You got to keep your strength up.

SARAH: I'm not hungry.

   (He looks down at the baby.)

FENTRY: Can I hold the baby?

SARAH: Sure.

   (He takes the baby in his arms. He cuddles it against his body.)
   Fentry...

FENTRY: Yes'm.

SARAH: If anything does happen to me, will you promise me you'll take care of the baby?

FENTRY: Nothing is going to happen to you.

SARAH: If it does?

FENTRY: Then you can rest easy. I'll always take care of him.

SARAH: The same as if it was yours?

FENTRY: The same as if it was mine.

SARAH: Thank you.

   (She watches him move around the room holding the baby.)
   Fentry...

FENTRY: Yes?

SARAH: If you still want to marry me, I'm willing now. My husband might be dead for all I know, and if he's not, he's gone so far, I'll never find him again. He told me that when he left, I'd never see him again or find him again and not to try. So even if we had the money for a divorce, it come to me lying here, how can you divorce a man you can't find? *(A pause.)* And so I thought why can't Fentry and I get married now, if he still wants to marry me.

FENTRY: I want to marry you.

SARAH: Can you get anybody to marry us right away?

FENTRY: Yes. Preacher Whitehead. He lives seven miles from here.

SARAH: Would you go get him now?

FENTRY: I will. *(He puts the baby beside her.)*

SARAH: How far does he live?

FENTRY: About seven miles. I'll have him here before morning.

SARAH: Thank you. Will you hurry?

FENTRY: I will.

> *(He hurries outside the door. She looks down at the baby beside her. Mrs. Hulie comes into the room.)*

MRS. HULIE: You know, I've placed you. Weren't you a Thorpe? Didn't you have a papa and three brothers and live with them on a farm back yonder? *(Sarah looks at her and nods her head yes but doesn't say anything.)* Don't you think they should be sent for at a time like this?

SARAH: I don't want them to know anything about me.

MRS. HULIE: I found some flour sacks over there that I split in two for you. When Mr. Fentry comes back, I'll show him how they can be used for diapers.

SARAH: Thank you.

MRS. HULIE: Do you have any money to buy the baby clothes?

SARAH: No.

MRS. HULIE: Have you picked a name to call your baby?

SARAH: No, I'll let my husband name him.

MRS. HULIE: Your husband?

SARAH: Mr. Fentry. We're going to be married. He's gone now to get the preacher.

MRS. HULIE: That's nice. *(She goes over to Sarah.)* Here, let me take the baby and I'll put him in this box Mr. Fentry and I fixed up for a crib, and you try to get some sleep now.

SARAH: Thank you.

> *(Mrs. Hulie takes the baby and puts him in a box in the corner of the room.)* Is it cold in here, Mrs. Hulie?

MRS. HULIE: No, honey. It's hot as everything.

SARAH: I'm cold. I'm so cold.

MRS. HULIE: Are you?

SARAH: Why am I so cold?

MRS. HULIE: I don't know, honey. But try and sleep. Maybe you'll forget about the cold if you can sleep.

> *(Sarah closes her eyes. Mrs. Hulie sits in the chair as the lights are brought*

down. The lights are brought upstage center. It is six hours later, and almost daylight. Mrs. Hulie is asleep in her chair. Fentry and Preacher Whitehead come into the room. Whitehead is in his fifties, a strong, kind man. Fentry lights a lantern. He goes over to Sarah's bed. He looks down at her asleep. She opens her eyes.)

FENTRY: I have the preacher here.

SARAH: All right.

(Mrs. Hulie has awakened. She sees Fentry and the preacher and she comes over to the bed.)

MRS. HULIE: Hello, Preacher.

PREACHER: Hello, Mrs. Hulie. *(The Preacher takes his Bible out of his pocket. He goes over to the edge of the bed and looks down at Sarah.)* Hello, Mrs.

SARAH: Hello, Preacher.

(Mrs. Hulie gets the lantern and brings it over and holds it by the preacher.)

PREACHER: "Dearly Beloved, we are gathered together here in the sight of God." Jackson Fentry, do you take this woman to be your lawful wedded wife?

FENTRY: I do.

PREACHER: What's your name, Mrs.?

SARAH: Sarah Eubanks.

PREACHER: Sarah Eubanks, do you take this man to be your lawful wedded husband?

SARAH: I do.

PREACHER: Then I pronounce you man and wife.

(Sarah closes her eyes. Mrs. Hulie and the preacher go to a corner of the room to look at the baby.)

SARAH: How is the fire, Fentry?

FENTRY: Are you cold?

SARAH: I'm so cold.

(He goes over to the stove and feeds it. He goes back to her.)

FENTRY: I don't dare put no more wood in it. It's red hot now.

SARAH: While you were gone, I had a terrible dream that I was freezing to death. I never seen snow and I don't know what it feels like or looks like, but in my dreams I kept saying I'm drowning in the cold, I'm drowning in the snow, and I was calling to you to save me.

(She shivers. He covers her.)

FENTRY: And didn't I save you?

SARAH: I don't know. I woke up when I was calling you, and there you were standing right by me. I want you to name the baby if you want to.

FENTRY: Thank you. I'd like to. When I brought the preacher here, I passed by the place where our house is going to be. It's going to have three rooms and a little porch for us to sit on. It'll have some pretty trees all around it…a hackberry tree and a chinaberry tree and an oak tree. *(He looks down at her.)* Are you feeling better now?

SARAH: Yes. Have you thought of a name for the baby yet?

FENTRY: No'm. I've been studying about it but I haven't thought of one yet.

SARAH: Will you bring me the baby?

FENTRY: Yes, ma'm. Are you all right?

SARAH: *(Weakly.)* Yes. Just get my baby, please.

(He goes over to the box and gets the baby. He comes back to Sarah and is about to give it to her when he looks down at her face. She is dead. He is not able yet to accept this.)

FENTRY: Sarah, I've got the baby here for you, Sarah. *(Calling.)* Mrs. Hulie. Preacher Whitehead.

(Mrs. Hulie and the preacher come to the bedside of the woman. Mrs. Hulie feels her pulse.)

MRS. HULIE: She's dead, Fentry.

FENTRY: No, she's not going to die. She is going to be all right. I'm going to save her.

MRS. HULIE: You can't save her now, Fentry. She's dead.

(Fentry doesn't protest any longer. He stands looking at Sarah. Mrs. Hulie takes the baby from him. The preacher puts his hand on his shoulder for a moment, then walks outside the boiler room. Mrs. Hulie puts the baby back in the box and goes outside after the preacher. Fentry stands for a beat longer looking at his wife.)

FENTRY: I don't know why we met when we did or why I found you when you was all wore out, and I couldn't save you no matter how bad I wanted to. I don't know why you wanted me to raise this baby instead of your people. I don't know what they done to you to make you turn so on them, but I don't care. I promised you I'd raise him, and I will. Like he was my own. *(He goes over to the box and looks down at the baby.)* Your mama is dead, son. But I'm gonna take care of you and see to you. I'll be your mama and your papa. You'll never want or do without while I have a breath of life in my bones.

(He goes outside. The preacher and Mrs. Hulie are huddled there. Day light is breaking in the east.)

PREACHER: Are you going to bury her or are you going to look for her people?

FENTRY: I'm going to bury her. I'm going into the woods now to look for a place. Will you help me?

PREACHER: I'll be glad to. When do you want the burial?

FENTRY: Right away. I'm going to take the baby and go back to my farm today.

MRS. HULIE: Have you ever taken care of a baby before?

FENTRY: No.

MRS. HULIE: Course you're gonna have to find a way to feed it. A cow's expensive to keep in the winter even if you had the money to buy one. I think you ought to get a goat to give you your milk.

FENTRY: Yes, ma'm.

MRS. HULIE: I have one I'll sell you cheap. Do you wanna go by my place and pick it up?

FENTRY: I sure do thank you.

MRS. HULIE: Do you know anything about goats?

FENTRY: No, ma'm.

MRS. HULIE: A goat ain't like a cow. You have to milk it every two hours.

FENTRY: Yes'm.

MRS. HULIE: That means nights, too.

FENTRY: Yes'm. I'd be much obliged if you all would wait here for me while I go pick out a place to bury her in.

MRS. HULIE: You go on. I'll go stay with the baby.

FENTRY: Thank you.

(Mrs. Hulie goes into the house and over to the baby. Fentry clears as the lights fade. The lights are brought up and the preacher and Fentry are standing by Sarah Eubank's grave. The preacher is reading from the Bible.)

PREACHER: "I am the resurrection and the life; he that believeth in me, though he were dead, yet shall he live: And whosoever liveth and believeth in me shall never die. Believest thou this?"

(He closes the Bible. He goes out. Fentry is left alone. Goes off as the lights fade. The lights are brought up in the cabin area. Mrs. Hulie is there beside the baby. We hear a goat "baaing" offstage.)

MRS. HULIE: Baby, I guess that's your papa come back with your goat.

(Fentry comes in the door.)

FENTRY: I tied my goat to the tree over there.

MRS. HULIE: Do you think you'll know how to milk her?

FENTRY: Yes, ma'm.

MRS. HULIE: Well, I'll be going on then.

FENTRY: Thank you for your kindness.

MRS. HULIE: It was nothing.

(*She leaves and exits left. Fentry begins to wrap in a newspaper the few things that belong to him. Isham Quick comes into the room from right.*)

ISHAM: I just heard about your wife, Fentry. I'm so sorry.

FENTRY: Thank you. I was just going to the house and tell your papa I have to quit. Me and the baby are going back to my pa's farm to live.

ISHAM: Are you going to walk them thirty miles?

FENTRY: No. I'm going to hire me a buggy to ride us.

ISHAM: Us?

FENTRY: Me and the baby.

ISHAM: Where is the baby?

FENTRY: Yonder.

(*He points to the box. Isham goes and looks down at it.*)

I'm taking a goat that's out there with me too. I just bought her from Mrs. Hulie because she says a goat's milk is as good as a cow's for a baby.

ISHAM: Come on. Get the baby and get the goat, and I'll have Pa loan me his buggy, and I'll drive you to your farm.

FENTRY: How much will you charge me?

ISHAM: It won't cost you anything.

FENTRY: No, sir. I want to pay. I can pay. I was counting on that.

ISHAM: It won't cost you anything. Come on. Get your baby.

(*Fentry goes to the box and picks the baby up. He holds the baby under one arm and the box under the other.*)

Give me the box and I'll carry that.

(*Fentry gives him the box. He picks up his newspaper package of clothes.*)

Where did you bury his mother?

FENTRY: Over yonder in the woods at the place where I was going to build the house. The preacher helped me.

ISHAM: Did she have a family anywhere around here?

FENTRY: She never said.

ISHAM: Her husband…

FENTRY: She never said…

ISHAM: Come on then.

(*Isham starts out. Fentry follows, carrying the baby, as the lights are brought down.*)

The lights are brought up on the Fentry porch yard and fields. Fentry's father, work worn, older than his years, is sitting on the porch. Fentry and Isham come into the yard.

FENTRY: Hello, Papa.

PAPA FENTRY: Hello, Fentry.

FENTRY: I'm home.

PAPA FENTRY: I see you are.

FENTRY: I'm home for good.

PAPA FENTRY: Is that so?

FENTRY: Papa, this is Isham Quick. His daddy owned the sawmill I worked in.

ISHAM: Howdy, Mr. Fentry.

PAPA FENTRY: Howdy.

> *(They shake hands.)*
>
> I was looking for you Christmas day, Fentry.

FENTRY: Yessir, I know but I couldn't get here Christmas day.

> *(Papa Fentry looks down at the baby.)*

PAPA FENTRY: Who does that belong to?

FENTRY: Me. It's my baby, Papa. I got married.

PAPA FENTRY: Where's your wife?

FENTRY: She died.

> *(Papa Fentry looks down at the baby.)*

PAPA FENTRY: Is this your baby?

FENTRY: Yessir.

PAPA FENTRY: Boy or girl?

FENTRY: Boy.

PAPA FENTRY: What you name it?

FENTRY: I thought I would name it after the two generals you served under. Jackson and Longstreet. If it's all right with you.

PAPA FENTRY: It's fine with me. *(He goes to the baby and Fentry. He takes him from his son.)* Come here to me, Jackson and Longstreet Fentry. *(He stands holding him and looking at him.)*

ISHAM: Well, you don't need me for nothing else now, so I'll be going on home.

FENTRY: I sure thank you.

ISHAM: That's all right.

> *(They shake hands.)*

ISHAM: Good luck.

FENTRY: Good luck to you.

(Isham goes off)

PAPA FENTRY: Is he a good baby, boy?

FENTRY: He is. How you been making out, Papa?

PAPA FENTRY: Pretty well.

FENTRY: How's that man I hired to help you been?

PAPA FENTRY: He's all right. I guess this is the reason I didn't see you Christmas.

FENTRY: Yes, sir.

PAPA FENTRY: I'm sorry I never got to meet your wife. What was her name?

FENTRY: Mary.

PAPA FENTRY: What did she die of?

FENTRY: She jus' died. She was poorly when I met her.

PAPA FENTRY: None of us Fentrys have luck with their wives. Your mama died when she warn't thirty. My mama didn't live to see thirty-four. How old was your wife when she died, son?

FENTRY: I don't know. I never asked her.

PAPA FENTRY: Think we can raise him?

FENTRY: I think we can.

PAPA FENTRY: My God, he's small. I'd forgotten how small they was. Well, if he's yours, he's welcome.

(Fentry takes the baby.)

FENTRY: His milk comes from that goat outside. You have to milk it every two hours. Nights too. A goat ain't no cow. I'll keep him in the room with me. As soon as he's old enough to take with me, I'll start helping around the farm again. You still have that man helping you out, don't you?

PAPA FENTRY: Yes, I do.

FENTRY: I asked the Pruitts to look in at you while I was gone. Did they do it?

PAPA FENTRY: They have. Near about ever day. One or t'other of them come over snooping around. What was the name of your wife again, son?

FENTRY: Sally...

PAPA FENTRY: That wasn't the name you said before, boy.

FENTRY: Wasn't it?

PAPA FENTRY: No, sir. I could have sworn before you said Mary.

FENTRY: I expect I did. She had a double name, Sally Mary. Sometimes I'd call her one and sometimes the other.

PAPA FENTRY: Sally Mary what?

FENTRY: Smith.

PAPA FENTRY: Did her people live up around Frenchman's Bend?

FENTRY: No, sir, she come from the northern part of the state.

(Mrs. Pruitt calls from offstage.)

MRS. PRUITT: Mr. Fentry.

(Papa Fentry goes over to Fentry.)

PAPA FENTRY: I think that's Mrs. Pruitt. You want her to know you're here?

FENTRY: I don't care, Papa.

PAPA FENTRY: We're right here, Mrs. Pruitt.

(Mrs. Pruitt enters.)

MRS. PRUITT: Hello, Jackson. Was that you come driving up in the buggy?

FENTRY: Yes'm.

MRS. PRUITT: Welcome home.

FENTRY: Thank you.

MRS. PRUITT: I see you have a new goat in your yard, Mr. Fentry.

PAPA FENTRY: It's Jackson's. He brought it home with him from Frenchman's Bend to feed his baby.

MRS. PRUITT: His baby?

PAPA FENTRY: He married him a wife while he was up at the sawmill, but his wife died and he brung his baby home to raise.

MRS. PRUITT: Where is your baby, Jackson?

FENTRY: Yonder in that box.

(Mrs. Pruitt goes over to the box and looks down at the baby.)

MRS. PRUITT: Boy or girl?

FENTRY: Boy.

MRS. PRUITT: How old is he?

FENTRY: Three days old.

PAPA FENTRY: His wife died when he was born.

MRS. PRUITT: What was the name of your wife, son?

FENTRY: Mary Sally Smith.

MRS. PRUITT: Was she from around there?

FENTRY: No'm. She was from down state.

MRS. PRUITT: I'm so sorry to hear about it. Have you named your baby?

FENTRY: Yes'm. Jackson and Longstreet Fentry. Pa fit under them both.

MRS. PRUITT: The baby doesn't have any clothes on, son.

FENTRY: No'm. I didn't have any for him. I'm going to have to make him some.

MRS. PRUITT: Have you got any diapers for the baby?

FENTRY: I've been using flour sacks. Mrs. Hulie, the midwife over in Frenchman's Bend showed me how to tear them in half so I could use them for diapers.

MRS. PRUITT: Well, I'll make some diapers for you, Fentry, and bring them over this evening.

FENTRY: Yes, ma'm. I don't want you to bother.

MRS. PRUITT: It's no bother. If there is anything I can do, will you let me know?

FENTRY: Yes, ma'm.

MRS. PRUITT: Why don't you let me take the baby on home with me?

FENTRY: No, thank you...

MRS. PRUITT: At least until it can be weaned?

FENTRY: No'm, I...

MRS. PRUITT: You can stay at my house, too, if you want to.

FENTRY: Thank you. But I can make out.

MRS. PRUITT: Well, all right. But you call me if you change your mind.

FENTRY: I will.

(She goes on out. He starts toward the baby. Papa Fentry watches him for a moment.)

PAPA FENTRY: Son, you'd better get the name of your wife straight. You told me it was Sally Mary Smith. You told Mrs. Pruitt it was Mary Sally Smith.

FENTRY: Well...

PAPA FENTRY: Which one was it?

(A pause.)

FENTRY: It wasn't neither. It was Sarah Eubanks. And she came from near Frenchman's Bend, though where, I don't know.

PAPA FENTRY: Well, why do you want to keep this a secret?

FENTRY: Papa, I'm not the baby's father. I met his Mama after his father had deserted her. She was sick and I took her into my house and took care of her. Right after the baby was born, we was married. I promised her I'd keep the boy and raise it, like it was my own. And I will, too.

PAPA FENTRY: Well, that's fine but what if some day her kin hear about this baby and try to find it and come and try to take him away from you?

FENTRY: That's never going to happen because I'm never going to leave him or let him leave me until he's grown. You'll have to make all the trips into town even to buy the groceries. I'll stay here and do the cooking and the washing and the cleaning and the nursing. *(He goes to the baby.)* Nobody is going to take him from me, Papa.

(Thornton Douglas appears again right.)

THORNTON DOUGLAS: And he raised that boy. I don't know how he was at sawmilling and he never had enough of a farm to find out if he was any good at farming, but he raised that boy all by himself. When the boy was old enough, he took him to the fields with him. In the late summer the boy could walk pretty good and he made him a little hoe out of a stick and a scrap of shingle and you could see Jackson chopping, in the middle high cotton, but you couldn't see the boy at all; you could just see the cotton shaking where he was. Mrs. Pruitt says the first time she saw him hiding in the fields that way she thought of a setter puppy or a fox or a wolf cub somebody had caught just last night. And then about three years later, the sheriff and Les and Dave Thorpe, the two brothers of Sarah Eubanks, moved in on Isham Quick at the sawmill. They wanted information on the child and Isham had no chance to warn him and no choice but to take them to Jackson Fentry.

(Thornton Douglas leaves the stage as Papa Fentry comes out of the house onto porch with milk. Fentry comes from cotton patch upstage left holding the boy. Hands glass to boy.)

FENTRY: Here boy, drink this. You know boy, it won't be long before it'll be time to go into Jefferson again to see about paying our taxes. Remember, son, to always pay your taxes. This land's all we got. It's gonna be yours someday to work it like me and your grandpa do. It isn't the best land in the world for sure, but it's ours to keep as long as we pay the taxes. You finished? Want some more? Going to be a fine morning.

PAPA FENTRY: Yes.

FENTRY: My boy here is going to be three years old tomorrow. Aren't you boy?

PAPA FENTRY: I hear yesterday the well gave out down the road. *(A pause.)* Jackson and Longstreet is small for three years old. He's quick though. He can run like the wind. *(Looks at Fentry.)* You was always small for your age too. Mrs. Pruitt said the other day when she came around "that boy is like Fentry. He don't talk much." He talks I said when he's got something to say. "He's never talked to me," she said. Well then he's got nothing to say to you I said. "Does he and Fentry ever talk to each other?" Not much I said unless they got something to say. "We call'm the son and moon," she said, "take away one you wouldn't have the other."
(Mrs. Pruitt enters from upstage right.)

MRS. PRUITT: How you folks this morning? Why he's gonna have black hair and I thought he was gonna be tow headed when I first seen him. Did your wife have black hair, Fentry?

FENTRY: No. She was fair.

MRS. PRUITT: Someone said the other day I vow Fentry never leaves the farm. I never seen him at all without that boy tagging behind him. I said you ain't likely to see them without each other. Why, I said, the only time I know Jackson and that boy to be separated as much as one full breath is when Jackson rides into Jefferson once a year to pay his taxes. I hope you won't mind my doing this, but I had some extra time and I had some cloth I couldn't use and I decided to make some clothes for your boy.

FENTRY: Thank you.

MRS. PRUITT: I hope you don't mind my interfering, but I knew how much you had to do without making his clothes and…

FENTRY: I don't mind that none. But I thank you, anyway. Come on, boy. We have to get to work.

(They exit into house.)

PAPA FENTRY: I hope he didn't hurt your feelings none. He wants to do everything for that boy himself. Sometimes I think he begrudges the earth itself for what the boy has to eat to keep alive.

MRS. PRUITT: I understand. I'm not sensitive. Well, I've got to get home and get on to my work. *(She goes.)*

PAPA FENTRY: I'm going out to the field now. *(He goes off behind house.)*

FENTRY: Yessir. *(He comes out holding his son. He looks up at the sky.)* Boy, look way up there. You know what this is flying around? That's a chicken hawk. And you know what they do? They catch and kill your chickens if you got any. And some day when you're big enough, I'm going to git you a gun, and we'll shoot chicken hawks together. *(He puts the boy down.)* Now run on and play, boy, while your daddy finishes his work. Don't go far, Jackson and Longstreet. Come over here and stay closer to me. *(Fentry starts to sharpen a sickle. Isham and the two Thorpe men come into the yard.)*

ISHAM: Howdy, Fentry.

FENTRY: Howdy.

ISHAM: Remember me?

FENTRY: Yes, I do.

ISHAM: How you been?

FENTRY: Pretty well. How you been?

ISHAM: That your boy? That Jackson and Longstreet?

FENTRY: Yes, it is.

ISHAM: Hi, boy.

FENTRY: Say hello to Mr. Isham, son.

ISHAM: When I got back home after bringing you all here, I went out to the woods and put a marker on your wife's grave.

FENTRY: Thank you for your trouble.

ISHAM: Ain't no trouble. I was glad to do it. These here are your wife's brothers, Dave and Les Thorpe.

FENTRY: Howdy.

LES AND DAVE: Howdy.

FENTRY: What can I do for you?

DAVE: I've come for the boy.

FENTRY: What boy?

LES: That boy.

FENTRY: You can't have him. He's my boy.

DAVE: I got a paper from the sheriff. We're gonna have him.

FENTRY: He's my boy.

LES: It's our sister's boy. She had a legal husband so your marriage don't count for nothing. His father gave him to us. He's our son. We want our own flesh and blood to raise ourselves. He belongs with us.

ISHAM: I'm gonna ask you one last time. Don't take the boy away from him. He took that boy as his own when nobody came to claim him. He has raised him, clothed, and fed him for three years. You can't walk up after three years...

DAVE: We want him and we aim to have him. We'll pay you for your trouble and for what the boy cost you.

FENTRY: Run, boy. Run to the field to grandpa.

(The boy runs off. Fentry takes the sickle and starts for the nearest Thorpe. Isham sees what he is about to do and grabs the sickle as a Thorpe grabs Fentry. Fentry begins a terrible struggle as all three men try to hold him down.)

ISHAM: Stop, Fentry. Stop. There's nothing you can do for now. They have the law on their side.

LES: Dave, catch and get the boy and take him to the surrey.

(Dave runs behind house, grabs boy, puts him in sack, and runs off. Fentry jerks until the boy is out of sight.)

FENTRY: *(Screaming.)* Jackson and Longstreet! Jackson and Longstreet!

(Then he collapses as though his bones have all turned to water. Isham and Les Thorpe put him down on the chopping block as though he had no bones at all.)

ISHAM: They can take the boy, Fentry. It's the law. Her husband is still alive. He gave the boy to them. I didn't want to bring them here but the Sheriff said he would find you...

FENTRY: I know it, I been expecting it. I reckon that's why it's taken me so by surprise. *(A pause.)* I'm all right now.

LES: We're sorry for it. We never found out about none of it until last week, but he's our kin. We want him home. You done well by him and we thank you. His mother thanks you. Here.

(He takes the money purse out of his pocket and puts it into Fentry's hand and turns and goes. Isham stays beside Fentry. He walks a few steps away, and then after a beat, he comes back to Fentry.)

ISHAM: They're gone.

(Fentry lies on the ground. He doesn't hear him.)

The sheriff come with them to the sawmill. They had a paper. But there's two sides to the law, Fentry. We'll go into town and talk to Captain Stevens. My pa knows him. I'll go with you.

(Fentry sits up. He gets up slowly. He is very stiff. He isn't panting so hard now and he looks better except for his eyes which are dazed looking. Then he raises the hand holding the money purse in it and starts to mop his face with it as though it were a handkerchief. It is then he realizes what is in his hand. He takes his hand down, looks at the money purse for about five seconds, and then tosses it as you would a handful of dirt. He gets up and walks across the yard toward the woods. He walks straight, not fast, offstage. Isham watches for a beat and then calls.)

Fentry! Fentry!

(Fentry doesn't answer him but keeps going. Papa Fentry comes in. He goes to Isham.)

PAPA FENTRY: Who are you?

ISHAM: I met you a long time ago, Mr. Fentry. I brought your boy home from the sawmill.

PAPA FENTRY: Where is Jackson?

(Isham doesn't answer him.)

Where's his boy?

ISHAM: A sad thing has happened, Mr. Fentry. His wife's brothers came and took the boy away from him. They say she had a husband. That the child is theirs.

PAPA FENTRY: Where did Fentry go?

(Isham points toward the woods.)

ISHAM: I'm sorry.

PAPA FENTRY: I thank you to go now.

ISHAM: I tried to talk them out of coming. I wanted to come on ahead and warn him, but I couldn't and they had the law…

(The old man turns and goes into the house. Mrs. Pruitt comes into the yard. She goes to Isham.)

MRS. PRUITT: Is there trouble, Mister?

ISHAM: They took the little boy from him.

MRS. PRUITT: Oh.

(She goes into the house. Thornton Douglas again appears right.)

THORNTON DOUGLAS: Yes. He saw happen what he had been expecting to see every time the sun rose for going on three years now and he had disappeared that morning—just gone. The house was empty and his Pa worked the place like he used to in the next five years because folks in this country haven't had time to learn anything but work.

(Papa Fentry enters from house. Sits on porch.)

Where Fentry was, God knows. Perhaps he got himself another day wage job not to get rich, just to earn a little extra money, against the life his grandpa led until he died between two plow handles one day, and his pa would lead—until he died in a corn furor and then it would be his turn and not even no son to come and pick him up out of the dirt. Five years and he came back just the way he had disappeared. There he was one morning.

(Thornton Douglas leaves as Fentry comes into yard. Fentry sees his father and goes toward him.)

FENTRY: Papa…

(His father goes to him.)

PAPA FENTRY: Welcome home, son.

FENTRY: Thank you. How have you been?

PAPA FENTRY: Pretty well. How have you been?

FENTRY: Pretty fair.

PAPA FENTRY: Where did you go Fentry?

FENTRY: All over. I farmed some cotton in Texas. I worked in some sugar fields in Louisiana. I… *(Walks to fields.)* How's the crop?

PAPA FENTRY: Pretty fair.

FENTRY: I'm home to stay. I'll start back to work tomorrow.

PAPA FENTRY: Are you hungry?

FENTRY: No.

PAPA FENTRY: How're things down in Texas?

FENTRY: Pretty fair.

PAPA FENTRY: What kind of land they got down that way?

FENTRY: It's good land. Place I worked in Texas would grow anything. They got two yields a year out of their cotton.

PAPA FENTRY: Black dirt or red?

FENTRY: Black.

PAPA FENTRY: What were the folks like?

FENTRY: Same as around here.

PAPA FENTRY: Did you see any cowboys in Texas?

FENTRY: I seen a man call himself one.

PAPA FENTRY: I hear they got mean horses down there.

FENTRY: I wouldn't know. We had mules place I worked.

PAPA FENTRY: I knew a man once went to Louisiana said he couldn't understand a thing people said. They didn't speak English. Could you understand them son?

FENTRY: Yessir. They had funny names but I could understand what they said.

PAPA FENTRY: I was over at Frenchman's Bend last month. I heard where
Jackson and Longstreet was living at. He lives on a cotton farm with his
uncles. I rode my mule over there after I heard and I seen him. I passed
him on the road. I knowed it was him. His hair was still just as black and
shiny. I said, "Hi, Jackson and Longstreet. Remember me?" "No, sir," he
said, "and my name ain't Jackson and Longstreet," he says. "It's Thorpe.
Buck Thorpe." *(A pause.)* He's eight years old now, son, and a fine-looking boy. But he didn't know at all who I was.

(He looks up at Fentry. Fentry's expression hasn't changed as he listened to the story.)
Are you home for good now?

FENTRY: Yessir.

PAPA FENTRY: I've been using the hired hand since you were gone. He's out
back. I reckon I'd better go fire him now.

FENTRY: Yessir.

*(Papa Fentry goes on back. Fentry looks at the house for a minute. Mrs.
Pruitt comes into the yard.)*

MRS. PRUITT: When did you get home?

FENTRY: I just came.

MRS. PRUITT: Where you been?

FENTRY: Texas. I don't know where all. *(He starts for the house.)*

MRS. PRUITT: You're looking well. *(A pause.)* I know your Papa was glad to see
you. It's looked lonesome over here since...I used to hate to come over
here it was so quiet and lonesome. Of course, I did come over every once
in awhile because I thought someone should see about your Papa. I didn't
know where you were. I said to my son, "last time Fentry went away, he
told us. This time I don't know what's happened." Fentry...

FENTRY: Yes'm.

MRS. PRUITT: What happened to him?

FENTRY: What happened to who?

MRS. PRUITT: The boy. Your Papa would never say. Did he die?

FENTRY: What boy?

(Fentry goes into house. Mrs. Pruitt goes off right as the lights fade. Thornton Douglas appears again downstage right.)

THORNTON DOUGLAS: What boy! If they ever mentioned the boy again, nobody ever heard it in the next twelve years. What boy! It don't take many words to tell the sum on any human experience; that somebody has already done in eight: he was born he suffered and he died—yes, what we seemed to have underestimated when he was asked to be a juror and why we now ironically doubt his fitness for it was his capacity for love. I reckon that coming from where he came from—he never had none at all, and for that same previous reason that even the comprehension of love had been lost out of him back down generations where the first one of them had had to take his final choice between pursuit of love and the pursuit of keeping on breathing. Maybe it's like the fellow says, and there ain't nowhere you can hide from either lightning or love.

(Thornton Douglas leaves as Fentry sits on his porch. His father comes out on the porch.)

PAPA FENTRY: The Pruitts tell me there is a lot of excitement over in Frenchman's Bend—there's a young bully shown up over there they say. He's drinking a lot the Pruitts say, fought everybody around—licked them, too, one way or another. Buck Thorpe they call him. I wonder—it comes to me it weren't Thorpe—Buck Thorpe.

(Fentry starts out.)

Where are you going?

FENTRY: I want to take a look at him.

PAPA FENTRY: What for?

FENTRY: To see for myself if it's him…to see if they won.

(The lights are brought up downstage left. Music is heard. Buck Thorpe is outside a roadside joint, dancing to the music. Fentry enters right. He stands in the shadows watching Buck. From the opposite side a girl enters. She stands in the shadows and for a second tries to get Buck's attention without calling. He doesn't hear her. Finally she whispers.)

MAYBELL: Buck. Buck.

(Buck still doesn't hear her, and she calls again even more urgently this time.)

Buck. Buck.

(Buck walks over and sees her.)

BUCK: What are you hiding in the shadows for? Come on over here, girl. Nobody is gonna bite you.

MAYBELL: No, Buck.

BUCK: Come on.

MAYBELL: No, Buck, please. You come here. I can't stay. If Papa knew I had slipped over here he'd kill me. I come to tell you not to come to the house tonight, and that I can't see you for a while.

BUCK: Why?

MAYBELL: Because Papa don't want me to. He says you're not to set foot in the yard again and if you do…

BUCK: Who's gonna keep me away?

MAYBELL: Papa says…

BUCK: He don't scare me.

MAYBELL: Oh, Buck. Listen to me. I'm scared. He talked wild tonight. He has a gun and he says he will kill you if you try to see me again.

BUCK: I gotta gun, too, honey. You tell him he better just remember that. *(He puts his hand on his pistol.)*

MAYBELL: Oh, Buck. Please, please, don't talk like that. Promise me you won't get in no more fights. I don't want nothing to happen to you.

BUCK: Ain't nothing gonna happen to Old Buck Thorpe. Now, come on…

MAYBELL: I can't stay. If Papa caught us together, why…

BUCK: Don't worry about him. I'll protect you.

MAYBELL: No. I don't dare.

   (He holds her. They kiss.)

   Buck, did you do what Papa says? Did you steal cattle and take them to Memphis?

BUCK: Is that what he said I done?

MAYBELL: Yes, and he says you're bootlegging and you're gonna get caught and sent to the pen. It's not true is it Buck?

BUCK: What do you think?

MAYBELL: You didn't do them things, did you, Buck?

BUCK: What do you think?

MAYBELL: I don't think you did.

BUCK: And what if I told you I did?

MAYBELL: Well, I…

BUCK: Come here to me.

MAYBELL: Did you…

BUCK: Come here to me.

   (He takes her and they embrace. She sees Fentry and breaks away.)

MAYBELL: What's that old man doing there watching, Buck? Oh, my God! Buck, I hope Papa ain't sent him here to spy on us.

BUCK: *(Walks over to Fentry.)* What are you looking at, old man?
(*Fentry says nothing. Buck turns back to the girl.*)

FENTRY: Jackson and Longstreet.
(*A pause. Buck looks around and then.*)

BUCK: What did you say?

FENTRY: Jackson and Longstreet.

BUCK: What the hell are you talking about Jackson and Longstreet? Are you crazy? Are you making fun of me or something? Now get out of here before I…
(*Buck pulls knife. A pause. Fentry grabs his arm, forcing knife to fall.*)

FENTRY: Boy. Look way up there. You know what that is flying around? A chicken hawk, boy.

BUCK: Let go of me you fool.
(*Fentry lets go of him. Buck grabs his gun. He points it toward Fentry. The girl runs to him and stops him from shooting.*)

MAYBELL: Put it away. Don't fight no more.

BUCK: *(Moving away from Fentry.)* Come on with me.

MAYBELL: I'm scared Buck.

BUCK: Come on with me.
(*They are out of sight but not for Fentry, who watches them and finally, embarrassed by what he sees, turns away and starts walking back toward his yard. He picks up his hoe and begins to work as if nothing ever happened. Thornton Douglas appears again right.*)

THORNTON DOUGLAS: And that night, her papa killed Buck Thorpe. Of course he wasn't going to vote Bookwright free. And you wouldn't have freed him either, don't forget that, if you had been Jackson Fentry— never. It wasn't Buck Thorpe, the bully, the brawler. Jackson Fentry would have shot that man as quick as Bookwright did if he had been in Bookwright's place. It was because somewhere in the debased and brutalized flesh which Bookwright slew there still remained, not the spirit maybe, but at least the memory of that little boy, that Jackson and Longstreet Fentry, even though the man the boy had become didn't know it, and only Fentry did. The lowly and invincible of the earth—to endure and endure and then endure, tomorrow and tomorrow and tomorrow.
(*The lights fade.*)

END OF PLAY

A COFFIN IN EGYPT

ORIGINAL PRODUCTION

A Coffin in Egypt was originally presented at Bay Street Theatre, Sag Harbor, New York, June–July 1998. It was directed by Leonard Foglia with the following cast:

MYRTLE BLEDSOE . . . . Glynis Johns
JESSIE LYDELL. . . . . Mindy H. Washington

PLACE
Egypt, Texas

TIME
1968

The lights are brought up on the sitting room of Myrtle Bledsoe. It is a small room with a few very handsome pieces in it: a red Chinese chest, a bookcase, a Chippendale American secretary, a small sofa, a small winged chair, a tea table in front of the wing chair. Myrtle, ninety, is still very handsome. Erect and tall, remarkably well-preserved. She is exquisitely dressed in a long, red, silk dress. Her skin is clear and still quite unwrinkled and her snow-white hair is worn up on top of her head, accentuating her long, graceful neck, the firmness of her facial structure. She has several handsome rings: a diamond dinner ring, a ruby and diamond ring. She wears a diamond bar pin and pearls around her neck.

This is the sitting room of the house she came to as a bride. The house is surrounded by cotton fields, and is part of a vast plantation. Myrtle, at rise, is seated in the wing chair looking out the window and listening to the singing which comes from a nearby Negro church. Her companion, Jessie Lydell, sits on the sofa looking at a fashion magazine. The two women listen to the music. Jessie turns the page of her magazine.

MYRTLE: I remember that night so well. How many years ago?

(Jessie closes the magazine.)

MYRTLE: It was a Sunday night, and across the fields I could hear the Negroes singing in their church. None of us ever went to church here in this house. Hunter had no religion one found in the churches in Glen Flora or Harrison. Can you hear the Negroes singing? I never cared for their singing, myself. I am not sentimental about Negroes and their religion as many whites I know are. I don't dislike Negroes. Some I like. Some I don't like; just as some whites I like and many, very many, I don't like. Oh, I know I am supposed to be bitter toward the Negro race, because of the colored mistress Hunter had as a young man. A young man? He preferred colored women until he was forty-five, and then he changed. "Why did you change?" I once asked him. The change almost cost him his life. But from the time he was forty-five on he only took white mistresses. Common and vulgar, mostly they were, too.

(Rear projection: a young, very lovely, mulatto girl.)

MYRTLE: I always thought the mulatto, Maude Jenkins, was the most beautiful, and in some ways the most refined, although when she left him for Walker, the gambler, she ran a house of prostitution, the vamp, across the tracks in Harrison. She has a house in California now, someone said. Left for there after the gambler, Walker, was killed. She's gotten fat, they say, and lost her looks. I only saw her twice when she was a girl, and she was beautiful then…Copper colored. She looked like the Tahitian girls in Gaugain pictures. She was a Jenkins. Maude Jenkins. Her mother was the mistress of Cy Merriweather and so she was his child, they say. She was some white man's child, that's for sure. Anyway, I went to Europe because of her.

(Rear projection: Myrtle, as a young woman, with her two daughters standing beside her.)

MYRTLE: I took my two girls and stayed eight years over there, traveling around from city to city.

(Rear projection: Algerian male in traditional sheik costume.)

MYRTLE: When I was in Algiers a Sheik fell in love with me and wanted me to divorce Hunter and marry him. He was dark complected and my girls thought he was a colored man. He was an African, of course, and perhaps he did have colored blood somewhere down the line, as they say. Anyway, we traveled all over: Paris, Rome. My girls took ballet lessons. In New York I met Mr. Frohman and he wanted to put me on the stage. I was a close friend of Lily Cahill's sister, and Lily was sweet to me when I was in New York.

(Rear projection: Lily Cahill as a young actress.)

MYRTLE: Lily Cahill is an actress. Was an actress. She's dead. She died of a broken heart in San Antonio, Texas, because she couldn't get a job in New York acting anymore, and she came home at the age of sixty-five to her sister in San Antonio, Texas and tried to start an acting company of some kind, but San Antonio was in the throes of all that mess about unpatriotic books being in the public libraries. And Lily said what you had to go through in San Antonio, Texas to put a play on was worse than ten Broadways. She died broke, they say. Proud, but broke.

(Rear projection: Cadmus portrait of Katherine Anne Porter.)

MYRTLE: Her cousin was Katherine Anne Porter, the writer. Do you know her?

JESSIE: No. I've never heard of her.

MYRTLE: You never heard of her? My! She's a very good writer, they say, although I've never read her. Lily thought highly of her talent. Did you see the movie *Ship Of Fools*?

(Jessie shakes her head to signify she hasn't.)

MYRTLE: No? Neither did I. But you've heard of it? Well, that was based on a novel of hers. I think it was a "Book of the Month Club" selection. I can't remember anything else she's written, although I have some of her books around here some place. *(She glances over at the bookcase, then back to Jessie.)* Anyway…I was gone a long time: New York, London, Paris, Rome. And then I came home. I took my girls and came home. I've never known why. But home I came. And it's like I was never, never away. It's like that person with those two young girls, floating around Europe, around Africa, was someone I read about, or was told about, someone I knew once a long time ago. *(She looks around at the room.)* This wasn't my home, you see.

(Rear projection of Hunter as a young man.)

MYRTLE: This is Hunter's home. He was born here. Not here in this house— he built this for me—but across the road in the old plantation house was where he was born. I was born not far away though, in Eagle Lake. In the town. Not in the country.

(Rear projection: photograph of Myrtle as a young woman.)

MYRTLE: And I was a beauty.

JESSIE: You're still beautiful. Very beautiful. A queen…a princess…

MYRTLE: Oh, thank you. Thank you. No, I'm not modest. I know I have a certain style now, a certain handsomeness, people tell me that, and I take care of myself, in spite of my age, but still, but still, it's not the same. Then I had remarkable beauty and I was much sought after by the eligible young men, and then this country bumpkin, short, strong as a bull, that's what my family kept telling me, oh, so very rich, came courting. Why? That's what I have asked him so often. "Why me? What did you see in me? My beauty? My intellect? My background?" And he stares at me and shrugs his shoulders and walks away, because he doesn't know. He found me cold, he told me once. My beauty was a cold beauty…too narcissistic, he said of me once when he wanted to hurt me…But I was beautiful. And I refused to live on here and be humiliated while he lived openly with his mulatto woman, Maude Jenkins, who he once told me he loved better than his wife, who he wrote love letters to. Love letters that she would read aloud when she was drunk to the young white boys in Harrison that came to her house of prostitution. *(A pause. She goes to the window.)* I'll tell you this though, when I came here as a bride, the country out here was extraordinary. I never tired of looking at its beauty. I would get on my horse early in the morning and ride for miles across the prairies; there was nothing here then for miles, no houses, no fences. The open prairie…in the spring the wild flowers blanketed the land, blue bonnets and Indian blankets and black-eyed Susans and buttercups and primroses, miles and miles of them thick and tall and I would head east and ride through the wild flowers toward the rising sun. In the late afternoon I would ride toward the west...toward the setting sun, and you have never seen such loveliness as there was then out here on these prairies. And sometimes when the girls were little and he would stay out all night with his mulatto mistress in Harrison...I would go across the prairies, when the moon was full, and cry and cry, because I didn't want to cry in the house where my girls or the Negro servants could hear me. Once, when I was young and couldn't stand the humiliation, or thought I couldn't, I went to visit a friend. I told her I could bear it if he denied it, lied to me even, but denied it, but he denied nothing. He told me he loved her. And when I asked him if he wanted me to divorce him, he said, "It doesn't matter to me. I can't marry her anyway, unless I left here, because there is a law in Texas against black and white marrying." And he wouldn't leave here. Like he said, he would put a fence around all this if he could and keep everybody but himself out. He wouldn't leave here to marry any woman, black or white, and so I left. I was gone seven years, off and on, but I told you that, didn't I? Some friend, some long-ago, very kind friend, once told me that his father, old Leon, once remarked, "I don't know why any of them want to marry when they can have any Nigger on the place for twenty-five cents." Or was it fifty cents? He thought, too, this was the world, this plantation, his father, old Leon, did...the beginning and the end of everything. He thought all you had to do was to ride your horse through the cotton fields all day and see that the tenants and the hands worked. He thought you should learn to read and write and count money, if you were white, but only if you were white. That any other kind of education was ridiculous and a waste of time. And that all the Negroes needed to know was to farm and work and he could teach them that. And, of course, he thought it would all stay the same. Once the Yankees had gone away, even though we lost the war, he thought since they had survived, that's the father I'm talking about, he was the son of the man that settled the land first, came here from Alabama with his slaves, a hundred and twenty, I believe. Anyway, he, the father, used to say since they had survived the war and the loss of their slaves, without losing an acre of their land, they could survive anything—low cotton prices, fires, drought, floods, storms, hurricanes—and they did until the thirties and the Depression and they couldn't give their cotton and their cattle away. That's when I had to leave Europe and come home for good. The girls were grown by then and Lois got married to a man from Atlanta. He was unfaithful; she found out during her second year of her marriage. It broke her heart, and Lorena married a boy from Houston and they went to live in the East. And, I came back here, alone in this big old house with Hunter. My father-in-law was dead by then, my brother-in-law and his wife lived in the original plantation house and my other brother-in-law and his wife, the one whose son killed him, built a house over there and my sister-in-law, Sally, built a house on the corner. And so when I came home, I was surrounded by them and their children, who were all younger than my children, but I wasn't congenial with the wives. Oh, I didn't dislike them but we weren't congenial and they thought I was snobbish and perhaps I was. Anyway, I went to Rockport and took some lessons and I came home and began to write poetry and paint.

(Rear projection: Degas ballet dancer.)

MYRTLE: I remember once this famous dancer from New York came out to see me. She was visiting someone in Harrison at the time and they were on their way to attend a service in a Negro church out this way; we have so many I forget which one. And they stopped by to see me and to see if I wanted to go with them. But I decided not to. I asked them back after the service for tea, and when they came back I had taken every picture in the house down and replaced them all with Degas prints of dancers I had, and I must say that dancer lady from New York seemed surprised and pleased. I told her my best friend in San Antonio was a cousin of Katherine Anne Porter's and she had never read Katherine Anne Porter either, but had heard of her. She spoke French and we talked together in French. Turk, our cook, called in all the servants to listen to me outside that door there, as they had never heard French spoken before. Always after that, until the day Turk died, and faithful she was too, every once in awhile she'd come up to my door and ask me to say something in French for her. I offered to teach her, and she said no. She was told it might put a spell on you if you learned something like that. I said to her, "Turk, it's put no spell on me." But she still wouldn't learn and I thought afterwards maybe she thinks there is a spell on me, and maybe there is. But if there is, it was there long before I learned to speak the French language, long before. Anyway, back here I was, Degas prints and all, and it was the Depression. Not that we had to do without, living out here, except we were short of money and Hunter said he couldn't afford for me to go traveling about the world, with or without my girls. And that I would have to be content out here in the country. And so I came back. I was lonely and I cried a lot, at first, but then Mrs. Carter moved out here with her children. She lived in one of the tenant houses and her husband managed the plantation store for Hunter. And they were poor as Job's Turkey, but she was an educated lady from Mississippi, whose husband was shiftless and had no ambition, spent his time away from the store raising gaming chickens and taking them all over Texas for fights. Anyway, she was sweet and friendly and she wrote poetry too. We got to visiting back and forth and she had so many troubles that it helped take my mind off of mine. I could confide in her, the way I couldn't to my sister-in-laws, or to my own family, about how bitter I felt over Hunter's neglect of me. And it was then I heard somehow that the mulatto, Maude, had left him for the white gambler, and that he had gotten drunk and gone over across the tracks in Harrison and cried and begged her to take him back, and it was then, I heard, she would get drunk and read his love letters to the white boys who came to her whorehouse. That everyone in Harrison was laughing about it, and I was too mortified to go into Harrison even to shop, and it was then I made Hunter get me my own car and a chauffeur so I could ride sixty miles into Houston to shop. Mrs. Carter used to ride with me and we would spend the day shopping together or I would, as she never had the money to buy the least thing. She wrote poems in Negro dialect and somehow she scraped up the money to get them printed. She thought it might be the beginning of her fortune, but my God, the poor thing didn't sell more than fifteen copies of her book. I bought ten of them—she had to give the rest away. Five hundred in all, as birthday and Christmas presents. She wasn't much of a poet, to tell you the truth, but she was sweet and loyal as a friend. Anyway, I felt no shame before her, and every time I would hear something about Hunter and Maude I would ask her to find out if it was true and she would. I never asked her who she asked to find out things from…asked her husband, no doubt. Anyway, that's when I knew that Walker, the gambler, was killed. Maude was drunk all the time grieving over him and was getting fat and losing her looks, they said. And Hunter was staying home for supper then, but he'd be in bed asleep by eight o'clock, as he was always up by four thirty in the morning. And that was the first time I remember his calling us old. He didn't say it to me, I overheard him talking to his brother and he said, "You know, Myrtle and I are getting old," and I looked up at him and I realized he was sixty and I was fifty-six. Although he rode a horse all day and worked as hard as ever, he was almost sixty and my hair was gray now and I was in my fifties. That was the age then when people considered you old at sixty. I thought it's 1934 and we've been married 34 years, and

I'll go crazy if I go on sitting out here with no one to talk to but Turk, the cook, and Mrs. Carter, and listen to her dialect poetry and so I told Hunter, Depression or not, I had to get away for awhile or I'd go crazy, and he'd have the expense of keeping me locked up in Austin in the asylum the rest of his life. And he said he couldn't understand that. He said if you wanted to drive him crazy take him away from here, as he had never been farther than Harrison but four times in his life. Twice to Houston and twice to San Antonio and he didn't ever care if he never even saw Harrison again now, and never left here. But, I guess he thought I meant it about going crazy, for the next day at breakfast there was a check for a thousand dollars by my plate and he said I could go off as long as that lasted and in those days it could last a long time. I went to visit both my daughters and I got a shock, because one of them, Lorena, told me that she and her sister thought my place was out there with Hunter and that if I hadn't gone off and left him to go traveling around Europe in the first place he wouldn't have acted the way he did and carried on so scandalously with a mulatto field hand, because that's all Maude was before he took up with her. You never knew my daughters did you? They're both dead now. They both died before you came here to be with me. Lois found out about husbands like I said, long before she died, and I often wondered too, then, if she still agreed with Lorena that it would have made a difference if I'd stayed home but I didn't ever say anything to her on the subject, except listen to her troubles when she told me how humiliated she was by her husband's unfaithfulness. Anyway, when my thousand dollars was finally gone and I had to come back here I found Hunter still eating his supper here every night and not going out, but getting to bed by eight and Turk said that's how he acted the whole time I was gone. He said to her he was an old man now and his roaming days were over. We were in the Second World War then…And we had German prisoners out at the fairground. I drove into town with my chauffeur, who could barely read or write, so the Army wouldn't take him, to see them. There were soldiers from all over, up North, and everyplace in Harrison then and I remember back to the First World War and I had gone to a dance at the Opera House with Hunter, although he wouldn't dance. He just sat on the side all evening and watched me dancing, and he was forty-two and I was thirty-eight.

(Rear projection: portrait of Captain Lawson.)

MYRTLE: There was a Captain, a Captain Lawson, who was in his early thirties, dashing and quite handsome and he gave me quite a rush all evening and he was a wonderful dancer and I know he was infatuated with me, because he wrote me a note telling me so, and I wanted badly to slip away somewhere and meet him. But I didn't dare and I got mad at Hunter and I told him what I wanted to do. That I thought it was unfair because he could openly go across the tracks and out to the cabins to his Negro woman and I couldn't be allowed to meet Captain Lawson, who was attractive and found me fascinating. And I told Hunter, hoping it would make him jealous, I suppose, and he said, "You don't fool with white women, white ladies," I believe he said…And I said, "Look at Miss Stella Dow, she is white and she gets drunk and sleeps with who she likes." And he says, "Do you want people to talk about you like they do Stella Dow?" And I said, "No, I guess I didn't." And I don't, of course, so I never answered Captain Lawson's note and he married Vivian Fairbain, who was a young widow in town with two children. It was her son that was so brutally murdered by Junior Dawson—cut from here to here and thrown on the steps of the Caney Valley Hospital and left to bleed to death. But that's another long and tragic story and anyway, Captain Lawson and Vivian were married and lived together three years, although without his uniform he didn't seem glamorous or handsome at all. He never could get much of a job and she divorced him and took her first married name back, which was sensible since it was the name of her two children. She behaved as scandalously with men then as Miss Stella Dow they say, and it must be something in her family, because they say Sooky, her oldest sister, went to Houston and became a prostitute. Anyway, where was I? In the Second World War riding out to see the German prisoners and thinking about Captain Lawson. And thinking these soldiers looked young enough to be my grandsons, most of them, and I had my niece, Baby Sister, with me and Elsie, her mother, says that's when I saw that girl, Iris, because when we came back from the ride Baby Sister told her mother that we had passed this Iris and she had waved to us, but of course, I didn't know who she was at the time and paid no attention to her at all. *(She looks at herself in the mirror.)* Mr. Frohman wanted to put me on the stage in 1910 when I met him in New York City at a fabulous party. With my beauty he said, "You must go on the stage." "Must I?" I said. "You must!" he said. But I didn't. I had my two little girls then I couldn't leave them even for Mr. Frohman. Lily Cahill went on the stage, you know, and became a famous actress. Her sister, who lived in San Antonio, was my best friend for many years. Her cousin was Katherine Anne Porter, the writer. Oh, but I've told you that. Oh, yes, where was I? Oh, yes. I was telling you about seeing the girl and not being aware I saw her. Or having known who she was if I had been aware of it. I never saw her, you know, when I would have known who she was. Anyway I didn't know who she was or what she was doing with Hunter until after the killing. The first I knew was that someone, I forget who, came running in here and said that Hunter had killed a man in Harrison. *(She goes to the window and looks out.)* It was in the house across the road there that Little Brother killed his father. They've torn the house down now, because no one could bear to live in it afterwards. I was sitting here when it happened. I heard the pistol shots and I thought someone was hunting close to the house and then I heard Elsie and then a Negro woman scream and then my cook, Turk, scream and she came running in here and she said Little Brother had killed his Daddy. "And he has a gun still and God knows who else he's gonna kill now. Lock the doors," she said. But I couldn't lock the door hearing Elsie scream across the street that way and I found the strength to go to her. Stevens' face was blown away and he lay on the floor of their living room. She hovered over him screaming and I went to the phone and called our doctor in Harrison and told him to find Hunter and the sheriff and by that time Little Leon and his wife came over, but Sally wouldn't come because she had stopped speaking by then to all her brothers. She wouldn't go to the funeral either and after Little Brother had been arrested and sent to the asylum, they said it was Sally sent him the money to bribe the guards to let him get away. That was a time let me tell you. He was loose from the asylum and all of us were afraid he'd come back to kill us. Especially Elsie, his mother, because as she says it was she he was trying to kill in the first place and not Stevens. She said he came out in his underwear with the gun and said he was going to kill her, when Stevens shoved her into the next room and the boy shot him instead. He was loose for five years before they caught him again. He got into a fight in a bar up North some place and shot a man and that's how they found him and they sent him to the penitentiary up there. *(A pause.)* In the North. *(A pause.)* Well, I outlived Hunter. That's one thing, I did. He rode horseback every day pretty near up to the day he died but I outlived him. *(A pause.)* Mr. Frohman met me at a party when I was only thirty. He told me I had great beauty and I should be on the stage. Mr. Frohman made Maude Adams a great star, of course. When he died she left the stage, she ended up teaching drama in college. Stephens College, in Missouri. *(A pause.)* A girls' school. *(A pause.)* They

say she always longed to be a nun. *(A pause.)* The day Hunter killed the girl's father I had been in my studio out back painting. I heard Hunter's car drive into the yard, and then I heard a lot more cars driving up, and I thought something is wrong out there, something I don't want to hear about or know about. But I knew sooner or later I would have to go out of my studio and see what all the commotion was about. But I put off going as long as I could and I began to clean all my paint brushes and to tidy up my studio, when Elsie came in and I closed the door behind her and she said she had something sad to tell me. That I must be brave, because we all had a lot of friends here and they would all stand by us. We could count on the rest of the family, too, except Sally. She knew and I knew that Sally wouldn't help any one of her brothers and sisters out. And I said, "Elsie, what is this trouble that's happened?" "Well," she said, "it's very serious and I am afraid Hunter's killed a white man. He said he did it," she said, "in self-defense, as the man was going to kill him." "What man?" I asked. "You know, the father of that high school girl." "What high school girl?" I asked. "I don't know what you are talking about." "The one," she said, "you passed going out to the fairgrounds with Baby Sister to look at the German prisoners of war." "I don't remember passing any girl," I said. "Oh, yes," she said. "You looked right at her, Baby Sister saw you do it." "I don't know what you're talking about" I said. "You don't?" she replied. "No," I said. "Oh, Heavens!" she said. "I'm sorry I'm going to have to be the one to tell you. I'm sorry for that." And then she proceeded to tell me. To tell me all about it. *(A pause. She points to a painting in the room.)*
(Rear projection: painting of a tree.)

MYRTLE: That's one of my paintings. These are trees. I usually paint trees. Someone said to me, "I've never seen trees that color, or that shape." "Haven't you?" I asked. "Well, I paint how they look to me." *(A pause.)* I love trees. They talk to me and tell me all their secrets. Have you noticed that pine tree in the front yard? I planted that. "You're wasting your time," people said to me. "Pine trees won't grow around here. Cotton will grow and sugarcane and pin oaks and live oaks but not pines. The soil is too rich." Well, they were wrong. *(A pause.)* The things Elsie told me. Hunter had been with a middle-aged white woman for four years, who had gotten sixty thousand dollars out of him and then she had run off with a twenty-year-old soda jerk, who worked at Outlar's Drug Store. And he had gotten very depressed and talked all the time about being an old man after the woman he gave sixty thousand dollars to ran off with the soda jerk. Elsie said they were really very worried about him. She and Stevens almost sent for me to come back home, when one day Baby Sister came home and said that a seventeen-year-old girl in the junior class, whose father painted houses for a living and was poor as a church mouse, drove up to school one day in a spanking brand-new, red convertible. And Baby Sister said when they asked her where she got it from she said it was a present from an admirer.

(A silent, almost sullen, old Negro woman brings tea in on a tray and places it in front of Myrtle. Myrtle pours the tea.)

MYRTLE: Thank you, Delia.

(Delia looks at her, sighs, and goes out without looking at the other woman.)

(Rear projection: Negro church.)

MYRTLE: When that lady dancer from New York came out here to visit the Negro church she said the pastor welcomed her as being from the North and after the sermon he had the choir sing Negro spirituals for her. She said she had never seen such poverty in her life. She said the poverty she saw around her in that church made her cry.

(Rear projection: a series of Negro portraits—men and women.)

MYRTLE: She said she hoped they thought it was their music that was making her cry and not the looks of them. They're still poor you know. They live, oh, I don't know how most of them live. Their houses leak, cold in winter; hot in summer. Maybe education will help. Think it will? I thought Hunter would die the day they let them go to school with the white children. You, of all people, I thought to myself, objecting to something like that. But I didn't say anything.

(Rear projection: Hunter—a series of portraits as a young man and as an older man.)

MYRTLE: I learned a long time ago not to bring up unpleasant subjects. It got you nowhere, and you could never win with him. He would just not answer whatever you said, or get up and leave the house and ride off some place on that horse of his. Oh, not that I always held my tongue. Sometimes the very sight of him would set me wild with hate and bitterness and I would begin just screaming at him of all the terrible things he'd done to me all these years, all the hurts and the humiliations and the neglect. But you know, the other night I couldn't sleep and I woke up and there was a terrible wind storm, and I thought for a moment the house would be blown away with it. But I was too tired to get up and I lay there listening to that terrible wind and thinking about Hunter and my life with him as I always seem to do in the night when I can't sleep and I thought of him dead and in his coffin and my living on, and no one now to blame my bitterness and my resentment on except a dead man. And lying in that bed, listening to the sound of that wind, the bitterness began to rise up inside me and I began to scream out again all my old grievances I held against him. I was screaming so loud that Miss Morisey, who was staying with me then, heard me over the sound of the wind and came in to me. She thought, she said, I was being murdered. "I am," I said. "Poisoned by the memories of him. It's been a long, slow poisoning I must admit," I said, "but it is poisoning me all the same." She sat by my bedside and I told her all about it, just as I'm now trying to tell you. And I thought to myself, if I can only even get it finally told, then I can die, too, get some rest perhaps from this burden of hate and bitterness. For I do hate him, you know, even though he's dead. I still hate him, or love him perhaps. One of his sisters said to me once: "No, you don't hate him, you love him, or you wouldn't feel such bitterness toward him." I used to tell him all the time, "God damn you, Hunter, I hate you!" But I don't believe he even cared then, what I thought or said. *(In the distance Negro church music is heard again.)*

MYRTLE: After Little Brother killed Stevens, his father, he ran across the prairie in his underwear still holding the gun. "It was him or me," he said as he ran across the prairie. That is what he'd heard Hunter say after he shot that seventeen-year-old white girl's father, "Him or me...I did it in self-defense...It was him or me." And Little Brother was screaming that, too, as he ran into the Negro church holding his gun over his head. "I did it in self-defense, it was him or me." And when the Negroes saw him run into that church in his underwear screaming, "It was him or me...I did it in self-defense," they almost killed themselves getting out of that church and ran in every direction in the night across the prairie. I've thought of that night a lot sitting here. And sometimes I can see that boy, he was only twenty, just as vividly, running across the prairie holding the gun and screaming, as if I had actually seen him. Why did he do it? I ask myself...Why did a twenty-year-old boy kill his father...who would have killed his mother if he could have first gotten to her? Once when I got mad at Hunter I said, "You are responsible...You gave him the idea when you killed the father of that seventeen-year-old whore you were keeping, and he heard you saying, 'It was self-defense. It was him or me.' And he saw that you got off scott free, no one punished you for anything, you never saw the inside of a jail or a court room for killing that girl's father." That was the only time I thought he might strike me when I yelled those things at him. He started to, but he didn't. He put on his hat and walked out into the yard and he stood looking across the road at the house where Stevens had lived, where he was killed, murdered, by his oldest son. And I went to the window and looked at him standing there in the yard, looking across at the house, and I felt sorry for him then, as I did when he came home after he killed the girl's father, surrounded by his friends and their wives, all of them saying they believed him that it was self-defense. He looked old and whipped-down for the first time that I can remember and in spite of their saying they believed why he did it, he just kept repeating over and over: "It was him or me." And after awhile he asked all his friends and their wives to leave. He asked me to stay alone in the room with him; they all left and I stayed alone with him and he said then he was sorry for all the misery and the unhappiness he had caused me and that he was going to make it up to me. He wanted to spend the rest of his life here on earth in peace. I said, I shouldn't have I guess, but I did: "What if they kill you? What if they kill you for killing that seventeen-year-old whore's father? You won't have many days to spend in peace then," I said. And do you know what he said? He said, "She wasn't a whore. Please don't talk that way about her. She loved me and I loved her." "You mean to tell me you're fool enough to believe a seventeen-year-old girl loves a sixty-eight-year-old man?" "She loved me," he said. "Does she love you now?" I said, "Now that you've killed her daddy?" "I don't know," he said. "I don't know about now." And then he began to say over and over like he did to his friends. "It was self-defense. It was him or me." And finally he stopped saying it, and looked up at me and he said, "You believe that don't you?" And I said: "Do you want the truth?" He said, "Yes." And I said, "No, I don't." "It's true," he said, "He told me to stop seeing her or he'd kill me." "He didn't even have a gun on him," I said. "But I didn't know that," he said. "I saw him coming toward me and I thought for sure he had a gun and I killed him. They believe me," he said. "Who does?" I said. "My friends," he said. "Do they?" I asked. "Yes," he said, "You heard them say they did." "And what about his friends?" I said. "What do they believe?" "What friends?" he said. "He's shiftless and no 'count and just a house painter. What friends does he have?" And I guess he didn't have many, if any. Anyway, they say only six or seven people came to his funeral when they buried him in Harrison and the day after the funeral they had some kind of hearing over at the courthouse which

Hunter didn't even have to attend. His brother, Stevens, and Little Brother went as his representatives. And he had a lawyer there, of course, and Stevens told the judge how Hunter said it happened. That the seventeen-year-old girl's father had threatened his life. What was that man's name? I can't remember…I think it was Gallagher or Gallaway or…Anyway, I remember her name, it was Iris. Anyway, he was acquitted at that hearing of any wrong doing. And someone said Hunter gave a hundred thousand dollars to Iris and her mother and they left town. But someone else told me it was ten and someone else five. I asked him once how much he paid them to leave. He said he had paid them nothing; there was nothing to pay them for. Anyway, they left, rode away in that red convertible he had given her, I reckon, rode away and vanished. *(Rear projection: a young white girl.)*

MYRTLE: I'd never seen her, of course, that I remembered in spite of what Elsie thought, until one day five or six years later when I was shopping in Foley's in Houston with Elsie. She said "There she is." "There's who?" I asked. "Iris," she said, "The girl who's father Hunter killed." She was working in the bridal department there in the store. It was her job, one of the clerks told me, to go around and show customers how to put on weddings, big, formal weddings, the clerk said. Sometimes she models different wedding gowns for the customers, the clerk said. Because of her beauty, she said, "she can make any gown, no matter how tacky, desirable. Don't you think she's beautiful?" the clerk asked me. "Do you want an honest opinion?" I said. "Why, yes," the clerk said. "Yes, I guess I do." "In a common sort of way," I said. "However, common beauty has never appealed to me." "She's had a very sad life," the clerk said. "Her father was murdered in cold blood by a rich man over in Harrison, who was in love with her and wanted to marry her. But he had a devil of a wife and she wouldn't give him a divorce and so her father said if that rich man couldn't marry her, she had to stop seeing him. The rich man got in a rage when he said that and killed him. Got off scott free, too. Then she came to Houston and married a man whose family had a lot of money. One of the Lee boys, Jack or Lester, I can't remember which." And then she turned to the sales girl next to her and asked, as if I cared, who Iris married…Jack or Lester Lee? And the girl said, "Lester" and then she said his family wouldn't give him any money, rich as they were because he drank so. So she had to go to work to support them, since he was born and raised a rich boy and didn't, consequently, know how to do anything and here she was. "Is she still married to Lester Lee?" Elsie asked her, as if it mattered. And the woman said, "No." She had to leave him finally on account of his drinking. She was being courted now by an oil millionaire and she heard the other day that somebody wanted to send her out to Hollywood and make her a movie star. Well, she never got to Hollywood, of course, at least if she did, she never made any pictures, not any I ever heard of, that is. God knows where she is now, or what's become of her. Her mother became a call girl they say. David Meyers told Elsie that and Elsie told me. She said he used to go to the Lamar Hotel to get women and they would always send four or five women up to your room for you to choose from and one night he said one of the women that came up was Martha Davis that used to slip off from her husband and children and go into Houston and work as a call girl. Although I'm not sure she really slipped off. Some people said her husband knew all about it and didn't care. Anyway, he said he'd hardly gotten over the shock of seeing Martha when he saw standing next to her Iris's mother. "How's Iris?" he asked her. "Gone to the dogs," she said. But that was just the mother talking, because Elsie told me, just before she died when she went to New Orleans for the Sugar Bowl Game, she saw Iris big as life and she was well-dressed and with a good-looking man who seemed to have lots of money. Elsie said she was still pretty enough to be in pictures. A little matronly looking now but very pretty. I was a beauty, too, many people think when I was younger. Mr. Daniel Frohman, I think he went down with the Titanic, didn't he? I believe so. And it broke Maude Adams heart they tell me and she retired from the stage after he died. He treated her like a princess, you know. He made a great star of her. I saw her do *Peter Pan* and *A Kiss for Cinderella,* and later, after he died and she retired, she decided to try the stage again and she teamed with Otis Skinner in *The Merchant Of Venice.* I went to see her in that when she came to Houston. Mr. Frohman begged me to go on the stage when he met me. "I have a husband and two little girls," I said. "No matter," he said, "your beauty should not be wasted, it belongs to the world." Anyway, once I got to thinking about the man Hunter killed, I went out to the graveyard in Harrison to look for his grave, but then I remembered I'd never overheard his name. So, I asked Red, my chauffeur, what was the name of the man that Hunter killed. "It was Davis," he said, "Lovell Davis." "Go out there and see if you can find his grave," I said. He looked around the graveyard for a better part of an hour and when he came back he said he had finally found it. I got out of the car and followed him to where the grave was and a tombstone had just been put up recently and marked on it was "Rest In Peace Daddy, Love Iris" *(A pause.)* And the date of his birth and the day he died. *(A pause.)* He was thirty-five when he was shot and killed by Hunter. She was seventeen, which meant he was eighteen when she was born. "Where did they come from?" I asked Red. "I don't know, ma'm," he said "nor where they gone to." "Well, we know where he's gone to," I said. "In a coffin in Harrison, buried deep in the ground." "Yes, ma'm," he said. And of course, that's where Hunter had ended—in a coffin, not in Harrison, but in Egypt. Like Joseph in the Bible. The difference between Joseph and Hunter was he would have lain with Potiphar's wife. Do you know how the First Chapter of Genesis begins? "In the beginning God created Heaven and Earth." And how the book ends? In a Coffin in Egypt. That's where I'll end too, of course, next to Hunter and my two daughters in a coffin in Egypt. Someone said the mulatto, Maude Jenkins, sent word from California to her people here that when she dies she wants to be shipped back here and buried in Egypt, too. Of course, she won't be buried in our graveyard, but with the colored people, with her family…which there were a lot of, and they say she's been wonderful to all her kin, her sisters and brothers and their children. Sent them food and clothes and educated them that wanted it. But no matter, she will end up, too, like the rest of us, won't she? Black and white. In a coffin in Egypt or some place. *(A pause.)* If I could have one day to live over before I die, do you know what I'd choose? *(A pause.)* I'd choose one of those lovely clear spring days, we used to have out here when I came here first as a bride and I'd get on my horse and ride across the prairie at sunrise to the east and ride all day on and on… *(She gets up, goes to the bookcase.)* Here are two books of Katherine Anne Porter… *Flowering Judas* and *Pale Horse, Pale Rider. (She takes them out of the bookcase and shows them to Jessie.)* This is her picture. She was quite beautiful, wasn't she? Lily Cahill was her cousin. Lily played with Jane Cowl in "First Lady," and she always knew how to dress very smartly, both on stage and off. And she toured, you know, all over America in *Life with Father.* Then she couldn't get work and she had to go back to San Antonio, Texas. I don't believe she was ever in a Frohman production. I could have been, you know. Mr. Frohman said he could have made a great star of me. He said I had the temperament to be a very great actress. And the beauty, and the poise. And the clothes…I always had, if I do say so myself, a remarkable sense of what looked best on me. Red was my favorite color. But I didn't wear it often, until my hair was white, and then I did and with great effect. Red hats, large brimmed, red coats, red dresses, red shoes. I adored red. I surrounded myself in red. Red clothes, red furnishings…"Red is a whore's color," someone said to me once. "But if I wear it, it's a lady's color," I said. "Oh, yes," she said, "for you are a lady, there is no mistaking that. Always a lady." "Except with Hunter," I said. He gets me so angry I forget myself, forget I am a lady, forget…

(The Negro music is heard again.)

MYRTLE: Turk was not in church that night Little Brother ran in there in his underwear, waving the gun, but her husband was and her sister was. She hadn't gone because she knew I was very despondent after Hunter had killed that man, Iris's father, and she said she was not going to leave me feeling like that. "Oh, I've been despondent a great deal of my life, Turk," I said, "I'm used to it." "Not like now," she said." I've never seen you like now," she said. And I think she was right. I felt a depth of humiliation those days that I'd never known before or since. And so I locked myself in my room and Turk brought me my meals. Not that I could eat anything at all, and I was in my room alone, not crying, but feeling a grief like I've never known before or since. When I heard Elsie scream and Turk ran in to tell me what the screams were about. *(A pause. She glances toward the window.)* "A Coffin in Egypt"…that's where Hunter is, and Stevens and my two girls all buried right out there with their father and grandfather and great grandfather and even Sally, who wouldn't speak to any of them for twenty years before she died, is buried out there beside them. But Little Brother, where is he? Up North some place in a prison…Minnesota, Wisconsin, Idaho… some place where it's cold and it snows all winter long. That's where they have him locked up. After they caught him finally living some way up there, who, as far as I know had never done a day's work in his life. Living up there, working up there, if he did work, which I doubt, since I think Sally was sending him money all the time. Just like I think it was Sally who paid off the guards to let him escape from the asylum in Austin. "Why in the name of God would she do something like that?" Turk said when I told her my opinion of the situation. "Because she's got a mean streak in her," I said. "Had since girlhood, hates her brothers and their wives, bitter, I've always thought that, because she couldn't have children of her own." The only one of the family she ever cared about was Little Brother. Doted on him. Absolutely…Always telling him how his mother and daddy favored Baby Sister over him and how he never got his fair share from his mother and father or any of the rest of us. Elsie says she thinks she poisoned his mind and that's why he went off that way and did what he did. Anyway, we were all scared to death, let me tell you, after he ran away from the asylum and we didn't know for five years where he was. It was a time of terror around here. No matter what happened or what you did always in the back of your mind was that this night might just be the night that he would take it in his head to come back here and kill the rest of us. I was scared as the rest of them. We were all scared except Sally, and she wasn't scared. I've always felt because she knew where he was and what he was up to, since she was sending him the money. "Can you prove that?" Hunter said once when I told him what I felt. "No," I said, "but there are a lot of things I know that I can't prove. Like, I know you haven't learned your lesson by getting caught running around with a seventeen-year-old girl. You already have yourself another woman over in Harrison some place." "How do you figure that?" he said. "Because I know you, Hunter," I said… *(A pause.)* I don't know where they buried Captain Lawson, or even where he died. Did he die in Harrison? I can't remember. Anyway, I don't think so. I think he moved away after Vivian divorced him. I have never seen a man change so in my life when he took that uniform off. Everybody still called him Captain, but it sounded funny because he was clerking in a grocery store for Mr. Sam Borden. Women would go in and say, "Captain Lawson, how are the mustard greens today?" Or the Irish Potatoes? Or whatever. And he'd click his heels and bow just like he was still in the army, only he looked funny clicking his heels and bowing with his butcher's apron on. Captain Lawson. What was his first name? Ernest? Albert? I can't remember. Captain Lawson. Long, long ago. He is dead and Vivian is dead. She's buried in the Harrison cemetery, but I'm not sure where he is buried. *(A pause.)* I was in this room when I heard a noise outside and said, "Turk, get in here and lock all the doors and windows, he's back." "Oh, My God!" she said, because she knew who I meant. I meant Little Brother. "Are you sure?" she said. "Yes, I heard his footsteps around the side of the house." But it wasn't Little Brother, because we read next morning in the Houston paper how he had gotten into a fight up North in a bar and tried to kill a man and the police came and arrested him and found out he was escaped from the asylum in Austin, Texas. Later the man died. I hear they gave Little Brother life. I am sorry about the man dying, but I'm glad they caught Little Brother, and locked him up for life. And not even Sally could get him out of there, no matter what she was willing to spend. His name was never mentioned after that, by his mother or his sister or his uncles. Now they're all dead. I don't know if they ever wrote to him, or heard from him ever again. I thought the other night…What does he think about being locked up in that prison in the North? I haven't seen him since he was twenty, and if he walked in this yard tomorrow, he would be an old man and I wouldn't know him. And I thought if he died who would they get in touch with? Me? Or would they? Maybe he is dead and buried in a coffin in wherever he is. What do they do with them when they die in those prisons? Do they send them home to their people like when they're killed in the army? Or do they bury them there in the prison? I'd write up there and find out if he was dead or alive, if I knew who to write to. Bud Jackson was sheriff then and might know where he was. Bud told me once in all the years he was sheriff catching that boy was one of the hardest things he ever had to do. He said it was even harder than going to California and getting Dude Borden when he was paroled out of San Quentin and bringing him back here, because he was raised with Dude and Dude was his best friend when he was a boy, although Dude was supposed to be off of dope in San Quentin, he knew he wasn't, and he knew that taking him to Houston was just like turning him over to the dope peddlers, which it was. Because Bud said in three weeks he was back on it full force. He never sold it again, though, which was what they arrested him for doing in California. Anyway, I was out in the yard when they told Bud about Stevens being killed and Little Brother running across the prairie somewhere, and he told Hunter that he would catch him, and he hoped he would come peacefully, because he didn't intend to get killed and he would kill him if Little Brother started shooting at him. Some Negroes came up then and told him he had come into the church hollering, "It was him or me." And as far as they knew he was still in the church so Bud and his deputies started for the church. They surrounded it first and then called for him to come out, but he didn't come out because he wasn't in it by the time they got there. They rode all night across the prairie, their lights flashing in every direction, until finally they found him sprawled across the ground so sound asleep he didn't hear the cars until they were up beside him. He didn't holler or struggle, he just looked up at Bud from where he lay on the ground and he said, Bud told us later, just as calm, "I want you to hear my side of it, Bud. I did it in self-defense. It was him or me." "That may be," Bud said he told him, "but get up now, Little Brother, like a good boy and come with me." "Where are you taking me?" Little Brother said. "Where I have to take you," Bud said, "to the jail in Harrison." "Why?" Little Brother asked him. "Because you killed your daddy," Bud told him. "I know that," Little Brother said. "But why are you locking me up? You didn't lock up Uncle Hunter when he killed that man." Hunter was standing beside me when he told me that, and I thought to myself, I hope you are listening Hunter, and I looked up at Hunter's face. His expression hadn't changed one iota. He just listened and nodded his head like he was one of the wise men from the East. They didn't have a trial for Little Brother either, but declared him insane. A colored man Turk knew said he had the cell next to Little Brother and he said on the day of his daddy's funeral Little Brother had gotten a funeral notice someway and he was reading it out loud from his cell. He said to that colored man that they were burying his daddy today and he had killed him in self-defense, but that nobody had come to see him in jail but his Aunt Sally. And she did come, too, because the colored man saw her and heard her say she was going to stand by him. *(A pause.)* The fall isn't much here. Oh, it's nice if you have pecan trees, and there is a good crop, but it's hot as summer a lot of the fall, except when a northern blows up across the prairie and then it can get cold let me tell you. It's the northers blow all the pecans out of these trees. And you can see people scurrying around raking through the leaves looking for the pecans. I never did, of course, the Negroes always picked mine up for me. Oh, and the winters. Deliver me! Rains, it seems to me, all winter long. But, oh, the spring is lovely. The wild flowers are beautiful then: primroses and buttercups and Indian blankets, but I told you about those. And did I tell you about Mr. Frohman wanting to put me on the stage? I told Hunter that. "He's some kind of a damn fool," Hunter said. *(A pause.)* "The Angel that talked with me came again, and waked me, as a man that's wakened out of his sleep." I woke up last night thinking of that, that's from the Bible some place. *(A pause.)* Lily Cahill got to be a star, too. Not under Mr. Frohman, though. Maude Adams was his star. Is she dead or alive? Someone told me the other day Katherine Anne Porter was still alive. If she is, she's as old as I am. As old as I am. I could write a book let me tell you. What a book I could write. *(A pause.)* "The Angel that talked with me came again…" That's in Zechariah some place, I think. *(A pause.)* The mulatto, Maude Jenkins, came back here one time in the forties they say. In a brand new Cadillac, more expensive than anything Hunter or I ever owned, and she drove it slowly around the Courthouse Square so everybody could see she was prospering out there in California. *(A pause.)* They tore the house down piece by piece where Little Brother killed his father. The plants that surrounded the house: the oleander and the crepe myrtle and rose bushes they left standing, and the trees in the yard. *(A pause.)* I left home the day they began to take the house down. Where did I go that time? *(A pause.)* Hunter called me when it was all done. "The house is down he said, you can come home now," and I did. *(A pause.)* Hand me that book yonder by Katherine Anne Porter, *Flowering Judas*. I think I'll read one of her stories.

(Jessie hands her the book. Myrtle opens it.)

MYRTLE: She had several husbands you know. Two or three, I don't remember. Lily Cahill never married. Mr. Frohman married, but Maude Adams never did. They say…Well, you know how they talk. Anyway, I don't believe a word of it. Mr. Frohman always behaved in a very gentlemanly fashion with me, and I think he had a very deep interest in spiritual things. *(A pause.)* The day Hunter died was a cold, bleak November day. He just went to sleep sitting in his chair there. We buried him the next day. It rained, so not many people came out from Harrison. Just his brother and his wife and his nephews and their wives, and me, of course, and a few neighbors and the rest were blacks. Every black out this way and there are enough of them. Why was that? He was mean as the devil to most of them. And not just the old ones: the young, too.

(The Negro singing is heard.)

MYRTLE: Who is left to come to my funeral? *(A pause.)* I'm older by twenty years than the mulatto, Maude Jenkins, but I've outlived so many, I might outlive her. Who will come to her funeral? There will be lots of Jenkins there, because they are still thick in the county and the blacks will come from everywhere from all the bottoms and the prairies, out of curiosity if nothing else. *(A pause.)* And I'd like to go just to get a look at her after all these years. But I couldn't, of course, even if I was still alive then. *(A pause.)* "The Angel that talked with me came again, and waked me, as a man that's wakened out of his sleep." *(A pause.)* "The Angel that talked with me came again, and waked me, as a man that's wakened out of his sleep." *(A pause.)* What was the name of Mr. Frohman's theater? The Empire. It was across the street from the Metropolitan Opera House. They're both torn down I read somewhere. I attended them both. Many times. I loved New York. I loved Paris. I loved Algiers. I loved Rome. I loved…Egypt. Not, Egypt, Texas, but Egypt. Egypt…Magic, Egypt. I used to tell Hunter that when I died I wanted to be cremated and have my ashes taken to one of the beautiful places I'd known as a young woman. But now, I don't care. Who is there left to take my ashes anywhere? Anyway, they have a place for my body between Hunter's grave and my two girls and that's where I'll end. In a coffin in Egypt. This Egypt. Out on the prairie. And in the spring our graves will be covered with the wild flowers, with primroses and Indian blankets and blue bonnets. *(A pause.)* What was the name of the man that Hunter killed? Gallagher? Or Gallaway? No…No… That's not it. I thought of it earlier. It wasn't an Irish name. It was English…Davis… Yes. Lovell Davis. That's right. Now who in the name of God was Gallagher or Gallaway? *(A pause.)* No matter. *(A pause.)* Mr. Frohman said, "I can't believe you are the mother of these two children…Why you seem more like their sister." Where is he buried? And Maude Adams? And Lily Cahill? And Katherine Anne Porter? And… Listen…Hear the wind out on the prairie? I think it will storm tonight. I never mind them you know. Storms comfort me somehow. *(A pause.)* Gallaway was the name of the first white child born in Harrison, someone told me once. *(A pause.)* Mr. Frohman said, "Tell us another one." Hunter said. *(A pause.)* "Another what?" I said. *(A pause.)* "Another one of your lies," he said "about Mr. Frohman and a Sheik being in love with you." "He was," I said. "And Captain Lawson…and…" *(A pause.)* Hunter…He never said he loved me. He said I can never say things like that, but he wrote them to Maude Jenkins, in those letters from him she would get drunk and read to the white boys. Oh, so long ago. "I hate you, Hunter." That's what I told him. Over and over…"I hate you." Did I? Was he ever here in this room? In that chair? Riding his horse across those fields? Was I young once? A girl? Was I in France and Algiers and New York? Was I? Was there a Captain Lawson and did he flirt with me? And Mr. Frohman? Did he want me to become an actress? And what if I had and left Hunter and my two girls? How would it all have ended? Anyway, I've outlived Hunter and Mr. Frohman and Lily Cahill and Maude Adams and Katherine Anne Porter… *(She closes her eyes. She opens them.)* Lovell Davis. Not Gallagher or Gallaway. Lovell Davis was the name of the man Hunter killed. Iris Davis was his daughter. She was the seventeen-year-old girl Hunter had an affair with when he was sixty-eight… *(A pause.)* I never saw Lovell Davis that I remembered. Not even a picture, but, of course, I might have passed him on the streets of Harrison without knowing who he was. I saw Iris once in Houston working in Foley's. But I told you that. *(A pause.)* "The Angel that talked with me came again…" And I visited the grave of Lovell Davis once, but I told you that. *(A pause.)* Renee Gordon's husband, Jason, got mixed up with a seventeen-year-old girl once in Harrison and the father of the girl threatened to kill him and he wasn't of Hunter's stripe at all, so he left town. Renee felt so disgraced over the whole thing that she killed herself. Hung herself. Not me. I felt disgraced all right, but I never once thought of killing myself. *(A pause.)* I wouldn't give Hunter that satisfaction. *(A pause.)* "Myrtle," she said, "this is Mr. Frohman. He asked to be introduced to you." "You are the loveliest one here tonight," he said. "Thank you," I said. "Have you ever considered a career in the theater?" Mr. Frohman said. "As an actress?" I asked. "Yes," he said. "Heavens no," I said. I was beautiful then, you know. I was a very great beauty then. I had exquisite hands and lovely tiny feet…and…I had style. "I can't teach you a thing about clothes," Lily Cahill said to me. "You have more style than anyone I know."

(The Negroes sing in the distance.)

MYRTLE: Running across the prairie in his underwear… "It was him or me. Self-defense." The Negroes scattered like partridges. They all disappeared into the night and left him alone in the church of God… Screaming, "It was him or me." *(A pause.)* Oh, the days and the years. summer and winter…spring and fall… *(A pause.)* The spring is my favorite time. In the spring…when I was a girl. A long, long time ago, when I was a girl, a bride and I came here, before…Anyway, I've told you all that. *(She begins to read again from the book. She closes her eyes.)* Yes, I've told you all that. What else? Hunter and me. I was nineteen when he proposed in a buggy taking me to my home in Eagle Lake, Texas. In a buggy, a surrey…and he was rich, they said, and I was beautiful and intelligent and… *(A pause. She opens her eyes. She turns and looks out the window.)*

(Curtain.)

END OF PLAY

LAURA DENNIS

ORIGINAL PRODUCTION

Laura Dennis was first presented at Signature Theatre Company (James Houghton, Artistic Director; Thomas C. Proehl, Managing Director; Elliot Fox, Associate Director) in New York City, on March 10, 1995. It was directed by James Houghton; the set design was by E. David Cosier; the costume design was by Jonathan Green; the lighting design was by Jeffrey S. Koger; the music coordinator was Loren Toolajian and the production stage manager was Bethany Ford. The cast was as follows:

PUD MURPHY	Victoria Fischer
LAURA DENNIS	Missy Yager
ANNIE LAURIE DAVIS	Stacey Moseley
MRS. MURPHY	Pamela Lewis
FAY GRISWOLD	Barbara Caren Sims
ANDREW GRISWOLD	Horton Foote, Jr.
HARVEY GRISWOLD	Peter Sarsgaard
LENA ABERNATHY	Becky Ann Baker
VELMA DENNIS	Hallie Foote
SEYMOUR MANN	Andrew Finney
ETHEL DENNIS	Janet Ward
STEWART WILSON	Eric Williams
EDWARD DENNIS	Michael Hadge

PLACE
Harrison, Texas

TIME
Fall, 1938

The play takes place in the fall of 1938 in Harrison, Texas. At rise the stage is divided into three areas: section of the Murphy living room, a section of the porch and yard of the Abernathy house, a section of the living room of the Griswold house. The lights are brought up on the Murphy house. Three girls, "Pud" Murphy, Annie Laurie Davis, and Laura Dennis, are there. It is the middle of September, and the day is warm.

PUD: Oh, I'm burning up. It's those cool mornings that always fool me. I think when I get up I'm gonna freeze, and I forget that as soon as the sun comes out it will get so hot you can't stand it. And all the sweaters and the wool dresses will make you feel like dying. I don't know why they have school in September anyway. Half the kids can't come until the cotton is picked. That's not until the middle of October.

LAURA: Sometimes as late as November.

PUD: Yep.

ANNIE LAURIE: Did you all ever pick cotton?

PUD: *(Screaming with laughter.)* No, I certainly have not. That's for the country people.

ANNIE LAURIE: Does everybody in the country pick cotton?

PUD: Where have you been, girl?

ANNIE LAURIE: Shreveport, Louisiana.

PUD: Don't they have cotton around there?

ANNIE LAURIE: Yes, but out in the country. I never got out there much and I never got to see who picked it.

PUD: Laura used to live in the country, but she never picked cotton.

ANNIE LAURIE: Who picks the cotton then? The Negroes and the Mexicans?

PUD: Whites, too. Poor whites. Laura is not a poor white. Her family owns acres and acres and acres and acres and acres of land.

ANNIE LAURIE: How many?

PUD: I don't know. How many Laura?

LAURA: I don't know. What difference does it make. None of it belongs to me.

ANNIE LAURIE: Yes it will someday.

LAURA: No it won't.

ANNIE LAURIE: But if your family owns it—

LAURA: They're not my family. They're my uncle and my cousins.

ANNIE LAURIE: Aren't uncles and cousins family?

PUD: Yes, but you don't inherit from uncles and cousins, goose, just from mamas and papas. *(A pause.)* If I get asked to the dance, Mama says I can buy a new evening dress. *(Calling.)* Didn't you, Mama?

MRS. MURPHY: *(Calling back.)* Didn't I what?

PUD: *(Calling.)* Say if I got asked to the dance I could buy a new evening dress?

MRS. MURPHY: *(Calling back.)* Yes.

PUD: Has Stewart Wilson asked you to the dance yet, Laura?

LAURA: No.

PUD: I'm sure he will.

(A car horn is heard.)

LAURA: I have to go.

PUD: Don't go. Stay and visit for a while longer. Sister will drive you home when she comes back with the car.

LAURA: I can't. *(She starts off the porch.)* Goodbye, Annie Laurie. Goodbye, Pud.

ANNIE LAURIE AND PUD: Goodbye.

LAURA: *(Calling.)* Goodbye, Mrs. Murphy.

MRS. MURPHY: *(Calling back.)* Bye bye, Laura.

(Laura hurries out. Annie Laurie looks out the window.)

ANNIE LAURIE: Is that her mother?

PUD: No.

ANNIE LAURIE: Who is that?

PUD: Mrs. Abernathy. She's the woman she lives with.

ANNIE LAURIE: Where's her daddy?

PUD: Dead.

ANNIE LAURIE: Is her mother dead too?

PUD: No. At least if she is I've never heard about it.

ANNIE LAURIE: Why doesn't she live with her?

PUD: Because she can't.

ANNIE LAURIE: She can't live with her own mother?

PUD: No.

ANNIE LAURIE: Why?

PUD: Oh, my God you ask a lot of questions. I don't know why. *(She calls.)* Mama!

(Mrs. Murphy appears.)

MRS. MURPHY: Yes.

PUD: Why can't Laura live with her mother?

MRS. MURPHY: What made you think of that?

PUD: I didn't think of it. Annie Laurie saw her leave with Mrs. Abernathy and asked me why she didn't live with her mother and I didn't know.

MRS. MURPHY: Well, I'll tell Annie Laurie's mother and if she thinks she should know she can tell her herself.

PUD: Why can't you tell us?

MRS. MURPHY: Because I don't want to.

PUD: Is it bad?

MRS. MURPHY: Pud, I'm not going to talk about it, so change the subject.

PUD: Does Laura know about it?

MRS. MURPHY: About what?

PUD: About why she can't live with her mother?

MRS. MURPHY: I wouldn't know, Pud. Let's change the subject.

ANNIE LAURIE: I bet that's why she's so sad. In all the time I've known her, I've never seen her smile once.

PUD: But you've only known her two weeks.

ANNIE LAURIE: Have you known her for a long time?

PUD: Sure, ever since she moved into Harrison.

ANNIE LAURIE: How long is that?

PUD: I don't know. How long has she lived in Harrison, Mama?

MRS. MURPHY: Let's see…thirteen years. She was four when she came here from out in the country.

ANNIE LAURIE: Was her father dead then, too?

PUD: No. He died last spring. April wasn't it, Mama?

MRS. MURPHY: Yes.

ANNIE LAURIE: What did he die of?

PUD: I don't know. You're the most inquisitive person I've ever known. What did Laura's father die of, Mama?

MRS. MURPHY: I don't know. *(She leaves the room.)*

PUD: She does too, but she doesn't believe in discussing things like that with me. You ask your mother to ask her. She'll tell her.

ANNIE LAURIE: Who is the boy you think will ask Laura to the dance?

PUD: Stewart Wilson.

ANNIE LAURIE: Do they go steady?

PUD: I guess. For now anyway. Laura told me it wasn't serious. She said he's going to marry Verna Kate Nelson.

ANNIE LAURIE: Why is he going with Laura, if he's going to marry Verna Kate?

PUD: I don't know. He used to go with Verna Kate. Then she started going with Harvey Griswold and Laura started going with Stewart. It is all very mixed up.

ANNIE LAURIE: I should think so. Does Verna Kate say she is going to marry Stewart?

PUD: I don't know what Verna Kate thinks or says and I don't care.

ANNIE LAURIE: Why?

PUD: Because she is a rich snob. She goes to Virginia to school. Not here. But personally, I think Laura is being used and I told her so. He's using you, Laura, I said, while Verna Kate is off in Virginia. Harvey Griswold is adopted. His mother and father couldn't have children of their own, so they adopted him.

ANNIE LAURIE: How old was he when they adopted him?

PUD: I don't know. *(Calling.)* Mama.

MRS. MURPHY: *(Calling back.)* Yes?

PUD: *(Calling.)* How old was Harvey Griswold when his parents adopted him?

MRS. MURPHY: *(Calling back.)* Just an infant.

ANNIE LAURIE: Does he know he's adopted?

PUD: Sure he does. He'll tell you in a minute he is. Come on. Let's go outside.
(They exit. As the lights fade on the Murphy living room they are brought up on the living room of the Griswold house. Fay Griswold is there with her husband Andrew. Harvey, their adopted son, comes in.)

HARVEY: May I have the car for the dance next week?

ANDREW: I suppose so Harvey. Do you have a date?

HARVEY: Not yet.

FAY: Do you need the car if you aren't going to take a girl to the dance?

HARVEY: I'm going to ask someone.

FAY: Who?

HARVEY: I was thinking of asking Laura Dennis.

FAY: She's a senior isn't she?

HARVEY: Yes.

FAY: Why don't you ask a girl in your own class?

HARVEY: I like her.

FAY: I really think you should be going with girls your own age.

HARVEY: Well, I go with Verna Kate Nelson when she's home and you don't argue about that, an' she's a senior. *(A pause.)* What do you have against Laura?

FAY: I have nothing against Laura personally. I just think…

ANDREW: Look. We still make the rules around here Harvey and if your mother doesn't want you taking a girl from the senior class to the dance that should be it. *(A pause.)* Personally, because of the circumstances of Laura Dennis's life and where she lives I would rather you not get involved with her or any of her family.

HARVEY: For God sakes, Dad, I'm only asking her to a dance. I'm not planning on marrying her.

FAY: Let's change the subject, please.

ANDREW: All right.

> (*Andrew exits. Fay picks up a magazine and starts to read as the lights fade. The lights are brought up on the porch of the Abernathy house. Lena Abernathy and Laura enter.*)

LENA: Your uncle is coming over sometime today to look over what I've spent on you this month. (*A pause.*) We need rain. Pecans are all falling off the trees. It's so dry.

LAURA: Are they still green?

LENA: Still green.

> (*A pause.*)

LAURA: I read where they had a tornado in South Dakota last week.

LENA: I'm scared of those things.

LAURA: Are they worse than Gulf storms?

LENA: I don't know. I'd hate to have to choose.

LAURA: Have you ever been in a tornado?

LENA: No, but I've been in plenty of Gulf storms, I can tell you.

LAURA: How many?

LENA: Six or seven. Three bad ones.

LAURA: I only remember one.

LENA: This is the month for them.

LAURA: I wonder if the tornado struck where my mother lives in South Dakota?

LENA: I don't know.

LAURA: Do you think anyone told my mother about Daddy's dying?

LENA: I don't know. (*A pause.*) I saw your cousin Ethel over here today. She said she and Velma were moving back.

LAURA: Who's Velma?

LENA: Ethel's daughter, another of your cousins. I said I was glad as I didn't like seeing the house all dark and shut up.

LAURA: I do have a lot of cousins.

LENA: Yes you do.

LAURA: I can't keep them all straight.

LENA: I guess not. (*A pause.*) Has Stewart asked you to the dance yet?

LAURA: No. Do you like him?

LENA: Yes, I do. I think he's very nice. Do you like him?

LAURA: Yes, I do like him.

> (*A pause. There is a sound of a Victrola next door, Gene Austin singing a song like "Sunday."*)

LENA: Somebody's over at Ethel's now. That's Gene Austin singing, remember him?

LAURA: Kind of.

LENA: I haven't heard a record of his in so long.

LAURA: Do you think my mother loved my father when she married him?

LENA: I don't know, honey.

LAURA: Do you think my father was in love with my mother?

LENA: Yes, I think so.

LAURA: Did he ever mention my mother to you?

LENA: No.

LAURA: Why do you think he loved her?

LENA: I just do.

(Velma, a woman in her early thirties, once beautiful, but now very dissipated, appears. She has her hands filled with phonograph records.)

VELMA: Heh.

LENA: Hello, Velma. Is that your Victrola I hear?

VELMA: Uh huh.

LENA: Welcome back, Velma.

VELMA: Thank you. Making a dress for yourself?

LENA: No, I'm making it for someone else.

VELMA: Who?

LENA: Mrs. Rockwood. Do you know her?

VELMA: I don't know if I know her or not. Why are you making a dress for her?

LENA: Because she pays me. It's how I make my living. Sewing for people.

VELMA: I can't even thread a needle. Mama can't either. Have you seen my mama?

LENA: I saw her earlier.

VELMA: Where in the hell is she? You never can find her when you want her. *(She goes on out.)*

LAURA: Is she drunk?

LENA: I think so. When I moved here Velma was fifteen, and I thought she was the loveliest, sweetest thing I'd ever seen. She had long blonde curls like Mary Pickford. That was the year they discovered oil here and the town was filled with young men working on the oil crews and her mother Ethel would have parties for them all the time.

VELMA: *(Calling.)* Mama! Mama!

LENA: And Velma was the life of those parties. One of the men, Charlie Deveraux, was over at her house morning, noon, and night.

VELMA: *(Calling.)* Mama! Mama!

LENA: Her father ran him off a couple of times.

LAURA: Why?

LENA: He was twenty-seven and he thought he was too old for Velma. Then Velma went to Houston and came back with her hair bobbed.

LAURA: Why did she do that?

LENA: I don't know. I tell you the whole town almost died because she cut off those beautiful curls.

VELMA: *(Calling.)* Mama! Mama!

LENA: Anyway, they soon forgot that because Velma ran off and married Charlie Deveraux and the parties stopped.

LAURA: What happened then?

LENA: After about six months she divorced him.

LAURA: Did the parties start again after she had divorced him?

LENA: No, because her father was sick by then, and after he died they closed up the house and moved to Houston.

(Velma comes back in with her records.)

Did you find your mama?

VELMA: No.

LENA: She probably went uptown for groceries or something.

VELMA: Look what I got? A bunch of old phonograph records. You want 'em?

LENA: No, thank you. This is Laura Dennis, Velma. She is your cousin.

VELMA: How are we cousins?

LENA: Your father's father and her father's father were brothers.

VELMA: You want these records? I've got Gene Austin, and Johnny Marvin and Ruth Etting. She sings "Ten Cents a Dance" an' I got someone singing "Am I Blue." I don't know who the hell that is. Oh, hell, there's a lot of 'em. You want 'em?

LAURA: No, thank you.

VELMA: That's all right. No hard feelings. *(She goes out.)*

LAURA: Do you think she's beautiful now?

LENA: Yes, in a way.

VELMA: *(Calling.)* Mama! Mama!

(Again the phonograph is heard next door. This time Ruth Etting singing a song like "Ten Cents a Dance" as the lights fade, and the lights are brought up on the Griswold living room. Fay Griswold is there. Harvey enters.)

FAY: Did you have a talk with your father?

(Harvey exits.)

Harvey, where are you going?

(Andrew enters.)

ANDREW: Where's Harvey?

FAY: I don't know. He just took off. He wouldn't tell me where he was going. *(A pause.)* Did you make it clear to him he could not ask Laura Dennis to the dance?

ANDREW: I think so.

FAY: You think so? You spoil him, Andrew. You spoil him rotten. You start out saying "no" to him about something and then you gradually begin to give in.

ANDREW: Well, so do you.

FAY: Maybe so. But this is one time we can't give into him. *(A pause.)* I hope we haven't spoiled him too much. *(A pause.)* He looks more like his father every day.

ANDREW: I know.

FAY: It's a wonder more people in town aren't aware of who his parents are.

ANDREW: I know.

FAY: When he asked you that time who his father was, what did you tell him?

ANDREW: I told him I didn't know, but that his mother lived in Pittsburgh, Pennsylvania.

FAY: What if one day he asks you for her name.

ANDREW: I'll say I don't know.

FAY: What if he wants to get in touch with the orphanage to find out.

ANDREW: Well... *(A pause.)* Maybe then I'll have to tell him the truth.

FAY: Maybe now is the time to do that.

ANDREW: Can we talk about this later, please? I have to go back to the office.

FAY: Andrew!

(Andrew starts out of the room as the lights fade. The lights are brought up on the porch of the Abernathy house. Lena and Laura are there.)

LAURA: Can I have a new dress for the dance if Stewart asks me to go?

LENA: I'll have to ask your uncle when he comes. He's your guardian. He tells me what I can spend. If he says yes, I'll make you one. We'll go downtown and pick out a pattern.

LAURA: What color do you think it should be?

LENA: What color would you like?

LAURA: Blue. Do you think he'll say I can have one?

LENA: I don't see why not. If I make it, it won't cost a whole lot.

LAURA: I went over to Catherine Lacy's two weeks ago, who was my mama's best friend. I got Mama's address in South Dakota and I wrote her a letter. I told her I wanted to come and visit her this summer. Why do you think she's never written me?

(A pause.)

LENA: I don't know.

LAURA: I asked her to send me a picture. Do you remember her?

LENA: To tell you the truth, Laura, I don't. I don't even remember having seen your mother.

LAURA: Catherine Lacy gave me a snapshot of her. She said it didn't do her justice. She said my mother was beautiful and was very vivacious. She said as quiet as my father was, my mother was just the opposite—always talking, laughing, and teasing. She said she was a cut up. *(A pause.)* She said my father wasn't always quiet. That she and her husband used to double date with them when they first were married and that he was lively then, too. Did my father seem quiet to you?

LENA: Sometimes. Sometimes he'd talk. Sometimes I had to do all the talking.

LAURA: My father always seemed very sad to me. Did he to you?

LENA: Yes, I guess so.

LAURA: Do you think that's why he drank so much because he was sad?

LENA: Maybe so.

LAURA: I told my mama in the letter he was dead.

(Screams can be heard from the house next door. Then the smashing of furniture. Ethel, Velma's mother, wearing a cowboy hat and boots comes in followed by a much younger man also wearing a cowboy hat and boots, Seymour Mann.)

ETHEL: Can I use your phone, Lena? Ours hasn't been connected yet.

LENA: Sure. The phone is in the front hall.

ETHEL: Velma is very drunk, and she's uncontrollable when she gets this way. I'm going to have to call a doctor to quiet her. They always have to give her a shot when she gets like this.

(Ethel hurries into the house. Seymour moves toward Lena and Laura.)

SEYMOUR: I'm Seymour Mann, Ethel's fiancé.

LENA: How do you do.

SEYMOUR: Sorry for all the trouble. Have you ever seen Velma in one of her fits? It is something. She had a bottle in her purse when we left Houston. I told Ethel about it, but Ethel is trusting and said Velma had promised her she would never get drunk again. Well, by the time we passed Sugarland she had started taking nips out of that bottle. Ethel tried to take it away from her and Velma hit her and said if she didn't get off her back she was going to jump out of the car and kill herself, so Ethel said go ahead and get drunk and I said that's another way of killing yourself and Velma cussed me out then and let me tell you she can curse.

(Stewart Wilson, seventeen, enters.)

STEWART: Heh.

LAURA: Hello, Stewart.

(Seymour goes to Stewart and extends his hand.)

SEYMOUR: I'm Seymour Mann.

STEWART: I'm Stewart Wilson.

SEYMOUR: Pleased to meet you.

STEWART: *(To Laura.)* Want to go for a ride? I have my mama's car.

LAURA: Where's your mama?

STEWART: Playing bridge.

(Velma appears.)

VELMA: Where's that old bitch?

SEYMOUR: Now come on, Velma. Let's go back inside the house.

VELMA: Where's that old bitch?

SEYMOUR: She's making a phone call. She's calling a doctor for you.

VELMA: Sure. Sure. Well, no sonevabitch doctor is coming near me. I'll tell
   you that. None. She needs a doctor. A head doctor.

(Ethel comes out.)

ETHEL: Velma! What the hell are you doing? Have you gone crazy?

VELMA: You old bitch.

ETHEL: Shut up, Velma. Come on, Seymour. The doctor is on his way.

SEYMOUR: Glad to have met you all.

(He and Ethel leave.)

VELMA: Where they going?

LENA: To your house, Velma.

VELMA: What the hell. *(She looks at Stewart.)* Who are you?

STEWART: I'm Stewart Wilson.

(Velma goes off)

   She's drunk and she's mean!

LAURA: May I go for a ride with Stewart?

LENA: All right. How long will you be?

STEWART: Not long. My mama has to have her car back by six.

LENA: Have a good time.

LAURA: Thank you.

*(She and Stewart leave. Lena goes into the house as the lights fade and are
   brought up on the Griswold living room. Harvey is there listening to a radio.
   Fay comes in.)*

FAY: Have you gotten your homework done?

(Harvey doesn't answer.)

FAY: Harvey.

> *(No answer.)*

> Harvey. I'm speaking to you.

HARVEY: What?

FAY: Turn the radio off so you can hear me.

HARVEY: I can hear you.

FAY: Well, then answer me. Have you done your homework?

HARVEY: Nope.

FAY: Then get to it. And turn that radio down.

> *(Andrew comes in. He has a letter. He hands it to Harvey.)*

ANDREW: Here's a letter from Verna Kate.

HARVEY: Thanks. *(He takes it.)*

ANDREW: Aren't you going to read it?

HARVEY: I'll read it.

FAY: What happened between you and Verna Kate? You used to ask every five
minutes if you had a letter from her.

HARVEY: I don't like her anymore.

FAY: What do you mean you don't like her anymore?

HARVEY: Just what I said.

ANDREW: Does she still like you?

HARVEY: I don't know. I guess so.

FAY: Have you told her how you feel?

HARVEY: Yeah.

FAY: Was she upset?

HARVEY: I guess so. *(A pause.)* I'm going to ask Laura Dennis to go to the dance.

ANDREW: Well, you'll have to walk, because you're not going to get the car.

HARVEY: All right, I'll walk.

FAY: I thought she was going out with Stewart Wilson.

HARVEY: So. There's no reason I can't ask her out too.

ANDREW: I bet she won't go with you.

HARVEY: Why?

ANDREW: Older girls don't like going with younger boys.

HARVEY: Verna Kate went with me. An' she's older than I am.

ANDREW: An' look where that got her.

> *(Harvey runs out.)*

> Harvey, come back here. Harvey did you hear me? Goddammit Harvey
come back here!

FAY: Andrew, don't lose your temper!

(Andrew starts out as the lights fade and are brought up on the porch of the Abernathy's. Velma comes into the yard. She has her records.)

VELMA: *(Calling.)* Lena.

(Lena comes out.)

LENA: Yes?

VELMA: I'm leaving, you know. I'm taking my records and I'm leaving. *(She sits down.)* Do you mind my asking you a question?

LENA: No.

VELMA: Did you? *(A pause.)* Oh, hell—I forgot the question.

(Edward Dennis enters. He is Laura's uncle and official guardian.)

EDWARD: Hello, ladies.

LENA: Hello, Mr. Dennis.

EDWARD: I've come for Laura's monthly accounting, Lena.

LENA: Won't you come in the house while I get the figures?

EDWARD: No. I'll just wait here.

(Lena goes into the house.)

How are you, Velma?

VELMA: All right. Who are you?

EDWARD: Now, you know who I am, Velma. I'm your father's first cousin, Edward Dennis.

VELMA: If you're my father's cousin, you must be mine, too.

EDWARD: Yes. Your first cousin once removed.

(Lena comes back outside with an envelope. She hands it to Edward.)

LENA: Here you are.

EDWARD: Thank you, Lena. How's Laura doing in school?

LENA: She does all right.

EDWARD: Is Laura taking any commercial courses?

LENA: Yes.

EDWARD: I'm glad. She has to be sensible. There will be no more money left from her father's trust when she finishes high school. She'll have to start earning money. I think she should start thinking about a job for the summer. How's your mother, Velma?

VELMA: She's getting married again to a boy younger than me. She loves men. All men, young, old, middle aged, fat, thin, hairy, bald. Just as long as they have you know what.

EDWARD: Where's Laura?

LENA: She's out riding.

(Edward starts away.)

Mr. Dennis.

EDWARD: Yes?

LENA: If Laura is asked to go to the dance next week she would like a new evening dress.

EDWARD: Let me think about it. Laura is seventeen now isn't she?

LENA: Yes.

VELMA: I was married at fifteen.

EDWARD: I remember, Velma.

VELMA: I eloped. What the hell was the name of my husband?

EDWARD: Charlie Deveraux.

VELMA: Right. I always regretted not having a church wedding.

EDWARD: What ever happened to Charlie Deveraux?

VELMA: I don't know. I'll ask my mama when we start speaking again. Maybe she knows.

EDWARD: Well, nice to have seen you ladies. I'll think about the evening dress. What will it come to?

LENA: Not much. Just the material and a pattern. I won't charge for making it.

EDWARD: That's very kind of you. *(He leaves.)*

VELMA: *(Calling)* Mama.

(She gets no answer. She calls again "Mama" and again now even louder, "Mama." Seymour appears. When Velma sees him she begins to laugh uncontrollably.)

SEYMOUR: What do you want, Velma?

VELMA: I want my mama. I want to ask her a question.

SEYMOUR: She's lying down. You've exhausted her.

VELMA: I want to ask her a question.

SEYMOUR: Tell me and I'll go ask her.

(She continues laughing.)

VELMA: I'm not going to tell you anything.

SEYMOUR: Suit yourself.

(He goes. Her laughter continues. She yells again, "Mama. Mama." No answer. Then again even louder: "Mama. Mama." She is laughing uncontrollably again. Ethel appears.)

ETHEL: For God sakes Velma. Do you want to drive me crazy? What in the name of God do you want?

VELMA: What happened to Charlie?

ETHEL: Charlie who?

VELMA: Charlie Deveraux. The man I married.

ETHEL: Is that what you got me out of bed for?

VELMA: What happened to him?

ETHEL: He's dead. You knew that.

VELMA: I didn't know that.

ETHEL: You certainly did. I told you.

VELMA: Then I forgot.

ETHEL: Please for my sake try to sober up. Seymour and I are getting married tomorrow.

(Again Velma goes into fits of laughter.)

VELMA: My God.

(Ethel leaves.)

I don't believe it. They're getting married.

(She leaves laughing as the lights fade and are brought up on the living room of the Griswold's. Fay and Andrew are there.)

ANDREW: Why do I have to tell him?

FAY: I think you should. You're the man. You're the one he's always asked about these things.

ANDREW: Well you be here while I tell him.

FAY: If you want me to be.

ANDREW: Yes. I would like you to be here. *(Calling.)* Harvey, will you come down here, please. *(To Fay.)* Oh, God. I dread this.

FAY: I know. I dread it too.

ANDREW: He seems so young and innocent. I know it's going to upset him.

FAY: What else can we do?

ANDREW: I know. It has to be done. *(A pause.)* Maybe we did the wrong thing in adopting him. Maybe…

FAY: Don't say that.

ANDREW: You know I don't really mean that. *(A pause.)* Oh, God. What's the right thing ever to do.

(Harvey enters.)

HARVEY: Well, you don't have to worry. I called my friend Bobby and he said that Stewart was asking Laura to the dance. *(A pause.)*

ANDREW: Sit down, son.

HARVEY: Why?

ANDREW: We need to have a little talk.

(A pause.)

HARVEY: What about?

ANDREW: Well… *(A pause.)* About your real mother and father.

HARVEY: I thought you didn't know who my father was?

ANDREW: I know. I lied to you. I do know.

(A pause.)

HARVEY: Why did you lie to me?

ANDREW: I don't know. I thought it was for the best for all of us. *(A pause.)* Your father was Harold Dennis, Laura Dennis's father's first cousin. Her mother, Cynthia Catherine Dennis, is your mother. Cynthia Catherine and Harold were having an affair, and she became pregnant with you. When Laura's father Roscoe found out about it, he killed your father. They were our friends.

HARVEY: Who were your friends?

ANDREW: Your mother and your father. We couldn't have children of our own and when we heard your mother had put you up for adoption we asked to be given you.

HARVEY: Does everybody in town know this?

ANDREW: Very few people, I think.

HARVEY: I don't believe you. I bet everybody knows it. That's why they always ask me if I know who my real parents are.

FAY: Honey, they ask that to all adopted children.

HARVEY: Does Laura know about this?

FAY: I don't know what she knows.

ANDREW: I'm sorry, son, we had to tell you all this, like this.

(Harvey begins to cry. Fay goes to him.)

FAY: Oh, come on, honey. Please don't cry. Please don't.

(Harvey composes himself. His father gives him a handkerchief, he wipes his eyes. He hands them a letter.)

HARVEY: I think you'd better read this.

(Fay takes the letter and reads it.)

FAY: My God.

(She hands the letter to Andrew. He reads it.)

ANDREW: How long have you known Verna Kate was pregnant?

HARVEY: Well…She wasn't sure until about three months ago.

ANDREW: Are you the father?

HARVEY: I don't know.

ANDREW: Does she think you are?

HARVEY: She says so. It could have been someone else.

ANDREW: Who?

HARVEY: A couple of other guys.

ANDREW: From here?

HARVEY: Yes.

ANDREW: How do you know?

HARVEY: They told me so.

FAY: Do her parents know?

HARVEY: I don't know. *(A pause.)* She wants me to marry her.

ANDREW: Do you want to marry her?

HARVEY: No.

FAY: You don't love her?

HARVEY: No.

FAY: Did you love her?

HARVEY: I don't know. I guess I did. At least I thought I did. But I don't think I'm the baby's father.

ANDREW: Who do you think is?

HARVEY: I don't know, but I don't think I am.

ANDREW: This is very serious, son.

HARVEY: I know it is.

ANDREW: We can't take this lightly.

HARVEY: I know that.

FAY: When is she expecting the baby?

HARVEY: Very soon, I guess.

ANDREW: Then her parents must know. *(A pause.)* We'd better go talk to them. You stay here until we get back.

(He and Fay leave. Harvey covers his face with his hands as the lights fade and are brought up on the porch of the Abernathy's. Lena is there. Laura enters.)

LAURA: Hi.

LENA: Hi. How was the ride?

LAURA: All right. Didn't get to go for long. His mother saw us as we were making the square and hailed us. She needed the car sooner than she thought.

LENA: Your uncle was here.

LAURA: I saw him driving away. I waved to him, but I don't think he saw me. Did you ask him about my dress?

LENA: Yes. He said he would think about it. He thinks you should think about a job for the summer.

LAURA: All right, I will. I don't think Stewart's mother likes me.

LENA: Why do you say that?

LAURA: I can tell. She barely speaks to me when she sees me. *(A pause.)* I like Stewart a lot. I don't know where liking Stewart is going to get me.

LENA: Does he know how you feel?

LAURA: Certainly not. *(A pause.)* He asked me to go to the dance with him.

LENA: There goes the doctor to give Velma her shot.

(A pause.)

LAURA: Is my Uncle Edward very rich?

LENA: I really don't know.

LAURA: Was my father rich before he killed his cousin?

LENA: I really don't know that either.

LAURA: I wonder if my mama has money?

LENA: And I don't know that.

(Seymour comes in.)

SEYMOUR: Do you mind if I use your phone again?

LENA: No.

SEYMOUR: I have to tend to some business for Ethel. I think we have an oil lease. Ethel's having to help the doctor with Velma. I think they're finally getting her quiet. *(He goes into the house.)*

LAURA: Here's the picture Mrs. Lacy gave me of my mother. *(She gives it to Lena.)*

LENA: She's very pretty.

LAURA: She's so young looking. She doesn't look a thing like I thought she would.

LENA: What did you think she'd look like?

LAURA: I don't know. Like me, I guess.

LENA: You look like your father.

(Ethel comes in.)

ETHEL: We finally got her quiet. Thank heavens! The doctor said the shot's going to last her until tonight at least.

LENA: Which doctor did you call?

ETHEL: I called Dr. White. He was very understanding. I've known him all my life. He delivered Velma.

(Seymour comes out.)

What did they say?

SEYMOUR: There's real interest.

ETHEL: Oh, wouldn't it be wonderful if we got a good lease. I could use the money.

SEYMOUR: Why stop with a lease. Why not have them find oil?

ETHEL: That would be wonderful, too. But don't get your hopes up. I've been through this too many times. You expect a well and you get a dry hole.

LENA: Are they drilling the well on your land?

ETHEL: Yes.

VELMA: *(Offstage.)* Mama! Mama!

(We hear offstage a recording of Ruth Etting singing a song like "Ten Cents a Dance.")

ETHEL: My God she's up again. The doctor was wrong. The shot didn't do her a bit of good. Seymour go call the damn doctor back and tell him to get back over here. He's going to have to give her another shot.

(Seymour goes back in the house.)

It's always something. *(Calling)* Velma, turn off that damn Victrola! *(She exits.)*

LENA: Well I'd better get supper on.

LAURA: I'll give you a hand.

ETHEL: *(Offstage.)* I said turn it off!

(The lights fade on the Abernathy area. The lights are brought up on the Griswold living room. Harvey is there. Fay and Andrew enter.)

HARVEY: How did it go?

ANDREW: It was very unpleasant. The Nelsons were very angry. They were demanding that you go with them to Virginia and marry Verna Kate, and then unfortunately I had to be very blunt. I said you weren't sure you were the father of the child and of course that infuriated them both. Mrs. Nelson began to cry and Mr. Nelson cursed you and called you a liar, and I had to remind him you were only sixteen years old and his daughter seventeen and that we thought after much consideration that the baby should be put up for adoption and they said they would never under any circumstances do that and then he said you would marry Verna Kate or he would kill you. I said where would that get us, that if he killed you I would have to kill him and then Mrs. Nelson cried and said he was just upset and would never do anything like that and then your mother cried and said we all felt so badly about it and then Mr. Nelson left the room and we all sat there a little while longer and then Mrs. Nelson said she thought you were fond of Verna Kate and would want to marry her and give the baby a name. And then I had to explain again that you were only sixteen and I was about to say once more you weren't sure the baby was yours, but before I could say that he came in the room again and said he would like us to leave. But before we left he wanted us to tell you that if you repeated in town that you couldn't be sure you were the father of the baby, he would kill you. And I tried to assure him you wouldn't even discuss it with anyone, but he stormed out of the room again without hearing me out. Have you ever discussed this with any of your friends?

HARVEY: Yessir, I told you.

ANDREW: Well, promise me you won't do it ever again. If they ask you about it, you will just say I don't want to discuss it.

HARVEY: Yessir.

ANDREW: This is going to be a very difficult time for all of us. They are obviously going to keep the baby and are going to bring it back here. We have to be very wise and discreet in how we act. I think for the next few months you'd better stay as close to home as possible.

HARVEY: Yessir.

ANDREW: Have you finished your homework?

HARVEY: Yessir.

ANDREW: It has been a long day. Let's all get ready for bed.

(Fay and Harvey leave. Andrew follows as the lights fade and the lights are brought up on the Abernathy yard. It is two days later. Laura is there. Edward Dennis enters.)

EDWARD: Hello, Laura.

LAURA: Hello, Uncle Edward.

EDWARD: You're looking well.

LAURA: Thank you.

EDWARD: I have some good news. When your father sold his land he, at my insistence, retained half the mineral rights which, of course, now belong to you. I am negotiating an oil lease for my share and your share of those rights. If they strike oil you will have a considerable income for a young woman.

LAURA: Yessir.

EDWARD: You have my permission to get a new dress for the dance.

LAURA: Yessir. Thank you.

EDWARD: As a matter of fact, your Aunt Gladys said, if you didn't want Mrs. Abernathy to make the dress, she would be glad to come into town and shop for one with you.

LAURA: Thank you, but I would like Mrs. Abernathy to make it.

EDWARD: Suit yourself. If oil or gas is found on our land you will have a nice little income for a number of years. *(A pause.)* Are you happy here with Mrs. Abernathy?

LAURA: Yessir.

EDWARD: She's kind to you?

LAURA: Yessir.

EDWARD: Well, I've often been concerned about that. She was brought up differently than we were, you know. She's from the country too, but she was poor. She used to work in the fields like a man. Her husband was thirty years older than she was. He brought her here from the country. We wanted to keep you out at our place with us, you know, when your father decided to move into town. But he wouldn't hear of it. He made me promise to never bring you back out there after he died. I think he felt that if he and your mother hadn't been living in the country none of those terrible things would have happened.

(Lena comes in.)

EDWARD: Hello, Mrs. Abernathy.

LENA: Hello, Mr. Dennis.

EDWARD: I told Laura she could go ahead with the evening dress. I didn't know if you've heard, but we have some oil interest out our way.

LENA: Ethel was telling us.

EDWARD: I'll keep in touch, Laura. *(He leaves.)*

LENA: We'll go down and buy the material for your dress this afternoon. I brought some patterns back for us to look over. *(She takes the patterns out of a bag.)* This is my favorite. I like the neck line. I think it will be very becoming. But you look them all over and see which one you like.

LAURA: Thank you.

(Ethel and Seymour enter.)

SEYMOUR: Hey Lena, hey Laura. We've just gotten married.

LENA: Congratulations.

SEYMOUR: Thank you.

ETHEL: We're leaving on a little honeymoon to New Orleans. We've agreed to let Edward represent us in negotiation for the oil lease, and nothing will happen with that for a week at least, so I figured it was a good time to get away. We wanted Velma to come with us, but she won't. She's not drinking now, but she's very depressed. I'd appreciate it if you'd keep an eye on her for me.

(Velma comes in.)

VELMA: I don't have a damn bit of money. You're going off on a honeymoon and leaving me with no money.

ETHEL: No money? I gave you two hundred dollars this morning.

VELMA: No, you didn't.

ETHEL: Yes, I did.

VELMA: No, you didn't.

ETHEL: Seymour, didn't you see me give her two hundred dollars this very morning?

SEYMOUR: Yes.

VELMA: Well, I don't have it now. I bet he took it.

SEYMOUR: I did not take it. I don't need your damn money. I have money of my own.

VELMA: Where did you get it from? You don't work. You only have what she gives you; money that belongs to my daddy.

ETHEL: Well, your daddy's dead now in case you haven't heard, and I'm his widow and everything he had belongs to me.

VELMA: Of course, you had him wrapped around your little finger; you made him think I couldn't take care of money.

ETHEL: Well, I don't think you can.

VELMA: I'm smart as you are. I'm smart enough not to give it to any man that looks twice at me.

SEYMOUR: Come on, Ethel. Give her money and let's go.

(Ethel opens her purse. She takes out some bills.)

ETHEL: Now try and behave yourself.

(Velma takes the money. Ethel and Seymour leave.)

VELMA: That's my new stepdaddy. Where does she find them. *(She sees the dress pattern.)* What's that?

LENA: Dress patterns. I'm making Laura an evening dress.

VELMA: Let me see. *(She looks at them.)* Which one are you going to use?

LENA: We haven't decided yet. Which one do you like?

VELMA: Honey, I can't tell anything by looking at patterns. I have to see it in a store. *(A pause.)* I'm very depressed. I'm going home. I'm going to bed. I may never get out of bed ever again. *(She exits.)*

LAURA: She seems so unhappy.

LENA: I know. *(She hands her one of the patterns.)* Do you like this one?

LAURA: Yes, I do.

(Stewart comes in.)

Hello, Stewart.

STEWART: Hello, Laura. I have to leave town suddenly and I can't be here for the dance. I wanted you to know in plenty of time in case someone else asks you to go.

LAURA: Where are you going Stewart?

STEWART: I'm afraid I can't tell you that now. I may be able to tell you when I get back and I may not. It all depends. Anyway, I'm sorry, and I hope you understand.

LAURA: Of course, I do.

STEWART: So long.

LAURA: Goodbye.

(Stewart leaves.)

LENA: That's too bad. I'm sure someone else will ask you to go.

LAURA: Maybe.

LENA: I think I'll go ahead and make the dress. Just in case.

LAURA: No, let's wait until I'm asked.

(We hear the record of a song like "Ten Cents a Dance" again from Velma's house. Lena and Laura listen as the lights fade. The lights are brought up on the Griswold area. Fay is there. Andrew comes in.)

ANDREW: What is it Fay?

FAY: I'm sorry to do this to you, but two friends called me just now and said that Jack Nelson is very distraught, and that Mrs. Nelson had to call their pastor to come and talk to him. According to them, he is blaming Harvey for everything. He says Harvey had told Verna Kate he was going to marry her, and that she had believed him.

ANDREW: I know. I've heard that too. They're leaving for Virginia in the morning. They won't be back, of course, until the baby is born.

FAY: Is Verna Kate still in school?

ANDREW: No. I hear she hasn't been in school for two months. She told the school she was ill and had to go home, but she stayed in Virginia with some friends. I guess finally they talked her into getting in touch with her parents.

(Harvey comes in.)

HARVEY: Hi.

ANDREW: Hello son.

FAY: How was school, son?

HARVEY: Okay.

FAY: Harvey, did you ever tell Verna Kate you were going to marry her?

HARVEY: No.

FAY: Will you swear to that?

HARVEY: Yes. Why?

FAY: She told her parents that you promised to marry her.

HARVEY: Well, I didn't.

FAY: Oh God, Andrew. What are we going to do?

ANDREW: We'll just have to wait it out. Nothing else we can do.

FAY: I want to leave here. I want us to take Harvey and leave this town.

ANDREW: Be sensible Fay. How can we leave here now, even if we wanted to.

FAY: I just can't stand it! I just can't stand it!

ANDREW: Fay!

HARVEY: Mama!

(Fay leaves the room, followed by Andrew and Harvey as the lights fade and

the lights are brought up on the Abernathy house—a week later. Laura is there reading. Velma comes in. She is very nervous and distraught, constantly humming half to herself a song like "Sunday." She wanders around the stage as she talks and hums.)

VELMA: Laura, honey, what day is it?

LAURA: Thursday.

(Velma continues to hum a song like "Sunday.")

VELMA: What time is it?

LAURA: Four-thirty.

(Velma continues to hum a song like "Sunday.")

VELMA: What are you doing?

LAURA: Studying for a history exam.

VELMA: I've slept around the clock every day since Mama has been gone. *(A pause.)* How long has she been gone?

LAURA: At least a week.

(Velma continues to hum a song like "Sunday.")

VELMA: Do you have any money?

LAURA: Two dollars.

VELMA: Two dollars? That won't do me any good. Mama gave me some money, but I can't find it. Is Lena home?

LAURA: No.

VELMA: Will she be back soon?

LAURA: In time to fix supper.

VELMA: Do you think she has any money?

LAURA: I don't know.

(Velma continues to hum a song like "Sunday.")

VELMA: You know what Mama did before she left on her honeymoon? She smashed all my records. Wasn't that mean? Do you remember my daddy?

LAURA: No.

VELMA: Too bad he had to be the one to die. When I cut off my curls he just cried like a baby. When I married Charlie Deveraux he said, "What have you done marrying at fifteen." Did you know my husband Charlie Deveraux?

LAURA: No.

VELMA: The last time I saw him he was bald. What happened to your hair Charlie, I asked him, you're as bald as a billiard ball. I knew your mama, did you know that? I was younger than she was, but I knew her. *(She continues to hum a song like "Sunday.")* How old would your mama be?

LAURA: I don't know.

VELMA: How old would your daddy be if he were living?

LAURA: I don't know that either. No one ever told me how old they were.

VELMA: Didn't you ever ask?

LAURA: No.

VELMA: Well, I'll ask Mama when she comes home. *(She continues to hum a song like "Sunday.")* She'll know. I remember the day your daddy killed our cousin, Harold Dennis. I was coming out of the drugstore and someone said, I forgot who now, "Your cousin Roscoe has just shot and killed his cousin right in front of the Queen Theater." Papa was with me and he said, "My God, what's next." He made me go home and he went over to the Queen Theater to see what he could do. *(She continues to hum a song like "Sunday.")* What's your mama's name? I forgot.

LAURA: Cynthia Catherine.

VELMA: Cynthia Catherine. That's right. Where's she now? *(She continues to hum a song like "Sunday.")*

LAURA: South Dakota. *(She reaches in her pocket and takes out the snapshot.)* Here's a picture of my mother.

(Velma looks at it.)

VELMA: Is that your mother?

LAURA: Yes, don't you recognize her?

VELMA: No I don't. *(She continues to hum a song like "Sunday." She gives the picture back to Laura and she gets up.)* I don't think Lena's ever coming back. I've got to get some money. I'm going back to look for the money Mama left me.

(She leaves. Laura looks at her mother's picture, puts it back in the pocket of her dress and resumes her studying. Edward enters.)

EDWARD: Hello, Laura.

LAURA: Hello, Uncle Edward.

EDWARD: Did you hear the terrible thing that happen to Verna Kate Nelson?

LAURA: No.

EDWARD: She died. Up in Virginia.

LAURA: Oh, I'm sorry.

EDWARD: It's quite a shock. I feel so for her mother and father. *(A pause.)* Would you like to have supper with me and your aunt tonight?

LAURA: I can't tonight, thank you. I have to study for my exams.

EDWARD: Another time, then?

LAURA: What did she die of?

EDWARD: I don't know. No one seems to know. It was all very sudden I understand.

(Lena comes in.)

LENA: Hello, Mr. Dennis.

EDWARD: Hello, Mrs. Abernathy. I came to take Laura to supper, but she has to study. I'll see you later, Laura.

LAURA: Yessir.

(Edward goes.)

A terrible thing happened. Verna Kate Nelson died.

LENA: I know. I just heard.

LAURA: Where did you hear?

LENA: At the grocery store. It's all anyone can talk about.

LAURA: I'm going over to Pud's. I'll be back in a while.

(She leaves as the lights fade and are then brought up on the Murphy living room. Pud and Annie Laurie are there. Laura enters.)

PUD: Did you hear about Verna Kate?

LAURA: Yes.

PUD: When did you hear about it?

LAURA: Just now.

PUD: Who told you?

LAURA: My uncle.

PUD: Isn't it terrible? I feel so bad about it. I'm sorry for every mean thing I ever said about Verna Kate.

ANNIE LAURIE: I never knew her, but I feel bad about it too.

PUD: Who told you about it?

ANNIE LAURIE: You did.

PUD: Oh, that's right. The whole town feels bad about it. I wonder if they'll still have the dance.

ANNIE LAURIE: Why wouldn't they?

PUD: Out of respect to Verna Kate and her family.

ANNIE LAURIE: Oh.

PUD: Do you think they'll still have the dance, Laura?

LAURA: I don't know.

ANNIE LAURIE: What did she die of?

PUD: I don't know. I forgot to ask Mama. Do you know, Laura?

LAURA: No.

PUD: *(Calling.)* Mama.

MRS. MURPHY: *(Calling back.)* Yes.

PUD: *(Calling.)* What did Verna Kate die of?

MRS. MURPHY: *(Calling back.)* I don't know.

PUD: I bet she does, too, but she just won't tell us.

(Mrs. Murphy enters.)

MRS. MURPHY: Yes, I do know and you're going to hear it sooner or later, so I might as well tell you. She died in childbirth.

PUD: My God, Mama. *(She begins to cry.)*

MRS. MURPHY: Now, come on, Pud. That's not doing anyone any good.

PUD: Who was the father?

MRS. MURPHY: *(A pause.)* Harvey Griswold.

PUD: Harvey Griswold.

MRS. MURPHY: That's what Verna Kate told her parents.

PUD: Harvey Griswold.

MRS. MURPHY: Yes, but I understand he says he wasn't, and his parents say they believe him, and they refuse to let him marry her.

PUD: Did she want to marry him?

MRS. MURPHY: I don't know. All I know is that the Griswolds said they wouldn't permit it. When Stewart Wilson heard about it…

PUD: Stewart Wilson? How did he hear about it?

MRS. MURPHY: Stewart? I don't know. Maybe Verna Kate's mother or father told him, or maybe Verna Kate called him from Virginia and told him. Anyway, I understand, he told her parents he loved her and wanted to marry her, and he and her parents left for Virginia, and she went into labor and died.

PUD: Did they marry?

MRS. MURPHY: I don't know. No one seems to know.

PUD: What about the baby?

MRS. MURPHY: It's a boy. They're bringing it home with them.

LAURA: When is the funeral?

MRS. MURPHY: I suppose as soon as they get her body here.

PUD: I hear you're gonna be rich, Laura.

MRS. MURPHY: Pud.

PUD: Didn't you say she was gonna be rich.

MRS. MURPHY: I certainly did not. I said I heard her uncle was negotiating for an oil lease, and, of course, if that happens and they drill for a well and they strike oil, Laura will be rich.

(The phone rings.)

Excuse me girls. There's my phone. *(She goes.)*

PUD: Has anyone asked you to the dance yet, Laura?

LAURA: No.

(Mrs. Murphy enters.)

MRS. MURPHY: The dance has been called off until next week. Verna Kate's funeral is day after tomorrow.

PUD: Mama, if Stewart married Verna Kate before she died, will he raise her baby?

MRS. MURPHY: I don't know, but I doubt it. I think her parents will raise the poor little thing.

PUD: Imagine being seventeen and being married and a father.

ANNIE LAURIE: Stepfather. He's not the real father.

LAURA: My cousin was married at fifteen.

PUD: Which cousin?

LAURA: Velma. She and her mother have just moved back here.

MRS. MURPHY: Are they back in their old house?

LAURA: Yes. She was divorced at sixteen. She had long blonde curls like Mary Pickford.

ANNIE LAURIE: The movie star?

MRS. MURPHY: Yes and she looked just like a movie star we all thought. It's been an emotional day, hearing about Verna Kate, and now thinking about Velma with her long blonde curls. *(A pause.)* It all seemed so simple then. You fell in love, you got married, you had children. *(She leaves.)*

LAURA: My cousin Velma has a lot of old phonograph records and she plays them all the time.

PUD: Why does she do that?

LAURA: I don't know. I've got to go. *(She goes.)*

PUD: All right. See you later.

ANNIE LAURIE: Why did she leave so suddenly?

PUD: I don't know.

ANNIE LAURIE: Do you think she's upset because she doesn't have a date for the dance?

PUD: Maybe.

ANNIE LAURIE: I've got to go too.

PUD: I'll walk you over to your house.

(They leave as the lights fade. The lights are brought up on the Abernathy porch and yard. Laura and Lena are there.)

LENA: How was the funeral?

LAURA: It was very sad. Verna Kate's mother and father were just heartbroken, of course. Stewart was sitting with them. It's the first time I've seen him; he hasn't come back to school yet.

LENA: Did you speak to him?

LAURA: No. *(A pause.)* I heard they were married in her room at the hospital, but she died soon after. *(A pause.)* Did you go by the post office today?

LENA: Yes, I did.

LAURA: No letter for me?

LENA: No. Of course, there is another delivery at four o'clock.

LAURA: You never get any out of town mail in the four o'clock delivery. To tell you the truth I don't know how I'll feel if my mother does write me and says come on to South Dakota. I'll be torn, I tell you that, because I won't like leaving you, and yet...I want to see my mother, I want to be with my mother, maybe even live with my mother. I guess what I really want is my mother to want me. *(A pause.)* I wouldn't want to live with my aunt and uncle even if they asked me to live with them, because I know my father didn't want me ever living out there again, and, too, because I feel in my heart my aunt and uncle don't really want me out there. Then, too, I want you to know that if I hear from my mother and she wants me to come to South Dakota, I'll probably go, but I'll feel sorry, very sorry to be leaving you, because I don't know what my daddy and I would have done if we hadn't been living here when he got so sick. *(A pause.)* Do you think my mother will answer my letter?

LENA: I hope so.

(A pause.)

LAURA: Harvey Griswold came back to school today, but none of the girls would speak to him. Even some of the boys wouldn't talk to him. Pud says her mother heard if Harvey didn't stop telling everybody in town who will listen to him that the baby wasn't his Mr. Nelson is going to kill him. *(A pause.)* I wonder what would have happened if my father hadn't killed his cousin, and if my mother hadn't fallen in love with his cousin. His name was Harold wasn't it?

LENA: Yes, I believe so.

LAURA: Harold Dennis. Did you ever see him?

LENA: Not that I remember.

LAURA: I went to see Catherine Lacy again yesterday. She said she hears from my mother every once in a while and I wanted to know if she had heard from my mother and if she had, had my mother mentioned getting a letter from me. She hadn't heard from her, she said. *(A pause.)* If I ask you something will you tell me the truth?

LENA: If I know the truth.

LAURA: Was my mother pregnant with Harold Dennis's baby when he was killed?

LENA: I don't know that.

LAURA: Had you ever heard it?

LENA: Yes. I've heard it. Who told you about it?

LAURA: A girl at school who lives out in the country told my friend Pud and Pud told me. Pud asked her mother and her mother said it was true and that the baby was born in South Dakota, but she didn't know if it was a boy or a girl. I wanted to ask Catherine Lacy if she knew, but I lost my courage.

(Ethel comes in.)

ETHEL: Hello.

LENA: Hello, Ethel. How are you?

ETHEL: Oh, I'm very depressed darling, very depressed, and worn out besides. I told Seymour I just had to get out of the house for a second at least. We have to watch Velma constantly these days. She says she is unhappy and going to kill herself. She won't get out of bed, she won't eat, she won't see a doctor when he comes over. She's not really going to kill herself, I know that, but like I told Seymour what if I'm wrong and she would kill herself. *(A pause.)* Why are you all dressed up Laura?

LAURA: I went to my friend Verna Kate's funeral.

ETHEL: Oh, yes. *(A pause.)* It's terrible to lose a child. I lost a little boy, you know.

LENA: I remember.

ETHEL: How old was your little boy when he died?

LENA: Five.

ETHEL: That crazy husband of yours. He used to come over to the house and rave and rant and say that damn child isn't mine. Be sensible, my husband used to say, Lena is a good woman. Whose child could it be if it wasn't yours? My husband, mild as he was most of the time, could on occasion have a terrible temper, and the day you were to bury the child your husband came over to our house and said I'm not going to the funeral. The child is not mine and I'm not going. And my husband said that's your business, but I'm going and my wife's going, and I thank you not to come around here any more with talk like that. But he wouldn't go, would he?

LENA: No.

ETHEL: The old fool, and you were so nice to him, too, my God, you were good to him. You waited on him hand and foot when he was sick and he was sick forever it seemed to me.

LENA: It was a long time.

ETHEL: Did you hear from your uncle today, Laura?

LAURA: No.

ETHEL: I said to Seymour I hope we haven't made a mistake turning the lease negotiations over to him. Excuse me for talking about your kin, Laura, but he can be arrogant and he always thinks you have to act tough when you negotiate.

LAURA: Excuse me. *(She goes into the house.)*

ETHEL: Edward told me that the money her daddy left is almost gone and if we don't get the oil lease, she'll have to soon get a job. Does she know that?

LENA: Yes.

ETHEL: You know the boy Harvey Griswold they say got the Nelson girl pregnant?

LENA: Yes, I know him.

ETHEL: He's adopted, you know.

LENA: Yes, I knew that.

ETHEL: You know whose child he is? *(A pause.)* Cynthia Catherine's and Harold Dennis's. Did you know that?

LENA: I'd heard it.

ETHEL: My husband arranged the whole adoption.

(Seymour comes to the edge of the yard.)

What is it, Seymour?

SEYMOUR: Velma's crying.

ETHEL: What's she crying about now?

SEYMOUR: I don't know. She won't tell me.

ETHEL: Oh, my God. Tell her I'll be there in a little.

(Seymour leaves.)

She's gotten so sensitive. Seymour probably said something to hurt her feelings. The least thing hurts her feelings. She didn't use to be that way, you know. When she was married at fifteen, my husband went to the school and said Velma is married, but we want her to finish high school and her husband agrees that she should, and the superintendent said that can't be, we can't have a married girl in school here. None of our teachers are married, and when they marry we ask right away for their resignation. But my husband said, I don't care about the teachers, Velma is going back to school, so they said, well, all right, but she can't leave the classroom once she gets there, not even for recess. But that didn't bother Velma. In those days nothing bothered Velma. She marched right up to that school as big as life. Of course, like I prophesied, she was sick of her husband before the year was out, and divorced him and in her senior year they let her go out during recess like all the other girls. Everybody in town was talking about her, you know, married and divorced by the time she was sixteen, but that didn't bother Velma either. But like I say, now, you can't look at her sideways without her starting to cry.

(Laura comes in.)

LAURA: I called the post office. There was no mail in our box.

ETHEL: Expecting a letter?

LAURA: Uh huh.

ETHEL: From your sweetheart?

LAURA: I don't have a sweetheart.

ETHEL: I don't believe that. A pretty girl like you.

(Velma enters. She is in her nightgown and robe.)

Well, I'm glad to see you out of bed, Velma. Come here and visit. It will do you good.

VELMA: I don't want to visit.

ETHEL: Now what do you want?

VELMA: I don't know what I want, I wish I did.

(Seymour enters.)

SEYMOUR: Ethel. Edward just called. He said Mr. Nelson just shot and killed the Griswold boy.

ETHEL: My God!

SEYMOUR: He said he was killed on the corner by the old Queen Theater. Almost to the spot where his father was killed.

LAURA: Who was his father?

ETHEL: Well, you're going to hear all of this now, his father was your cousin and Velma's cousin Harold Dennis. His mother was your mother.

LAURA: Then Harvey was my half brother?

ETHEL: Yes.

(Laura goes to Lena. Lena holds her.)

LAURA: Does my Mama know he's here?

ETHEL: I think so.

LAURA: Is someone going to tell her he's dead?

ETHEL: I expect your uncle will.

(Laura is crying now. Lena holds her.)

VELMA: What's wrong with Laura?

ETHEL: She's upset Velma. My God didn't you just hear what we said? Her half brother was just killed. Now come on. Let's go home.

(She takes Velma by the hand and they start out as the lights fade. The lights

are brought up center on the Griswold living room. Fay enters. Andrew,
Edward, and Laura come in. Edward goes over to Fay. Fay is crying.)

EDWARD: We're awful sorry.

FAY: Thank you. Hello, Laura.

LAURA: Hello. I'm very sorry.

FAY: Edward why did we ever bring him here?

EDWARD: This was your home. You did what you thought was best for the boy.

ANDREW: Has anybody been in touch with Cynthia Catherine?

EDWARD: I haven't.

ANDREW: I'll reach her. I'm sure Catherine Lacy has her address.

LAURA: I have her address.

ANDREW: I'll get it from you later.

FAY: We didn't want him to leave the house, but he had to go back to school, and we asked him not to discuss this with anyone.

ANDREW: But he said the boys in school kept teasing him and they kept saying they had seen the baby and he looked just like him and that Stewart Wilson was going to beat him up when he came back to school, and how many more children had he fathered. You know how cruel boys can be. Anyway, he was distraught and wanted to go to the picture show just to be off by himself and against my better judgment I gave him the money to go, and Jack Nelson saw him going toward the picture show and called to him and said I told your parents to tell you not to discuss our daughter or our grandchild, and Ned Stansbury said he was on the corner and heard Harvey say I didn't discuss her with anyone, and Nelson said you're lying and he took a pistol and shot him. Ned said he was killed by the first shot.

EDWARD: Did you ever tell him who his father was?

ANDREW: Yes and his mother. Just a few days ago. We felt we had to when all this started. *(A pause.)* Laura.

LAURA: Yessir.

ANDREW: Did you hear what I told your uncle?

LAURA: Yessir.

ANDREW: He knew he was your half brother.

LAURA: Yessir.

ANDREW: His body's at the funeral parlor now. The undertaker says he'll be ready for viewing tonight. I hope you can see him. He looks very peaceful.

LAURA: Yessir.

EDWARD: When will the funeral be?

ANDREW: Friday afternoon.

EDWARD: Will he be buried in the old cemetery or the new?

ANDREW: The old.

EDWARD: I'm glad of that. I much prefer the old cemetery. His father is buried there, you know.

ANDREW: Yes. I know.

EDWARD: Will he be buried with his father?

ANDREW: No. We're getting our own plot. Fay and I will be buried beside him in time.

(Ethel and Velma enter.)

FAY: Ethel, I remember the day you called to tell me that the adoption had been arranged. We were so happy.

ETHEL: I remember that day well. Joe and I were happy for you, too. We were all so glad the boy was going to have a good home with people we knew.

FAY: I keep thinking if we had told him from the start who his parents were, but then I remember, Edward, you felt it would be an unnecessary burden for him.

EDWARD: Yes, I did. I still do.

FAY: We had to finally tell him, Edward. Under the circumstances.

EDWARD: I understand that.

FAY: We had to tell him. Didn't we Andrew?

ANDREW: Yes.

EDWARD: You should have no regrets. You gave him a good home. A wonderful home.

ANDREW: We tried to.

FAY: How are you Velma?

VELMA: I'm all right, I guess.

ETHEL: Velma has been ill for more than a week. This is the first time she's gotten dressed in I don't know when.

FAY: I appreciate your coming, Velma.

VELMA: Thank you.

FAY: You're married again, Ethel?

ETHEL: Yes, just got married.

FAY: Well, I hope I can meet your husband one day.

ETHEL: You will.

ANDREW: I hear you're negotiating an oil lease for your family, Edward.

EDWARD: Yes, they all put me in charge.

ANDREW: How is it going?

EDWARD: Slow.

FAY: We're taking the book for people to sign over to the funeral parlor tonight. Would you like to sign it now?

(Ethel signs, then Velma. When they finish signing they move away and Edward signs and then joins Ethel and Velma. Laura signs and as she finishes Fay goes to her and holds her for a moment. Then Laura joins Edward and the others and they leave followed by Andrew and Fay, as the lights are brought down. The lights are brought up on the Murphy parlor. Pud and Annie Laurie are there. They are in their new evening dresses.)

PUD: I thought for sure when Harvey was killed they would call off the dance again, but they didn't.

ANNIE LAURIE: Did you go to his funeral?

PUD: No. Mama went. She said very few people were there. She said Laura was there. He was her half brother.

ANNIE LAURIE: I heard that, too.

LAURA: *(From off calling.)* Pud! *(Laura enters.)*

PUD: Hi, Laura.

LAURA: Hi. I came by to see your dresses and they're beautiful.

PUD: Thank you.

ANNIE LAURIE: Thank you.

(Mrs. Murphy enters.)

MRS. MURPHY: Hello, Laura.

LAURA: Hello.

MRS. MURPHY: Don't the girls look pretty?

LAURA: Yes, they do.

PUD: I'm sorry you aren't going to the dance, Laura.

MRS. MURPHY: I don't think Laura would feel like going to the dance tonight under the circumstances.

ANNIE LAURIE: Under what circumstances?

(A pause. No one answers her.)

Oh, yes.

(A pause.)

MRS. MURPHY: I hear your uncle signed the oil lease for you all.

LAURA: Yes, ma'am.

MRS. MURPHY: I hear your share of the lease is seven thousand.

LAURA: Yes, ma'am. I think so.

MRS. MURPHY: And if they strike oil—my goodness you'll be worth all kinds of money.

PUD: Don't forget your old friends when you get rich, Laura.

LAURA: *(Laughing.)* I won't. I have to go. Have a good time at the dance.

PUD: We will.

(Laura leaves.)

ANNIE LAURIE: Oh, I felt terrible asking what the circumstances were that kept her from going to the dance. I just forgot.

MRS. MURPHY: I know, honey. We all make mistakes like that.

PUD: Laura looks so sad. I don't feel like going to the dance at all now, Mama.

ANNIE LAURIE: Come on Pud. We'll have a good time.

MRS. MURPHY: That's right. Come on. We'll sit on the porch and wait for your dates.

(She starts out and Pud and Annie Laurie follow as the lights fade. The lights are brought up on the Abernathy porch. Laura is there with Lena. In the distance we can hear the dance music.)

LENA: Sounds like a nice orchestra. Who is it? Do you know?

LAURA: I think someone said it was Red Cornelson. They're from El Campo. Did you ever go to dances here?

LENA: No. I came here as a married woman. I don't think my husband even knew how to dance.

LAURA: Did my father ever dance?

LENA: I don't know. Not when I knew him, anyway.

(Edward enters.)

EDWARD: Evening.

LENA: Evening.

LAURA: Hello, Uncle Edward.

EDWARD: I brought some papers for you to sign, Laura, for the oil lease.

LAURA: Yessir.

EDWARD: We'd better go into the light.

LAURA: Yessir.

(She and Edward go into the house. Ethel comes in.)

ETHEL: Is Laura signing the lease papers?

LENA: Yes.

ETHEL: I just signed mine and happily too I might add.

LENA: Congratulations. I'm happy for you. Hear the dance music?

ETHEL: Yes.

LENA: I'm surprised they're having a dance the same day as Harvey's funeral. When I was a girl growing up in the country, people thought it was sinful to dance. My mother had danced as a girl, and she taught me how. But we had to keep it secret from my father.

(Seymour comes in.)

SEYMOUR: Ethel, do you know Velma is drinking again?

ETHEL: Yes, but what can I do about it? When I get my lease money I'm going to send her away for a cure.

SEYMOUR: I'm going to need a cure if she keeps this up.

(Velma comes out with a bottle of whiskey.)

ETHEL: Give me the bottle, Velma. You don't want people seeing you drinking out of a bottle.

VELMA: Go to hell.

(Seymour starts out.)

Where are you going?

SEYMOUR: Away from you.

VELMA: Go to hell. Everybody go to hell. *(She looks at Lena.)* You know that old husband of yours was always saying you were sleeping with Laura's daddy, my cousin.

ETHEL: Velma. Come on.

VELMA: What was his name? Roscoe. Cousin Roscoe. There's Cousin Edwards and Cousin…

ETHEL: Velma, just shut up.

VELMA: My apologies. I meant no offense.

ETHEL: Now, come on home.

VELMA: No thank you. I like it over here.

ETHEL: Well, you can't stay here. Lena doesn't want you over here.

LENA: It's all right, Ethel.

(A pause.)

VELMA: There is a dance at the opera house. I don't have a date. You can't go without a date, if you're a girl. Now, a boy can go without a date and they call him a stag, but a girl can't go without a date, because if she did you know what they would call her. W-H-O-R-E! You know what that spells?

ETHEL: We all know what it spells, Velma.

VELMA: I'm going to get Seymour to take me to the dance. He's been making passes at me, you know.

ETHEL: Oh, Velma. Hush up.

VELMA: He certainly has and I told him to bug off. You are married to my mother. *(She goes out calling: "Seymour I want you to take me to the dance.")*

ETHEL: Oh God. How do I stand it?

(She goes out. Laura and Edward come out of the house.)

EDWARD: Well, everything is signed. Let's hope this time next month we'll have a producing well. Wouldn't that be fine? *(He starts out.)* Thank you, Laura.

LAURA: Yessir. Thank you.

EDWARD: Goodnight, Mrs. Abernathy.

LENA: Goodnight, Mr. Dennis.

(*Edward leaves.*)

LAURA: Looks like I'm going to get to go to college if I want to.

LENA: Do you want to?

LAURA: To tell you the truth I don't know what I want. (*A pause.*) He wants me to go to Sophie Newcomb.

LENA: That's in New Orleans.

LAURA: Yes. My aunt went there, he said. (*A pause.*) He said my mother got in touch with him. She asked him to ask me not to write her anymore. She doesn't want to see me. She wants to forget about everything that happened here. She's married again now and has a family. A boy six and a girl four.

(*Music from the dance can be heard.*)

Hear the music from the dance?

LENA: Yes.

LAURA: I bet they're having a good time. (*A pause.*) I saw Stewart this afternoon as he came out of the jail. I think he had been to see Mr. Nelson. He didn't see me. Somebody said he's not going back to school here, that he's going to finish out the year at Allen Academy. (*A pause.*) Do you know I've lived here with you eleven years? I was counting them up just now.

LENA: I expect it has been.

LAURA: When we first came to town Daddy got a house and a colored lady to cook for us and take care of me when he wasn't home. I remember when he came home and said there's a nice lady in town here that has rooms to rent and serves meals and will look after you when I'm away and we're going to move in there. You know I remember the first time I saw you.

LENA: Do you?

LAURA: You were standing in the room there watching when Daddy and I drove by in his car and he said that lady standing in the door is the one that we're going to live with and then I saw Mr. Abernathy sitting on the porch and I said who is that and he said that's her husband, he's not well. I don't remember ever seeing him again. Why didn't I ever see him again?

LENA: That was the last time he left his room. He had been very sick a long time. We had to take him to the hospital a week after you and your daddy came. He died there.

LAURA: How long were you married to him?

LENA: Twelve years.

LAURA: Do you realize if my mother walked into this yard right now, I wouldn't know her. She would have to say, "Laura Dennis, I'm your mother," before I'd know who she was. *(A pause.)* I went to school with my brother for I don't know how many years and I didn't know who he was and he didn't know who I was.

(She is crying. Velma comes in.)

VELMA: Seems like I owe my mother an apology and my stepfather an apology, but they're locked up in their room and won't permit me to apologize. *(A pause.)* I thought my mother out of meanness had destroyed all my records, but I was mistaken. I found them in a closet half an hour ago, and soon after that I found the two hundred dollars I thought my stepfather had stolen. I am so sorry for the false accusations. *(She begins to cry.)*

LENA: It's all right, Velma. It's all right.

VELMA: Nothing is all right. Nothing at all is all right. I try to stay sober and I get so depressed I can't stand it and I get drunk and get crazy.

(The record stops playing. The dance music is again heard.)

The dance music is pretty isn't it? I used to love to dance. I was very popular, too. I had long blonde curls. Everybody said just like Mary Pickford...sweet and innocent and... *(A pause.)* I was always very popular when I went to the dances. Even after I was married and divorced I was still very, very popular. *(A pause.)* Do you think Andrew Griswold will kill Mr. Nelson? Mama says he won't, she says it will all blow over. Mama is usually right about these things. She says she's seen a lot of killings in her time. *(A pause.)* What's your opinion? Do you think Andrew Griswold will kill Mr. Nelson?

LENA: I hope not, Velma.

VELMA: I saw Laura's daddy kill our cousin Harold Dennis as he...

(Laura is crying now.)

Laura's crying.

LENA: She'll be all right, Velma.

VELMA: What's the name of the song the orchestra is playing?

LENA: I don't know.

LAURA: "Dream a Little Dream of Me."

VELMA: "Dream a Little Dream of Me." That's a sweet song isn't it?

(There is silence then as they listen to the dance music and the lights fade.)

END OF PLAY

VERNON EARLY

ORIGINAL PRODUCTION

Vernon Early was first presented at the Alabama Shakespeare Festival, Montgomery, Alabama, May–June 1998. It was directed by Charles Towers with the following cast:

MILDRED EARLY	Jill Tanner
VERNON EARLY	Philip Pleasants
VELMA	Sonja Lanzener
MISS ETHEL	Mary Fogarty
ERMA	Elisabeth Omilami
LOU ANN	Lanier Walker/Blaine Wise
DOUGLAS	Danno Allgrove/Cameron Doucette
JACKIE	Yvette Jones-Smedley
GERTRUDE MAYFIELD	Fiona Macleod
HARRY REAVIS	Barry Boys
REENIE REAVIS	Monica Bell
GRANT	Virgil Wilson
SOLOMON	Jeff Obafemi Carr
SHERIFF	Reese Phillip Purser

PLACE
Harrison, Texas

TIME
Fall, 1950

Bedroom of the Earlys. It is three in the morning, the room is in darkness except for a night light. A phone rings. Neither of the two occupants of the bed wake. The phone rings again and again. Finally, Mildred Early, fifty, raises up to where she can reach for the phone, does so, takes the receiver off of the hook, brings it over to where she lies on the bed and speaks into it with a sleepy voice.

MILDRED: Hello. Yes. Hello. Yes. Oh. May I ask who's calling? Oh. All right.
(She pokes her husband. He is in a sound, sound sleep and she can't wake him. She speaks again into the phone.)
Miss Ethel, he's so sound asleep it's going to take me awhile to wake him. I'll have him call you as soon as I can get him awake. I know it. Yes'm. As soon as I can.
(She turns on the reading light hanging on the bed, and she turns to her husband, who is now snoring ever so slightly and shakes him with great force. He still doesn't respond and she gets out of the bed throwing the bed clothes back angrily, looking at the clock.)
My God. It's three-thirty in the morning. The drunken fools.
(We can get a fairly good look at Mildred now in the darkened room. The phone rings again. She answers it, almost crossly this time.)
Yes. Yes. No. I haven't gotten him awake yet. I know that. Yes'm. I'm trying. Yes ma'm. I promise. *(She hangs the phone up. She lifts her husband by the arm. She shakes him again and again, almost screaming at him as she does so.)* Vernon! Vernon! Wake up! For Godsakes!
(He still doesn't wake. She lets his arm fall back.)
I am so sick of being awakened in the night this way. There's not a doctor in this town but this jack ass I'm married to will allow himself to be called any time of the night. *(She takes him by the shoulders now and shakes him yelling.)* Vernon! Vernon!
(Vernon begins to stir, he mutters something, she shakes him again and again, calling over and over.)
Vernon. Vernon. Vernon.
(At last he raises his head, opens his eyes and looks at her.)
VERNON: What?
MILDRED: My God. You don't hear the phone. You don't hear me. You're killing yourself for these damn people. Killing yourself. And for what? I'd like to know. You've got all the money any man on earth could wish for. And don't talk to me about a doctor's duty. What about your duty to me? I've put up with this for nearly thirty years. Getting up in the

middle of the night. Waking you up. If it's a doctor's duty, why are you the only doctor in town or the State of Texas, as near as I can make out, killing himself this way? And I wouldn't care if it were for the sick or the dying. But not for those crazy drunk Dennis's. You're gonna get killed out there one night, getting into the middle of one of their crazy, drunken brawls.

(The phone rings again.)

Oh, my God. There they are again. Vernon, are you awake? You answer the phone. I'll be damned if I'm going to.

(He tries to rise up from the bed. He is exhausted and falls back on the bed.)

VERNON: Tell them I'm on my way.

MILDRED: Are you crazy? You're not going out there. You're half dead. You look like a skeleton, getting no sleep.

(He somehow gets the energy and the strength, in defiance of the near hysterical woman, and takes the receiver off the hook.)

VERNON: Yes? Yes, ma'm. That's all right. *(He talks a little loudly as if the person he was speaking to was deaf.)* Yes. I see. Mildred was telling me. I was just getting ready to call you. All right. Yes, ma'm. I'll be there in about half an hour. Yes, ma'm. I'll hurry. *(He puts the phone down. He sits for a moment on the side of the bed and then he gets up groggily. He is thin, his body stooped and bent, and he seems excessively frail standing there in his shorts and undershirt. He is awake now though, and he dresses himself, not hurrying but deliberately.)*

MILDRED: I guess you're going. I guess nothing that I can say will stop you. Nothing. Well, a bullet will stop you or a knife. You're a pediatrician. Why do they call you? I know the answer to that. You're the only one crazy enough to go out there to that hellhole. Answer me, Vernon. Why are you going?

VERNON: Miss Ethel needs me. Velma is drunk and they can't control her. She's threatening to kill them. They want me to give her a shot to quiet her.

MILDRED: Go on then. I know there's nothing I can do to stop you. You're the one she's gonna kill one of these nights. You're the one. Not Miss Ethel. Not those poor pitiful children, not the nigras. You. Old good-hearted Vernon. *(A pause.)* Why do you do it? Why do you go every time the Manns or the Dennis's or the Jervis's or the Galbreaths call for one of their crazy drunks? Why? When you're half dead yourself, work all day at the hospital and half the night at the clinic when everyone else is gone home?

(He is dressed now and has started out the room. She screams after him.)

Don't tell me it's devotion to your profession. It's not that. It's something else. I think you're sick. I think you're crazy. That's what I think. If they don't kill you, you'll fall over the wheel of your car some night going out to call on some drunk or fool that no medicine can help. None.

(He goes out. We can hear the car starting. She turns around in despair and looks at the room. The phone rings. She answers it.)

Hello. Yes, ma'm. He's on his way. Yes.

(She hangs up as the lights fade. The lights fade up on the living room of the Dennis's country house. The room is in shambles, disorder everywhere, tables, chairs overturned. Hanging on the wall, slashed, is an oil painting of a young girl, fourteen or fifteen. The girl in the portrait is dressed in white organdy has long blonde curls, worn in the Mary Pickford manner. Standing under the portrait, back to it, is Velma, forty-five with a black eye patch over her left eye. She is drunk, holds a bottle of whiskey in her hand (right), and after a moment has a swig from it. A door opens slowly, carefully down right, and her mother, Miss Ethel, seventy, peers into the room. Velma sees her and throws the bottle at her. The bottle goes wide of its mark, and Velma falls, collapsing onto the sofa. Miss Ethel watches from the door. Then comes in cautiously and goes over to her daughter. She peers down at her for a moment and then calls.)

ETHEL: Erma! Erma!

(A black woman in her late fifties comes into the room.)

She's passed out.

ERMA: Is she out for sure?

ETHEL: Yes. She's out for sure.

ERMA: I tell you right now drunk or sober, the next time she calls me a black nigger I'm leaving.

ETHEL: She calls me worse than that. She called me a whore and a bitch.

ERMA: But she's not my daughter and I don't have to take it.

ETHEL: She's drunk. She doesn't know what she's saying.

ERMA: Sure, she knows what she's saying.

ETHEL: She doesn't.

ERMA: She does too. She knows exactly what she is saying. And anyhow, if you want me to work on here she better know what she's saying when she talks to me.

ETHEL: Don't be uppity now. You weren't raised that way. Your mother didn't raise you that way.

ERMA: I'll be like I want to. If you don't like how I talk, I can go.

ETHEL: Oh, shut up Erma.

ERMA: You shut up. I'm tired of being awakened in the middle of the night by your drunken fights.

ETHEL: Did the children get back to sleep?

ERMA: I guess so. Nothing keeps them up anymore. They're used to hearing their mother hollering and carrying on like a drunken fool.

ETHEL: Hand me her portrait.

(Erma takes it down from the wall.)

ERMA: It is wrecked this time for sure. You're not going to be able to fix it this time. *(She looks at it.)* She gouged out the eye. She said to me while she was doing it: I'll fix it this time to look like I do right now.

(Velma mutters drunkenly from the couch.)

ETHEL: That's all right, Velma. Everything's going to be all right now. Go over and get that knife from her.

ERMA: No, ma'm. She might just be playing possum and she'd cut me as soon as look at me.

ETHEL: Oh, I don't think so. I think it's all just bluff.

ERMA: Then you get the knife from her.

ETHEL: I'll let Vernon get it when he comes. He is always able to make her behave. I don't know what we'd do without him.

ERMA: I don't either, and that's the truth.

ETHEL: He's been a dear friend of ours for a long time.

ERMA: He sure looks bad. I don't think he's going to be here much longer the way he looks.

ETHEL: He works so hard. He's very dedicated.

ERMA: If you got the money.

ETHEL: Now, that is not true. Why do you always say things like that?

ERMA: Like what?

ETHEL: Things to make one feel bad. To hurt one.

ERMA: I'd like to see any of my friends call him in the middle of the night and see what would happen. I can tell you what would happen. Nothing.

ETHEL: Didn't he come last month out here when you had the flu?

ERMA: That's because you called him. An' he knowed you'd pay the bill if I didn't. *(There is a knock at the door. Erma goes. She opens it. Vernon is there. He comes into the room.)*

ETHEL: She's passed out. Just a few minutes ago. It was terrible before then, Vernon. Wasn't it Erma?

ERMA: It sure was.

ETHEL: She said she had a gun and that she was going to kill me and the children.

ERMA: And me. Don't forget me. She said she was goin' to kill me too.

ETHEL: I got the children into my room and locked the door. Erma was outside getting the car keys so she couldn't leave and she had to come around to the back and climb in the window. All the while we could hear Velma saying she would shoot the door down. I kept thinking she would quiet down, but she didn't and we could hear her breaking all the things in here. *(She points to the picture.)* She ripped this all up again. I don't think I can repair it now. Maybe it's just as well. She says I keep it here to mock her. Oh, my God. She said she never looked like that.

ERMA: That's not what she said to me. She said she never was like that. She said that picture was an angel and she was born a devil.

ETHEL: Well, she wasn't. Why do you say things like that?

ERMA: I said nothin'. I'm only repeatin' what she said.

ETHEL: Well, she's drunk and she didn't know what she was saying. She looked like that and she acted that way too, didn't she Vernon? She looked like an angel and she acted like one. She was fifteen the summer the portrait was painted. We were living in our house in town then, remember? *(To Vernon.)* Just a stone's throw from the Santa Fe Depot, and had that big palm tree in the side yard and that was the year the oil crews arrived in the country and they were finding oil everywhere and everybody was hoping they would discover oil on their land.

ERMA: We had oil on our land but Dr. Thomas got to us before the oil men did and he cheated us. He bought up our mineral rights for a hundred dollars and the mineral rights of all the colored people around us and then he turned around and sold them to the oil companies for millions.

ETHEL: Why do you always bring up stories like that? All that is past. Dr. Vernon and I had nothing to do with that.

(A boy, six, and a girl, five, come sleepily in the room. They look at Velma.)

LOU ANN: What's wrong with Mama?

ERMA: She's drunk. That's what's wrong with her. Now you know that. Why do you ask a question like that?

DOUGLAS: Did Dr. Vernon give her a shot to keep her quiet?

VERNON: Not yet, Douglas.

DOUGLAS: Are you going to?

VERNON: I'll see.

ERMA: You all go on back to bed now.

(They turn and go.)

ETHEL: I don't remember, Vernon, did they find oil on your papa's land?

VERNON: No.

ETHEL: Thank God they found gas wells out here or we'd be starvin' to death. Do you remember when the oil crews first came to Harrison?

VERNON: Not really. I wasn't here. I was off at the university.

ETHEL: Well, we'd never known such excitement as there was in Harrison then. Everyone was having parties. We had open house at our home most every night. We had an early spring that year, and it was warm and we opened all the windows and had Japanese lanterns on the porch and in the yards and every room of the house lit up and we entertained the young men on the oil crews. Velma was fifteen then. Do you remember how beautiful she was? She had those long blonde curls, and there was one young man in particular practically lived at our house. Ben Lacque. Leland was so jealous of him. He thought he had a crush on me, because he was always at our house. Morning, noon, and night. He's got no crush on me, honey, I said. It's Velma. Don't be silly, he said, she's only a baby. She's fifteen, I said, and he's in love with her. Then I'm going to throw him out of my house. He's old enough to be her father. And he was too, almost. He was twenty-eight. But I liked him. I did have a little bit of a crush on him myself. He was the one who talked me into getting Velma's picture painted. We had it painted right before school was out. She was in the ninth grade, and I remember I had to ask Professor Autrey to excuse her from her last two classes of the day. And the day the picture was finished, she and Ben Lacque came and asked me to ask her daddy to let them get married, and I did and they were married in June and she went away with him in July to another oil field, and then he lost his job and they came back here in September and the next month her daddy had the marriage annulled. Ben Lacque is dead. Did you know that?

VERNON: Yes, I heard that.

ETHEL: Erma, go check on those children.

(Erma goes.)

Velma came home this afternoon half drunk ranting and cussing and calling me all kinds of names. She told me I ruined her life. That I had no morals and no decency and I wasn't fit to be a mother and I made the mistake of asking her if she thought she was a fit mother and that did it and she spat at me and tried to claw me and then I told her how sorry I was to have ever said a thing like that, and she quieted down for a little and then she got the bottle out and I begged her not to drink anymore, but she wouldn't listen, of course, and she took her glass eye out and held it up and cursed me because she had one and I said it wasn't my fault, she got drunk and drove her car into a cotton truck and lost her eye and that really got her going. She said everything was my fault. That I had ruined her, that I broke her daddy's heart and was the cause of his drinking himself to death. That I talked her into marrying John Borden for his money, and I interrupted her there. I said what would have happened to you if you hadn't married him and he hadn't had the marriage annulled and given you a hundred thousand dollars? Of course, it's all been spent long ago and…

(Vernon is nodding off. He's heard all this many times before.)

Vernon.

VERNON: Excuse me, Miss Ethel. I'm just so tired. *(He shakes his head.)* I'm just awful tired.

ETHEL: And selfish women like me wake you up during the night and drag you out of bed and keep you up telling you their troubles.

VERNON: *(Wiping his eyes.)* I'm glad to help if I can. I think I better go now. It is almost daybreak. Do you want me to give her a shot so she'll sleep on?

ETHEL: Oh. I don't know. I don't think she'll wake up now. She has a knife on her. Would you get it before you go? She said she had a pistol, too, but I don't believe that.

(Vernon goes over to Velma asleep on the couch.)

VERNON: Here's the knife. *(He takes a long handled knife from under her body, and then he brings out a pistol.)*

ETHEL: My God. She did have a pistol. It's a wonder she didn't kill us all.

(Erma comes in.)

ERMA: Do you want some coffee, Dr. Vernon? I made a pot.

ETHEL: Maybe you'd like some breakfast too.

VERNON: No, thank you. I'll go on back to town now. Charlie Johnson and I are having breakfast together. His wife is out of town this week.

ETHEL: She did have a pistol, Erma.

ERMA: My God.

(Vernon is looking around her.)

ETHEL: What are you looking for now?

VERNON: Her glass eye. She's taken it out.

ETHEL: Help him, Erma.

(They begin to look around on the floor. Vernon sees her clutched fist. She is holding the glass eye. He takes it from her.)

VERNON: Here it is. You'd better take it and put it away some place, Erma.

(Erma takes it and starts away.)

VELMA: Give me my eye. Give it to me. I'm blind. I can't see without my eye.
(Erma gives the eye back to Vernon. Vernon motions Ethel and Erma to leave. They go quietly.)

VERNON: I think you better leave it out for awhile, until you've finished your sleep.

VELMA: I've finished my sleep. I want a drink.

VERNON: We've nothing to drink. We're going to fix you up, so you will have a nice long sleep now. You'll feel ever so much better.

VELMA: Vernon, I'm sick. I'm sick. I'll never be well. I feel so rotten. (She begins to cry.)

VERNON: Oh, now. You're not so bad.

VELMA: Everything around me is rotten. Mama is rotten. You know she's rotten. What's to become of my children? Why in the name of God did I ever have children? Rotten. No good—slut that I am.

VERNON: Now. Now. Come on. (He opens his bag. He takes out a hypodermic needle.)

VELMA: Are you going to give me a shot?

VERNON: Yes. So you can sleep.

VELMA: Give me one, so I'll never wake up. Then give Mama one and the children and burn the house around us. Some night I'll set this house on fire. I told Mama that when I'm drunk and she and the children are...

VERNON: Sh. Sh. Now just don't talk.

VELMA: You wait and see. One night you'll wake up and you'll see a fire way out on the prairie and you'll say she's done it. Velma has set their place on fire; they're all burning up out there. (She screams.) I can't sleep. I can't rest. Give me something in the name of Christ. I need so to rest. I need so to...
(He gives her the shot in her arm. She falls back. A pause. Velma is drifting into unconsciousness. She is almost mumbling the next speech.)
Oh, I haven't done so bad. No, by God. I've had three husbands. I've got two lovely children. You've done all right, Vernon. You've got all kinds of money and you're a respected doctor. You have a hospital and five cotton farms and...My God you've done all right. Why...
(She has fallen asleep. Ethel comes in.)

VERNON: She'll sleep on now.

ETHEL: Thank you. I don't know what we'd do without you.

VERNON: That's all right.
(He takes his black bag and starts out. Erma comes in.)

ERMA: Your wife is on the phone doctor. She wanted to know if you were coming home for breakfast.

VERNON: No. Tell her I have a number of calls to make. That I'll get breakfast in town.

(He goes. Erma goes to the phone. Ethel goes over to her daughter. She looks at her for a moment and then Velma spits at her mother and Ethel leaves the room as the lights fade. The lights are brought up on the bedroom of the Earlys. Mildred is there still in her night gown and robe. Jackie, a middle-aged black woman, comes in with coffee. She hands it to Mildred.)

JACKIE: You want some breakfast, Miss Mildred?

MILDRED: No, just coffee. Thank you.

JACKIE: Doctor have breakfast in town?

MILDRED: I guess so. He said he was going to.

(The phone rings.)

You get it please?

(Jackie goes to the phone and picks up the receiver.)

JACKIE: Early residence. Jackie. Yes'm. No ma'm, the doctor is not here. Just a minute. *(She hands the phone to Mildred.)* It's the clinic looking for the doctor.

(Mildred takes the phone.)

MILDRED: Hello, Mrs. Pratt. No. I don't know where he is. He left here at about four this morning. He had to go out to Miss Ethel's. Yes. Out in the country. I called out there an hour or so later and he had gone. She said he was eating breakfast in town and had some early calls to make. If I hear from him I will. Mrs. Pratt can't you talk some sense into him. He'll kill himself if he keeps on going this way. I know. Don't tell me anything. I've been married to him you know for almost thirty years. I know. Well, I'd appreciate that. Of course, I know that. I know he's a fine man. I know. I know he's tired. I know he works too hard. Yes. I know that. All right. Thank you. *(She hangs the phone up.)* I get so sick and tired of hearing what an angel he is. Oh, Doctor is a saint. Doctor's an angel. Oh, my. My. Well, he's no saint Jackie, you know that.

JACKIE: Yes'm. He works too hard.

(A voice calls from outside: "Mildred.")

MILDRED: Come on in Gertrude. The door is unlocked.

(Gertrude Mayfield, in her fifties, comes in.)

GERTRUDE: Hey, Mildred. Hey, Jackie.

JACKIE: Good morning.

MILDRED: I'm still in my night gown. Jackie, heat some coffee for Miss Gertrude.

GERTRUDE: I'd prefer a Coke if you don't mind.

MILDRED: No. Bring me a Coke too, Jackie.

JACKIE: Yes'm. *(She goes.)*

GERTRUDE: Well, what's new?

MILDRED: Nothing is new here. Same old thing. Vernon went out to Miss Ethel's at four this morning. Velma was drunk. I'm mad enough to kill him.

GERTRUDE: Well, he doesn't cheat on you we know that. Lena Davis came over the other day and she said Mildred will never have to worry about her husband being unfaithful. Why do you say that, I asked her. She said because Jeannie Wright has had a terrible crush on him for a long time and the other day when she went to him for an examination she took off all her clothes and told him she loved him and couldn't live without him and he just walked out of the room and when he came back in he had his nurse with him.

MILDRED: Jeannie Wright?

GERTRUDE: Yes. Jeannie Wright.

MILDRED: Well, she's not the only one. I'm very friendly with his nurse you know and she tells me everything that's going on. You'd be surprise how many women in the town have made a play for him. That's why, she says, she is always in his office with him when he's examining one of his woman patients.

GERTRUDE: My God! Can't women be terrible. Talk about men.

(The phone rings.)

MILDRED: Jackie answer that.

JACKIE: *(Calling.)* Yes, ma'm.

GERTRUDE: You going to Mae's party this afternoon?

MILDRED: Yes, I am.

JACKIE: *(Calling back.)* It's the clinic.

(Mildred picks up the phone.)

MILDRED: Hello. No. I haven't heard a word. I don't know. Well, let me know when you hear from him. *(She hangs the phone up.)* I don't know where in the name of God he is. I'm going to try to get him to go on a cruise. That's the only way I can ever get him to relax.

GERTRUDE: You love cruises, don't you?

MILDRED: Yes, I do.

GERTRUDE: Do you think you can get Vernon to go on one?

MILDRED: I'm going to try. I got him to go twice, and he enjoyed it, although he won't admit it.

GERTRUDE: You all going to the Shepherd's tomorrow night?

MILDRED: I'm going, but he won't go. He says he's going, but I know what will happen. Fifteen minutes before it's time for us to leave he'll call...

(Jackie comes in with two Cokes and gives one to Gertrude and one to Mildred.)

...and say he has to see a patient in some God forsaken place and can't make it. Oh, well. I'm used to it. I decided a long time ago I won't just sit here and wait for him to come home. No. I was going to go and have a good time. And if he wants to work like a fool and kill himself, I can't help it.

GERTRUDE: Thank you for the Coke, Jackie.

JACKIE: Yes, ma'm.

MILDRED: Help yourself to a Coke, too, Jackie.

JACKIE: Yes'm. Thank you. I already did.

(She goes out. The phone rings. Mildred answers.)

MILDRED: Yes? No, I haven't heard. Look. Don't keep calling here. There's nothing I can do about it. If I hear anything, I'll call you. Yes, I'm concerned. But what good does that do? *(She hangs up.)* I guess I should be worried.

GERTRUDE: Hasn't he done this before?

MILDRED: Yes. Several times. He'll just disappear. He goes to friends in Houston or Galveston and crashes out. Sleeps for a day and then back at it again. Excuse me, while I get dressed.

(Mildred goes offstage to dress. Gertrude sees photographs lying on the floor.)

GERTRUDE: What are these photographs?

MILDRED: *(Offstage.)* Oh, just some pictures I had taken while at the university. I was cleaning out some drawers yesterday and came across them.

(Gertrude picks them up and starts to look at them.)

GERTRUDE: These were when you were on the Beauty Page of the Texas year book?

MILDRED: *(Offstage.)* Uh. Huh. And some pictures when I went on the university sponsored tour with Bert Sparks. I was his dancing partner. You know we toured picture houses and auditoriums for six weeks, even went as far as Mexico.

GERTRUDE: Were you chaperoned?

MILDRED: *(Offstage.)* Yes. Mama was along.

GERTRUDE: And you were on the Beauty Page on the A&M annual the same year weren't you?

MILDRED: *(Offstage.)* Yes, I was.

GERTRUDE: What kind of dancing did you do on your tour?

MILDRED: *(Offstage.)* Ballroom. Charleston, Tango, Foxtrot.

(A pause. Gertrude continues to look at the pictures.)

GERTRUDE: Mildred, what was the name of the woman that took her baby away from you and Vernon?

MILDRED: *(Offstage.)* What do you want to know that for?

GERTRUDE: Was it Myrtle?

MILDRED: *(Offstage.)* Yes.

GERTRUDE: And the name of the man that was the father of the baby. Was it Hayhurst?

MILDRED: *(Offstage.)* Yes. Why in the name of God do you want to know?

GERTRUDE: I read in the paper last night that a Myrtle Hayhurst had committed suicide.

MILDRED: *(Offstage.)* In what paper?

GERTRUDE: The *Chronicle.* They said she had a husband and a son and a daughter. Did you know she had a daughter?

MILDRED: *(Offstage.)* No. After what she did to us I never wanted to hear about her again. *(Mildred comes back into the room. She is dressed. Calling.)* Jackie.

JACKIE: *(Offstage.)* Yes'm.

MILDRED: Last night's *Chronicle* is in the breakfast room. Would you bring it to me?

GERTRUDE: Are you ever curious how the boy turned out?

(Mildred begins to cry.)

I'm sorry, Mildred. Maybe I shouldn't have told you about it. I'm sorry.

MILDRED: I wonder why God did that to us, Gertrude?

GERTRUDE: Did what?

MILDRED: Send that little boy to us and then take him away.

GERTRUDE: Oh, I don't know about things like that. I'm sorry. I thought this all happened so long ago that you never thought about it anymore.

MILDRED: I don't really. Maybe once in awhile.

(Jackie comes in with the paper and hands it to Mildred. Mildred gives the paper to Gertrude.)

Find me the story please.

GERTRUDE: Are you sure you want to read it?

MILDRED: Yes, I do.

(Gertrude takes the paper and turns its pages until she finds the story. She hands the paper to Mildred, who begins to read as the lights fade. The lights are brought up on a room in the small Houston apartment of Harry and Reenie Reavis. Vernon is there asleep on a couch. Harry Reavis comes in. He's Vernon's age. He goes over to him and shakes him.)

HARRY: Vernon. Vernon.

(Vernon sleeps on. Harry goes to the phone. He dials.)

Dr. Early's office, please. Hello. This is Harry Reavis. Yes. Dr. Early is here at my apartment. He's sound asleep. Yes. Will you call his wife and tell her he's here? Thank you. *(He puts the phone away. He looks over at Vernon. He checks his wrist watch and then he goes and shakes Vernon again.)* Vernon. Vernon.

(Vernon stirs and looks up at him.)

Man how long have you been here? Half of Harrison has been trying to reach you.

VERNON: What time is it?

HARRY: Almost seven o'clock.

VERNON: Have you eaten?

HARRY: Yes. I ate on the way home from work. There is a wonderful little cafeteria around the corner. It is real cheap. Delicious food. Are you hungry?

VERNON: Where's Reenie?

HARRY: She had to work late. Are you all right?

VERNON: I'm all right. I was exhausted, but I'm all right.

(The phone rings.)

If that's the hospital, I'll talk to them, but if it's Mildred, say I'm already left and you don't know where I am.

(Harry goes to the phone.)

HARRY: Hello. Yes. Oh. Mildred. How are you? No. Yes, he was. He left as soon as I woke him. I don't know. No. He didn't say. Uh. Huh. I know, Mildred. Yep. Sure. I understand. Sure you do. Uh. Huh. I'll tell him if I see him. I just don't know, Mildred. Sure, anytime. *(He hangs up.)* Are you going home tonight?

VERNON: I don't know. Are you coming over to Dr. Thomas's funeral?

HARRY: Yes. They asked me to be an honorary pall bearer. Are you going?

VERNON: Yes.

HARRY: Are you going to be a pall bearer?

VERNON: Honorary one. I'll see you there.

HARRY: All right.

VERNON: Tell Reenie, hello.

HARRY: I will.

(Vernon goes to the door, pauses.)

HARRY: Are you all right, Vernon?

VERNON: I'm all right. Tired.

HARRY: Are you going back to Harrison now?

VERNON: I think so.

HARRY: Maybe I should drive you.

VERNON: No. I'll make it. You've worked hard all day, too. *(A pause.)* I'll tell you what. I'm going to the Drake for supper first. Will you call the hospital and ask them to get S.L. to come for me?

HARRY: S.L? S.L. is dead. He committed suicide a year ago.

VERNON: *(Laughing.)* My God. That's right. That's how tired I am. Call Grant.

HARRY: Grant?

VERNON: Grant. He's the one I get to drive for me now when I'm tired. Call the hospital and ask them to find him.

HARRY: Can they find him this time of night?

VERNON: Yes. And he's a faithful devil. He'll come wherever he is, or whatever he's doin'. I wish everybody in the world was as faithful as Grant. Did you hear the latest? Jack Grayson has his oil wholesale company out in the Quarters near where Cassie lives and...

(Reenie comes in.)

REENIE: Hello. *(She kisses Harry.)*

VERNON: Hello, Reenie.

HARRY: You got home earlier than I thought.

VERNON: Maybe you'd like to come and have supper with me.

REENIE: I'm sorry. I've eaten.

HARRY: Where did you eat?

REENIE: At the cafeteria. Did you eat?

HARRY: Yes. What were you sayin' about Cassie, Vernon?

VERNON: Oh...well...

HARRY: You know who Cassie is, Reenie?

REENIE: Yes. She's the colored woman that worked for Vernon's mother.

HARRY: Forty years wasn't it, Vernon?

VERNON: Forty-five.

HARRY: Forty-five. Well, what's the story and I promise not to interrupt this time, but I always have to be sure Reenie knows who we're talking about when we get into stories about Harrison.

REENIE: Speaking of Harrison. Do you all remember a John B. Cookenboo?

HARRY: Sure. He lived next door to Vernon until his father died, then he and his mother moved into Houston. Why?

REENIE: He and his wife Ada something or other.

HARRY: Ada B.

REENIE: I guess so. They were in the restaurant. He came over and spoke to me. He said we'd met. I had no memory of it.

HARRY: You sure did meet him. You met him at two funerals. Mrs. Vaughn's and Vernon's mother.

REENIE: Maybe so. Are they rich?

HARRY: I think so. Don't you Vernon?

VERNON: I guess so.

REENIE: Was their family rich?

VERNON: No. Mr. Cookenboo worked at the Freight Depot. When he died all he left was the house and five thousand dollars. Mrs. Cookenboo sold the house for another five and moved to Houston. She gave the insurance money to the oldest boy Henry to study to be a dentist but he didn't amount to anything.

HARRY: The second boy Elwood did all right.

VERNON: I guess so. He worked for the railroad.

HARRY: John B. is an accountant. He's way up in his company. *(He laughs.)* My God, we've never let Vernon finish his story about Cassie.

VERNON: Oh, it's nothin'. She lives in one of Mama's houses down in the Quarters that I inherited, rent free, and Jack Grayson came to me and said I ought to be ashamed of myself not fixing the steps that lead to the privy. I said let that old trifling son of hers fix them. You know how Jack is. Since his son became an Episcopalian minister, he's become a regular bleeding heart. He won't even wear silk.

REENIE: Why won't he wear silk?

VERNON: Because of some liberal ban on silk.

HARRY: Yeah?

(The phone rings. Reenie goes to answer it.)

If it's Mildred for Vernon he is not here.

REENIE: What?

HARRY: He doesn't want to talk to her now.

REENIE: Then, you'd better answer it. I don't want Mildred mad at me.

(Harry answers the phone.)

HARRY: Yes. Oh. Mildred. No. You haven't heard from him yet. No. I don't understand that. No, I wouldn't honey. I'm sure he's fine. Sure. Goodnight.

(He hangs up. Vernon starts out of the room.)

VERNON: Don't forget to call Grant.

HARRY: I won't.

(Vernon pauses. He starts away. Again he pauses, thinking.)

VERNON: I heard the other day that Dolores Stewart died.

HARRY: When?

VERNON: I don't know exactly. The last week or so, I guess. I met a cousin of hers and she told me.

HARRY: She was living in New Orleans?

VERNON: Yes. *(Again he starts out of the room. Pauses.)* You know what I was thinking about all the way drivin' over here? Teddy. Every once in awhile I think I'll just dig around and find out where he is and what's become of him.

HARRY: Do you know his name now?

VERNON: Oh, sure. Leroy.

HARRY: Leroy?

VERNON: Yes, Leroy Hayhurst.

HARRY: How old would he be now?

VERNON: Twenty-three. If I passed him on the street I doubt if I'd even recognize him. Of course, he wouldn't know me from Adam.

HARRY: Teddy was the little boy Mildred and Vernon almost adopted.

REENIE: Oh, yes. I remember you're telling me. That was so sad.

VERNON: I tell you that was a terrible day when the agency called just a month before the adoption became final and said the mother had changed her mind and wanted the boy back.

REENIE: Why did she change her mind?

VERNON: Well, she'd had the baby without her mother's knowing it, and then just before the legal time was up, her grandmother died and the girl got stricken by remorse during the wake and confessed to her mother what she had done and the mother went to the boy that got her daughter pregnant and made him marry her daughter and then they went to the agency and asked for the baby back and the agency called me and said it was their legal right to do so, but I decided to take it to court and I spent a fortune let me tell you fighting for him in the courts. I finally went to the girl and her mother and offered her fifty thousand dollars if she would let us keep the baby. *(A pause.)* But no. No way. The day we gave him back it was like a funeral. Mildred cried for months. I never thought I would get over the hurt, but I did, of course, I did. That was almost the hardest thing I had to get over. Almost. *(He starts out again. He pauses.)* I guess maybe the worst was when Jack Henry died from lock jaw. I was his doctor. In those days we didn't automatically give tetanus shots when you broke your arm, and this boy was always falling and breaking something and getting well, mending so fast, but this fall was by a stable and he got an infection. *(A pause.)* And the Henrys have never let me forget the death of that boy. Never. When Steve Henry was trying to build a filling station across from our house, and Mildred was trying to stop him, he turned on her one day in the drugstore and said your husband killed one of my children and now you're trying to take bread away from the mouth of the other one. *(A pause.)* And things get back to you. That hurt. When I refused to fix Cassie's steps, that preacher son of Jack Grayson's told someone that we'd learned nothing when God took the little boy from us, that all we thought of was the almighty dollar—that nothing else mattered. I sent a carpenter out to Cassie's and had the damn steps fixed but all time that no good son of Cassie's was telling everybody would listen—everybody, black or white, how Cassie had worked for my mother for forty-five years for three dollars a week and how my mother had always promised to leave her money when she died to take care of Cassie, but left her nothing and that all I did, with all my money, was to let her stay rent free in a leaking nigger shack that I couldn't get anybody to pay rent for. *(A pause.)* What he didn't tell was how we fed half the nigras of Harrison from our kitchen, Cassie, her son and all their kin and the ones they didn't feed in the kitchen, they would take her food to give to their friends in the quarters. I was sitting in my breakfast room one noon and I saw that old no count son of Cassie's coming out of Mama's kitchen totin' enough food to feed all of the quarters and I ran out of the house and I ordered him to take every bit of that food back. He did, too, by God. Anyway, once when Jack Grayson's preacher son was here on a visit we invited him out to supper and he declined. I heard later he said he felt like telling me to give the money we would spend on his food to Cassie.

HARRY: What was the name of Cassie's son? I forgot.

VERNON: Solomon. I used to say to Mama get rid of him. Tell him to stay away from your kitchen. What good are you doin' him feeding him this way. Oh, I can't do that to Cassie's son she'd say. The truth was it had nothin' to do with Cassie, but Mama's brother, who she supported too, whenever he would get on one of his drunks and go wanderin' across the track to the quarters, she'd call Solomon day or night and he'd go find him for her and bring him home or else take him to his house until he slept off his drunk. *(A pause.)* Last night I went out to Miss Ethel Dennis's in the middle of the night because Velma was drunk again, and I'm the only one that can quiet her, and I thought, I am so tired, I will never make it out there, and when I left I was to have breakfast with Charles Johnson, but I was too tired to make it back to town and I pulled up by the side of the road and I went to sleep and the sun woke me up and I decided to come here and really sleep. *(A pause.)* Do you realize, Harry, Mildred and I are the only family now left living on that once quiet street of ours? All the other houses on the street have been abandoned.

HARRY: I know and it was a lovely street too, beautiful old houses.

VERNON: It has turned into an inferno now—an inferno of all-night food stands, filling stations, used car lots, the cotton and the oil trucks roaring by day and night, and the people—our friends, Harry, that once lived in the houses. Think of the terror that has pursued all of them. Even after they sold their houses and left. The Vaughns, the Taylors, the Johnsons, the Watts, the Gayles, the Gautiers. The most evil, vengeful fiend could not have imagined the horrors that have descended on our friends and their children and their children's children, as if some evil spirit was determined to not only scatter the people living on that street but to pursue them vengefully, eternally.

HARRY: Now not everybody.

VERNON: Well, almost everybody.

HARRY: John B. Cookenboo has done well. You've been a great success, Vernon. You're an honored man in your community. You're…

VERNON: Am I? But think of our friends. The boys we grew up with. Jack and Buster and Tom and Leland and Henry—and I don't honor myself, Harry—at fifty, mortally tired. Mildred is always after me to go on another cruise. She says the phone can't ring there in the middle of the night. She thinks a cruise is the cure for everything. And maybe she's right. Maybe I should go. I don't know.

(The phone rings.)

I'm going so you won't have to lie to Mildred.

HARRY: I don't mind lying to Mildred. I don't want you by yourself when you're upset like this Vernon.

VERNON: No. Don't worry. I'm tough, you know that. I'll live. I'll survive. *(Vernon starts out of the room. He pauses at the door.)* Don't forget to have the clinic call Grant.

HARRY: I won't.

(Vernon leaves. Harry picks up the phone.)

HARRY: Hello. No, Mildred. No. I'm sorry. No, I wouldn't lie to you. No. *(He hangs up. He dials a number on the phone. Into phone.)* I'm calling for Dr. Vernon Early. Yes. He asked that you get in touch with Grant and ask him to come and pick him up at Drake's Restaurant in Houston. Yes. Anytime. He's on his way there now. *(He puts the phone down.)*

REENIE: He looks terrible.

HARRY: He was up half the night, he said. He was asleep when I got here. He'll be all right. He's gone on like this for years.

REENIE: Why does he go on this way, Harry?

HARRY: Partly ambition. Partly…

REENIE: Greed?

HARRY: I guess so.

REENIE: He's made so much money, besides what he inherited. He spends nothing, except when he and Mildred go to a medical convention or on a cruise. She says he always spends a great deal then. I don't see how Mildred stands it. I know I couldn't stand their life.

HARRY: Mildred can take care of herself. She's no angel, you know.

REENIE: Oh, I know. She's self-centered and vain and selfish.

HARRY: She's never grown up. She's still back at the sorority at the university.

REENIE: Was she very beautiful then?

HARRY: Yes, she was beautiful. She was chosen as one of the seven beauties her senior year at both the university and at A&M. Oh, he's always been a difficult person. Moody, ambitious, proud. We've always kept our friendship because I was no competition for him.

REENIE: You've had a much happier life.

HARRY: That may be. But I don't think he's very interested in happiness or contentment. He drives himself so. He wanted to be a surgeon, you know, the worst way in the world, but that's the one thing he couldn't make himself do. The day he tried his first operation, Dr. Murray and Dr. Cox were beside him in the operating room. He took the knife and started to make an incision on the patient, but he began to tremble with fear and he couldn't go through with it, and he had to give the knife to Dr. Cox and let him do the operation. And that ended his chance of ever becoming a surgeon. *(A pause.)* And, I believe, perhaps it's just a sentimental fancy, but I believe he was once very much in love with Dolores Stewart.

REENIE: The woman he said just died in New Orleans?

HARRY: Yes.

REENIE: He was in love with her?

HARRY: In high school.

REENIE: Why didn't they marry?

HARRY: I don't know. Everyone blamed his family. I know Dolores did. It is easy to blame his family. They did oppose it, but I think there was something in him that made him hold back. Something that said marry that wild, unconventional girl and you'll go wild like the rest of your friends. Oh, he had a wild streak then. He drank a great deal and Dolores did. Mildred has said if it hadn't been for her, he could have ended up a drunkard. I don't know. I do know she watched him closely after they married whenever he began to drink. I remember in the thirties after Dolores had married, divorced gone to New Orleans then moved to New York and lost her job during the Depression and was forced to come home and live with her mother and her stepfather because she had no money and no job, he came to me one day and he was all upset because he had been standing in front of the drugstore with some men and she came down the street and one of the men said she'd sleep with you for money, and another man said he didn't believe it, and the man told him to go ask her and he'd find out, and the man went up to her and spoke to her and he came back to the men and said it was true. She would. And Vernon came to me and told me about it and he seemed hurt and puzzled that she would do such a thing. He said, "I don't understand her doing something like that. If she needed money she could have come to me and I would have given it to her." And I remember thinking at the time, you still have some feelings left for her.

REENIE: Do you think Mildred ever suspected this?

HARRY: I don't know. She always hated Dolores. She was living in another town when she began to go with Vernon. When she married Vernon and moved here Dolores had gone, but when Dolores returned in the thirties Mildred attacked her in every way she could, but no more then the rest of the good women of the town, until Dolores married again and left. I bet he hasn't seen her more than twice in the twenty years since then and I doubt he ever thinks of her at all now. *(A pause.)* And yet…I think sometimes when he goes out in the middle of the night to Miss Ethel and Velma or one of the other old-timers that are in some kind of trouble, he goes because of Dolores and himself as if he were tending that part of himself that he has stifled and that part of Dolores that destroyed her. *(A pause.)* The only time I ever saw him deeply hurt was when they took the child from them.

REENIE: That was cruel.

HARRY: Yes, it was cruel and it almost killed him. He sobbed when he saw me. He said it was killing him to give the boy back.

REENIE: And yet—he can be so cold. So unfeeling. Imagine anyone having to shame him into fixing Cassie's steps.

HARRY: That's the selfishness of him, and of all, or most all of the ones, I grew up with. They can ride through the quarters to pick up their maids and cooks and yardmen, look at their houses unpainted, falling in, unpaved streets, no sewage, nothing much changing in all these years while white Harrison looks the other way.

(The phone rings.)

Yes. No, Mildred. No. Believe me.

(He hangs up the phone as the lights fade. The lights are brought up on the front seat of Vernon's car. Grant, a black man, fifty-five, is driving.)

VERNON: How is your family gettin' on, Grant?

GRANT: They're all fine.

VERNON: Your children are all doing well?

GRANT: Yes, thank God.

VERNON: Some live in Houston?

GRANT: Yessir.

VERNON: I know you're proud of your children.

GRANT: I am. I am.

VERNON: They all went to college?

GRANT: Yessir, everyone of them.

VERNON: They all graduated?

GRANT: Yessir, thank God.

(A pause.)

VERNON: We need rain.

GRANT: Yes, we do.

(A pause.)

VERNON: Were you the one who found S.L.'s body when he committed suicide?

GRANT: Yessir.

VERNON: I was talking about him tonight to Harry Reavis. S.L. used to drive me, you know.

GRANT: I remember. How's Mr. Harry?

VERNON: He's all right. *(A pause.)* Why do you think S.L. killed himself?

GRANT: He was depressed. He had eight children, you know, just stair steps. He made twenty-five dollars a week working at the drugstore and whatever else he picked up driving you and the other white folks. He just was behind all the time. He used to come to my house, because my kids were all grown and gone and it was quiet there and we'd talk awhile about growin' up in Harrison and how could he make it with so many children and so little money and after awhile he'd say sing me a song, and I'd say what kind of song and he'd say a church song. And I would sing, "I Believe" or "The Sweet Bye and Bye" or "Precious Lord," and that would quiet him and he would close his eyes and fall asleep.

(A pause.)

VERNON: How are you going to get your car in Houston tomorrow?

GRANT: I'll get a cousin of mine to drive me in.

VERNON: I'll pay for all that you know.

GRANT: Yessir. Thank you.

VERNON: I'm a rich man, you know.

GRANT: That's what they tell me.

(A pause. Vernon's body trembles convulsively.)

You all right, Mr. Vernon?

VERNON: I'm all right. I'm tired.

GRANT: Yessir. You work hard.

VERNON: No harder than you do.

GRANT: I expect that's right.

(A pause.)

VERNON: It's goin' to be a full moon.

GRANT: Looks like it.

(A pause.)

VERNON: Look at the sky. They'll be no rain tonight. You remember my papa, Grant?

GRANT: Yes, I do.

VERNON: The cotton farms I own I inherited from him.

GRANT: Yessir.

VERNON: An' every night when I was a boy, I could see him walking up and down in the front yard worryin' over the cotton crop, lookin' up at the sky tryin' to figure out if it was goin' to rain or not. *(A pause.)* Everything's changed, Grant. Nothing is like it used to be when we were coming along.

GRANT: I know that's right. Everything's changed.

VERNON: I am tired, Grant. I am so tired. I'm bone tired.

GRANT: Yessir. You work hard. *(A pause. They drive on in silence. Grant begins singing half to himself "Precious Lord Take My Hand.")*

"Precious Lord take my hand,
Lead me on and let me stand.
I am tired, I am weak,
I am worn."

VERNON: Is that one of the songs you used to sing to S.L.?

GRANT: Yes.

VERNON: How are S.L.'s children getting along without him?

GRANT: They get along some way. Their mama has two brothers and they help out. I don't hear a lot about them. They moved out in the country with one of her brothers. *(Again there is silence. After a beat, Grant continues singing.)*

"Through the storm through the night,
Lead me on to the light.
Take my hand Precious Lord,
and lead me on."

(Vernon falls asleep as the lights fade. The lights are brought up in the Early bedroom. It is later the same night. Mildred is there watching television. Vernon enters. Mildred glances up at him, doesn't speak and goes on watching television. Vernon takes his jacket off, unloosens his tie, then takes his shoes off and puts them to one side.)

VERNON: Aren't you going to speak to me, Mildred?

(She doesn't look at him or answer.)

Mildred…

MILDRED: No, I don't think I'm ever going to speak to you again.

(She shuts off the television and starts out of the bedroom.)

VERNON: Mildred?

MILDRED: What?

VERNON: I'm sorry.

MILDRED: The hell you are, you're too selfish to be sorry. You have no heart, no feelings, you are without feelings. Well, I'm not. I've been half out of my mind all day, not knowing if you were alive or dead. Not one phone call, not one word all day or night out of you, and then you walk in here so calmly as if nothing had happened. Nothing at all. And you expect me to pretend that nothing has happened. *(A pause.)* Solomon came over earlier this evening. Cassie's sick. He came to the front door bold as anything. He could see me in the kitchen, too, and I had to walk across the whole house to answer the front bell. When I saw who it was, I said, didn't you see me in the kitchen? And he said, yes, and I said, why didn't you come to the back door and save me walking clear across the house, and he looked at me in that sullen way of his and didn't answer, and I started to say there was a time not too long ago when you had to go to the back door. If you'd gone to the front door you would have been horse whipped.

VERNON: Why didn't he take Cassie to the hospital?

MILDRED: I don't know. I didn't ask him. I just said you weren't home and I didn't know where you were or when you'd be here. *(She hands Vernon the newspaper.)* Read this.

VERNON: What?

MILDRED: This.

(She points to the announcement of the death. He reads it.)

What do you think of that?

VERNON: What is there to think?

MILDRED: I wonder how the boy is.

VERNON: God knows. Anyway, he's not a boy now, he's a man.

(A pause.)

MILDRED: Are you hungry? You want something to eat?

VERNON: No. I ate in Houston before I left.

MILDRED: Where?

VERNON: Drakes.

(A pause.)

MILDRED: Vernon?

VERNON: Yes.

MILDRED: Why do you think she committed suicide?

VERNON: God knows.

(A pause.)

MILDRED: Vernon?

VERNON: Yes?

MILDRED: Do you ever think of him?

VERNON: Once in a while. I did tonight. I don't know why.

MILDRED: Would you ever be curious to see him again?

VERNON: Not really. Not now.

MILDRED: He's twenty-three now.

VERNON: I know.

(The phone rings. She answers it.)

MILDRED: Hello. Yes. He's here. Just a minute. *(She puts her hand over the receiver.)* It's Miss Ethel. She says Velma won't eat anything and just sits and won't talk. She wonders if you'd come out and speak to her.

(He takes the phone.)

VERNON: Hello, Miss Ethel. Yes, ma'm. No, ma'm. I can't tonight. Yes, ma'm. Try not to worry about it. She's just trying to get attention is all. She'll eat when she gets hungry. Yes, ma'm. *(He hangs up the phone.)*

MILDRED: Well, hooray! Thank God you didn't go running out there.

VERNON: I couldn't go. I'm too tired to go another step.

MILDRED: I thought you slept all day.

VERNON: I did. I'm still tired.

MILDRED: I told Gertrude today I think we should go on another cruise. You got so relaxed on the last one. You remember? We had a good time. Didn't we have a good time? Will you at least think about it, Vernon? *(He has fallen asleep.)*
Vernon. My God. *(She looks at him for a beat.)* Sometimes, I swear, I think you are trying to kill yourself. Why are you trying to kill yourself? *(The phone rings. She answers it.)*
Yes. Yes. Oh, hello, Miss Ethel. He's asleep. No, ma'm, I'm not going to wake him. He's worn out. Yes, ma'm. I'll tell him. *(She hangs up the phone. She goes to Vernon. She shakes him.)* Vernon. Get up now and undress. You can't rest properly sitting on a chair. Come on now. Let's go to bed. Vernon. Vernon.
(He doesn't answer. She is shaking him as the lights fade. The lights are brought up on Ethel and Velma's living room. Velma lies on a couch. Ethel is listening to country and western music on the radio. The two children are playing with toys on the floor. Erma is asleep in a chair.)

VELMA: Turn off the damn radio. It's making me nervous.
(Ethel does so.)
Erma.
(Erma opens her eyes.)
Take those two kids out of here. They're makin' me nervous.

ERMA: What's wrong with you. They ain't botherin' anybody.

VELMA: They make me nervous I told you.

ERMA: Everything makes you nervous. I make you nervous. Your mama makes you nervous. The poor little children make you nervous.

VELMA: I'm goin' to give them away, you know.

ETHEL: The hell you are.

VELMA: The hell I'm not. I'm gonna call their daddy and say come and get 'em. If you don't I'm puttin' them in an orphan asylum. Put them up for adoption.

ETHEL: Oh, shut up, Velma.

VELMA: You shut up. *(She screams at the children.)* Get the hell out of here!

ERMA: Shame on you. You ought a be ashamed of yourself.

VELMA: Shut up!

(Erma goes to the children. She holds them.)

ERMA: Don't pay any attention to her.

(There is a knock on the door. Erma, carrying the children, goes to the door and opens it. Vernon is there.)

Come on in, Doctor.

(He enters.)

VELMA: Who the hell sent for you?

ETHEL: I did, Velma.

(Vernon goes to Velma.)

VERNON: Hello, Velma.

(Velma turns her back to him.)

What's this I hear about you not eating?

ETHEL: She hasn't eaten for three days. She's so weak she just staggers around the house.

ERMA: She mostly jus' stays on that couch. She won't even drink whiskey. She says we're trying to poison her. Now she's talking about givin' her children away.

(A pause.)

VERNON: Velma.

(She doesn't answer.)

Velma.

VELMA: Get out of here, Vernon, and let me alone.

VERNON: You have to eat you know.

VELMA: I don't have to do anything.

VERNON: Be sensible, Velma.

(A pause.)

ETHEL: What are we gonna do?

VERNON: She'll come around. She's like a child tryin' to get attention. I would suggest just go on about your business an' try not to pay attention to her.

VELMA: Who's like a child?

ETHEL: You are Velma.

VELMA: Who says so?

ETHEL: Vernon. He says you are just trying to get our attention.

VELMA: Well, he's a fool and you can tell him that for me.

(A pause. Vernon goes to the children sitting by Erma.)

VERNON: Hello, children.

CHILDREN: Hello.

VELMA: Take them out of here.

ETHEL: Shut up, Velma.

VELMA: *(Screaming.)* Take them out of here!

ERMA: You ought to be ashamed of yourself.

   (She takes the children and leaves.)

ETHEL: Please, talk to her Vernon. She always listens to you. *(A pause. He goes over to Velma.)*

VERNON: Velma. Don't do anything you'll be sorry for.

VELMA: All right, Mr. Jesus. Dr. Thomas that took out my eye. The nigras all called him Mr. Jesus. Is that who you are, the new Mr. Jesus?

VERNON: No, I'm not Velma. But I'm fond of you and I want to help you if you'll let me.

VELMA: I don't want anybody to help me.

VERNON: All right. *(He starts away.)* You know where I am if you want to see me. *(He starts away.)*

ETHEL: I hear you are going on a cruise.

VERNON: I'm thinking about it. Mildred wants me to go.

ETHEL: How long?

VERNON: She'd like it to be three weeks, but I don't think I could take more than two weeks if I go.

VELMA: I want my children. Where are my children?

ETHEL: You gave them away, Velma. Remember. They're gone.

VELMA: *(Screaming.)* I want my children! I want my children!

ETHEL: *(Calling.)* Erma. Bring the children in.

   (Erma comes in with the children.)

   She wants them.

VELMA: Come here to me, children.

   (The children cling to Erma.)

   Come here to your poor old mama. Come here to me, please. I'm sorry. Forgive me children. I'm sorry, so sorry.

   (The children don't budge. They cling to Erma. Vernon goes to the children.)

VERNON: Come on children. Let's go to your mama.

   (He takes them by the hand. He leads them to Velma. They allow themselves reluctantly to be led to her. Velma embraces them.)

   Erma, do you have any soup?

ERMA: Yessir.

VERNON: Bring me some.

   (Erma goes.)

ETHEL: If you go, where would you go?

VERNON: Mexico, I suppose. I don't know. I don't care really. Mildred has been on about sixteen cruises since we married. She's been everywhere.

ETHEL: How many have you been on?

VERNON: Two. Bermuda. Panama Canal.

ETHEL: I've never been on a cruise. Are they fun at all?

VERNON: If you like cruises. Mildred loves them. Mildred loves to travel. I wouldn't care if I never left here again as long as I live. I was born here. I'll die here. Mildred doesn't understand that, since she wasn't born here.

ETHEL: Mildred wasn't from here?

VERNON: No. She's from Brazoria County.

ETHEL: Of course that's right. I know that.

(A pause.)

VERNON: Dolores Stewart died last week in New Orleans, I heard.

ETHEL: Dolores Stewart. My God. I haven't thought of her in the longest kind of time. What did she die of?

VERNON: I don't know any of the particulars. I just met a cousin of hers the other day and she told me.

ETHEL: Was she still married?

VERNON: I believe so.

ETHEL: Will they bury her here?

VERNON: No, in New Orleans.

ETHEL: Velma.

VELMA: What?

ETHEL: Did you hear what Vernon said?

VELMA: No. What.

ETHEL: Dolores Stewart died.

VELMA: Who's that?

ETHEL: Now you remember Dolores Stewart. She had red hair.

VELMA: Was it natural or was it dyed?

ETHEL: It was dyed.

VELMA: I still don't remember her.

ETHEL: Yes, you do. Why…

VELMA: I do not. I don't remember her at all. I only remember one red-haired woman. Mrs. Cordray who was with Bubba Jackson when he killed Grayson Templeton.

ETHEL: Mrs. Cordray. My God I haven't thought of her in years. How did you remember her? You were only seven at the time.

VELMA: She had red hair.

ETHEL: She certainly did. Vernon and Dolores were sweethearts at one time. Weren't you Vernon?

VERNON: I guess you could say so, for awhile anyway.

ETHEL: Were you and Dolores the same age?

VERNON: I was a year older.

ETHEL: She came back here from New York during the Depression and went to work for the government. She used to go from house to house asking questions.

VELMA: What kind of questions?

ETHEL: My God. I don't remember what kind of questions. She came to our house once to ask her questions and we gave her a Coke while she sat on our porch and rested. You sat with her, and you asked her all kinds of questions about New York City and New Orleans. Now do you remember her?

VELMA: No, so be quiet.

ETHEL: Velma.

VELMA: Be quiet I said. I'm praying. I'm holding my little children in my arms and I'm praying that God will make me a good woman and a good mother. *(She closes her eyes.)* Help, me Father. *(She holds her children close to her.)* Pray children with your mama. Pray that God will make me a good woman. *(She continues holding them, her eyes closed as if in prayer.)*

ETHEL: How old was Dolores when she married the first time?

VERNON: I don't remember exactly. Twenty-two or twenty-three.

ETHEL: Right after you got married?

VERNON: Yes.

ETHEL: It didn't last?

VERNON: No.

ETHEL: Then she got married the second time to that man from New Orleans. What was his name?

VERNON: Cummings, I believe.

ETHEL: I think so. Anyway, she got married in the Episcopal church and everyone in town was wondering if she'd wear white.

VERNON: Did she?

ETHEL: I don't remember. I wasn't invited to the wedding. Weren't you invited, Vernon?

VERNON: No.

ETHEL: Anyway. We heard at the time he was rich and he took her away to New Orleans and…

VELMA: Please be quiet, Mama.

ETHEL: Why?

VELMA: I'm praying.

(Erma comes in with the soup. Vernon takes it and goes to Velma.)

VERNON: Velma, Erma fixed some good nourishing soup for you. This will make you feel better. Open your mouth now and take a sip of this good soup. *(He takes a spoonful of soup and holds it close to Velma's mouth.)* Come on, Velma. Just a swallow.

(She swallows the spoonful.)

Isn't that good? Now one more.

ETHEL: Vernon. How old are you?

VERNON: Fifty.

ETHEL: My God. Is it possible. I watched you grow up. Now Dolores must have been forty-nine.

VERNON: Yes. All of that.

VELMA: How old are you, Mama?

ETHEL: Old enough to know better.

VELMA: What does that mean?

ETHEL: You figure it out. I always heard in high school Dolores went skinny dipping with the boys. Was that true?

VERNON: I don't remember. *(He holds a spoonful of soup up to Velma.)* Come on, Velma. Have another swallow.

(She does so.)

Now, wasn't that good?

VELMA: Not particularly. *(A pause.)* My papa has been dead a long time. Do you remember my papa?

VERNON: Yes, very well.

VELMA: He worshipped me.

VERNON: I expect, he did.

VELMA: He cried the day I cut my curls off didn't he, Mama?

ETHEL: Yes, he did. Cried like a baby.

VELMA: I'm glad he didn't live to see me like this. One eye gone.

VERNON: All right, Velma. One more spoonful.

ETHEL: Who was all in your high school crowd, Vernon? Let's see. There was Dolores and Bob and Jerry and Elizabeth and Alice.

VERNON: Alice wasn't in our crowd. She was older.

ETHEL: You're right. But there was Grayson.

VELMA: He got killed.

ETHEL: Yes, he did. It tore this town apart too.

VELMA: What did?

ETHEL: His death.

VELMA: Why?

ETHEL: Because he was killed by his cousin and everybody was asked to take sides.

VELMA: Who asked them?

ETHEL: The family of the boy that killed him and his family.

VELMA: Did you take sides?

ETHEL: No. I stayed out of it.

VELMA: What's today?

ETHEL: Monday.

VELMA: I'm going to church next Sunday. I'm going to church and I'm going to get down on my knees and ask God's forgiveness. I'm going to take you with me, Mama, and I'm going to ask God to forgive you too.

ETHEL: You won't get me to go to church, thank you. I don't need forgiveness.

VELMA: Like hell.

ETHEL: I don't. I have a clear conscience, thank you very much.

VELMA: Yes, you do too need forgiveness.

ETHEL: No, I don't. I don't need forgiveness.

VELMA: Like hell you don't. *(She knocks the soup out of Vernon's hand. It spills on the floor.)* Like bloody hell.

ETHEL: Velma.

VELMA: Velma yourself, you old bitch.

ETHEL: Did any spill on you, Vernon?

VERNON: No.

ETHEL: *(Calling.)* Erma. Bring some rags. The soup got spilled.

(Erma comes in with rags and begins to clean up the spilled soup.)

VELMA: Did you go to church, Vernon?

VERNON: No.

VELMA: Never?

VERNON: Sometimes, Easter—Christmas.

VELMA: I'll pray for you, too, then. I'll pray for you too.

VERNON: Thank you.

(They sit in silence. Velma closes her eyes and continues her silent prayers. Erma continues to clean up the soup as the lights fade. The lights are brought up on the Early bedroom. Mildred is there with Gertrude. She has lots of cruise literature around. Gertrude is looking at some of it.)

GERTRUDE: When is he going to decide whether he will go or not?

MILDRED: I don't know. I don't press. I know him well enough not to. I pretend like I'm indifferent one way or the other. If I seem too anxious that he goes, he'll be determined not to. He's stubborn as a mule. But so am I. We're both stubborn God knows.

GERTRUDE: If he goes, where do you think he'll want to go?

MILDRED: God knows. I pretend I don't care about that either. I hope we go to Bermuda, but he keeps eyeing some places in Mexico. *(She laughs.)* Not that it makes any difference where we go. He never leaves the ship. The last one we took together was to Bermuda, and when we docked I said I was going ashore to shop and he said he'd prefer waiting as usual on the ship. So off I go and wandered farther than I should and I decided I'd get a taxi back to the ship, and I hailed one and got in and we rode a few blocks and it stopped and picked up another passenger, and we rode a few more blocks and we stopped and picked up another passenger and then another and by this time I was getting very nervous and anxious and I told the driver I had little time and he told me to relax and not worry, and he began driving to what seemed like a very strange section of the city and the driver stopped and let one passenger off and then another off and I looked at my watch and the time of departure for the boat was getting closer and closer and then he let another passenger off and then another and by this time I was in a panic, not only did I think I would miss the boat, but I was afraid he was taking me some place to rape me or rob me. And so I began to cry and pleaded with him to get me right to the boat and he turned the car around after giving me the most disgusted look and raced through the town and got me there just in time. My God I was very relieved. And Vernon was scared to death too, although he wouldn't admit it. He was standing on the deck looking at his watch. *(She laughs.)* I just hope, if he decides to go, nothing comes up at the last minute, like a sick patient to keep him from going. When his mother was alive and we'd go to New York or Chicago for medical conventions, she'd call him the minute he got there about some patient that was refusing to see any other doctor and he'd feel guilty and go on back home. "Darling, I'm sorry to bother you," she'd say, "but I thought you'd want to know." The truth is she was jealous of me. She couldn't stand his being off alone with me. Do you know the whole time she was alive he went over to her house every night and sat on their front porch and visited for at least two hours. He expected me at first to go with him. But I soon put him straight about that. No way I said was I going over and sit on that porch every night with his mother or anyone else. No way, Jose. No way. She's not my mother I told him. So, I had my mother move here from Brazoria and she built a house just a block away from ours and while he went to sit with his mother I would get in my car and I would pick up my mother up at her house and we'd ride around town until I'd see his car back in our drive and then I'd take my mother home and I'd go home. That went on until his mother died and after she died he began staying late at the clinic, so I was determined not to sit here by myself and wait for him then either and I'd go and get mother and we'd ride around town, until I'd see his car in the drive and I'd take Mama home and come on home. That went on until my mama died, now I just get in the car and ride by myself.

(Jackie comes in.)

JACKIE: Solomon is here.

MILDRED: What's he want?

JACKIE: He won't tell me.

MILDRED: Well, go tell him I said to tell you. *(A pause.)* And Vernon had his mama fooled, you know. She thought he was an angel. When I first met him and he was still going with that Dolores...

GERTRUDE: She died, you know.

MILDRED: Who did?

GERTRUDE: Dolores Stewart.

MILDRED: When?

GERTRUDE: I don't know. I heard up town yesterday.

MILDRED: Well anyway when I first knew him he was still going with her and he would get so drunk at the dances he could hardly stand up straight. And when I began to go with him I'd try to get him to stop but he wouldn't. And his mama would look you straight in the face and say darling has never touched whiskey in his life, because he took the temperance pledge when he was six years old and he's never broken it, and I know he never will; and she believed it too, and her daughter smoked like a fiend behind her mother's back and I have seen cigarettes fall out of her purse before her mother and her mother would look you right in the eye and say her daughter has never smoked, and even when she was kicked out of Baylor Belton after she had been caught smoking, still according to her mama she had never smoked.

GERTRUDE: Did you think she was attractive?

MILDRED: Who?

GERTRUDE: Dolores Stewart.

MILDRED: No. I never did. Did you?

GERTRUDE: Yes and no.

MILDRED: What in heavens name was attractive about her?

GERTRUDE: Oh, I don't know.

MILDRED: I couldn't stand her.

(*Jackie comes back in.*)

JACKIE: He won't tell me. He says it's about a white boy.

MILDRED: Stubborn thing. What white boy?

JACKIE: I don't know. That's all he said.

MILDRED: Stubborn thing. Well, ask him to come on back.

(*Jackie goes.*)

Oh, Vernon's mama was always so jealous of me. When we first married her husband had just died and we had to live with her for a year, the most miserable year of my life. And during that first year he was going to New York for a medical convention and I was to join him there, and the day before I was to leave she rared and pitched a fit and began pulling out her hair and saying I wasn't to go, but that didn't bother me. I said, pull all your hair out if you want to. I'm going to New York to be with my husband. I'm married to him. Not you. And I went too. And I had a grand time. While Vernon was in classes and medical meetings I went to all the shows. I saw Ruby Keeler in a musical and I forgot the name of it, but she was married to Al Jolson then and the day I saw the play much to everybody's surprise Al Jolson suddenly rose up out of the audience and went up on stage and he begin to sing while she tap danced.

GERTRUDE: Oh, sweet. What did he sing?

MILDRED: I think the song was called "Liza," but I can't remember.

(*Jackie comes in with Solomon.*)

JACKIE: Here's Solomon.

MILDRED: Hello, Solomon. You know Miss Gertrude.

GERTRUDE: Hello, Solomon.

(*He nods.*)

MILDRED: What's this about a white boy.

SOLOMON: Where's the doctor?

MILDRED: Why?

SOLOMON: I think he should hear what I have to say.

MILDRED: Well, tell me and I'll tell him.

SOLOMON: Do you know a white boy named Leroy Hayhurst?

MILDRED: No. (*A pause.*) Oh, yes, I do too. I don't know him. I mean I used to know him when he was a very little boy. He wasn't called Leroy then. We called him Teddy. You must remember him Solomon. Teddy. He was with us until he was almost three years old.

SOLOMON: I remember.

(Vernon comes into the room.)

VERNON: Hello, Gertrude. Hello, Solomon.

MILDRED: Solomon was about to tell me something about Leroy Hayhurst.

VERNON: Who?

MILDRED: Leroy Hayhurst. You know, Teddy.

VERNON: Oh, yes. What about him?

SOLOMON: He got killed this afternoon.

VERNON: How?

SOLOMON: He was stabbed by a colored man. Joe Gray.

VERNON: Why did he kill him?

SOLOMON: They got into a fight over in that gambling joint in the quarters called the Club 90. He has been over in the quarters drunk every day for the last three or four…

VERNON: Who has?

SOLOMON: Leroy Hayhurst. I took him home one day drunk and kept him until he sobered up, but he came back the next day drunk again. He said he had come over here to your house twice to find you, but you were never home. He was going all over the quarters saying you had offered his mama fifty thousand dollars to let you adopt him, and that now that she was dead he was going to find you, so you could adopt him and he'd be rich.

VERNON: When was he killed?

SOLOMON: Today.

VERNON: What time was he killed?

SOLOMON: I don't know exactly. Rosie Jackson came over to the house to tell me he'd been stabbed, and by the time I got to the Club 90 he was on the floor dead.

VERNON: Where is his body now?

SOLOMON: I don't know. Soon after I got there the sheriff came and took it away. They put Joe in jail. He cut him bad. He was bleeding like a hog.

VERNON: Do you know if his family has been notified?

SOLOMON: No. That's why I came to tell you. I thought you might want to get in touch with them.

VERNON: I wouldn't know how to.

(Jackie enters.)

JACKIE: Excuse me. The sheriff is here.

VERNON: Have him come on back.

GERTRUDE: I'm so sorry. I think I should go. I'll call you.

(She starts out as the sheriff appears.)

Hello, Sheriff.

SHERIFF: Hello, Gertrude.

(Gertrude leaves. The sheriff comes into the room.)

Vernon, they told me over in the quarters that you knew a Leroy Hayhurst?

VERNON: No, sir, Sheriff, not really.

SHERIFF: Oh, I thought Booger Red that owns the joint where he was killed said…

VERNON: I used to know him. A very long time ago. He was the boy Mildred and I tried to adopt. That was twenty-three years ago. We read in the *Chronicle* a week ago that his mother committed suicide. She lived I believe in Conroe. Didn't the paper say she lived in Conroe, Mildred?

MILDRED: Yes. It did. Conroe.

SHERIFF: That's right. It was Conroe. He had his parents' address on him. I called the father before I came over here and he said they were estranged and Leroy told him he was coming over here to live with you, and his father said he wanted nothing to do with him, and I told him he had been killed and did he want to send for the body and he said no. He said he didn't care what we did with the body, we could throw it in the river as far as he was concerned. That he had been nothing but misery to him all his life. And since I thought you knew him, and maybe he was staying here, I thought maybe you'd want to do something about his body. Otherwise, the county will bury him.

VERNON: No, I don't want that. I'll take care of the burial.

SHERIFF: Do you want to see him? His body is over at the jail. I should warn you though that he's pretty cut up.

VERNON: No, I think not.

(Mildred is crying now.)

MILDRED: Oh, my God. That sweet little boy. That sweet, precious little boy.

(The sheriff and Solomon leave. Mildred continues crying.)

VERNON: Don't cry, Mildred. There is nothing in this world we could have done. I think I better call the funeral parlour to come for the body. *(He starts for the phone. He pauses.)* I think I will go and see him first. I'll call the funeral parlour from there. You want to go?

MILDRED: No. I couldn't bear to see him all cut up.

(Vernon leaves. She continues crying as the lights fade. The lights are brought up on the Early bedroom. Mildred is there looking through a mail order catalogue. Vernon comes in. He seems extremely tired.)

VERNON: I didn't get to see him. His body was gone when I got there. His father had changed his mind and come for it. The hearse was leaving with him as I got there.

MILDRED: Was the father there?

VERNON: Yes.

MILDRED: Did you get to speak to him?

VERNON: Yes. The sheriff introduced us. I told him we were very sorry. There was a young woman there with him. No one introduced us, but I think it was his daughter. She seemed very grieved.

MILDRED: What was the father like?

VERNON: I couldn't tell much. He had on khakis. He's much younger then we are.

MILDRED: I think he was eighteen when Teddy was born.

VERNON: Something like that.

MILDRED: I know the mother was sixteen.

VERNON: Yes.

(A pause.)

MILDRED: What time do you want supper?

VERNON: It doesn't matter.

MILDRED: Are you hungry?

VERNON: Not very.

(A pause.)

MILDRED: Vernon?

VERNON: Yes.

MILDRED: Have you thought anymore about the cruise?

VERNON: I've thought about it.

(Jackie comes in.)

JACKIE: What time do you all want supper?

MILDRED: Neither of us are very hungry Jackie. You go on home. I'll fix something later.

JACKIE: Yes, ma'm.

(Jackie goes. Vernon goes to a chair and sits down.)

MILDRED: Jackie says she saw a drunken white boy wandering around the quarters twice. She said she thought to herself he's heading for trouble. *(A pause.)* Vernon?

VERNON: Yes?

MILDRED: I know you don't like me to bug you, I know I can be a nag, and I don't ever mean to be. I do get concerned about you and I do want you to get away from here for awhile so you can get some real rest.

VERNON: I guess I should.

(A pause.)

MILDRED: If we go on a cruise, have you thought anymore about where you'd like to go?

VERNON: No. You decide. I'll be happy wherever you want to go. I never leave the boat anyway.

MILDRED: Well, if you don't mind I'd like to go back to Bermuda.

VERNON: That's fine with me.

MILDRED: When do you think you'll decide if you want to go?

VERNON: My God, I don't know, Mildred. I'm so tired now. I can't think about anything. (A pause.) All right. I've decided I will go.

MILDRED: I'm glad. How soon do you want to go?

VERNON: You can decide that too.

MILDRED: Can we leave this weekend?

VERNON: This weekend?

MILDRED: Yes.

VERNON: Oh, I don't know. Can you arrange everything that quickly?

MILDRED: I've already started arrangements. They know me well at my travel agency. I had them book several dates tentatively. I have one this weekend or next Wednesday.

VERNON: Well all right, let's go this weekend.

MILDRED: Oh, that's wonderful. (A pause.) That boy.

VERNON: Leroy.

MILDRED: Yes. Do you think he ever really came here looking for us?

VERNON: I don't know.

MILDRED: Are they burying him in Conroe?

VERNON: I guess. I didn't ask.

MILDRED: I suppose he'll be buried next to his mother?

VERNON: I imagine. (A pause.) I stopped by Cassie's and I gave her a check for the amount that Solomon has told all over town that my mama promised Cassie to leave her after she died. I explained to Cassie she never told me about it and didn't have it in her will, so I had no way of knowing about it. And I told Cassie I wish she had come to me and told me what she had been promised. That it upset me to hear it the way I did. That Solomon had told some of my friends and they had come to me about it. Solomon was there and I said to him I wish he had come to me himself.

MILDRED: What did he say?

VERNON: Nothing.

MILDRED: Did Cassie thank you?

VERNON: Yes, she did.

MILDRED: Did Solomon thank you?

VERNON: No. All he said was, I only know two people that I'm sure will get to heaven. My mama and your mama.

MILDRED: That's all he said?

VERNON: Yes. Leroy's father asked me if he had been living with us. I said no we hadn't even seen him. We didn't even know he was in town until...

MILDRED: I found a picture of Teddy taken when he lived with us. I showed it to Jackie. She said the man she saw looked nothing like that. I hadn't seen the picture myself in so long. He was a sweet-looking little boy. Would you like to see it?

VERNON: No.

(A pause.)

MILDRED: Miss Ethel called twice while you were gone. She says Velma is driving them crazy. They could hear her praying last night all night long. An' she said she started in again this morning. She said she took her into Harrison to shop for groceries hoping to get her mind off the praying and she was quiet for awhile, but when she got inside the grocery store, she got on her knees and she began to pray out loud and nothing could stop her not even the manager of the store. She said she was going to call you to come over and talk to her, but she didn't know what you could do in the middle of a grocery store. She said she was just desperate when a little Mexican boy went over to Velma and took her hand and for some reason that hushed her up. *(A pause.)* Gertrude told me Dolores Stewart died in New Orleans.

VERNON: Yes, I heard that.

MILDRED: Why didn't you tell me?

VERNON: I don't know. It slipped my mind.

MILDRED: I remember the first summer I came here to visit my aunt. I met Dolores and she asked me to go riding with her and I did and we passed you in the car and she said she was going steady with you and had been for two years. I didn't tell her that you had asked me for a date that very night. Well, she never had any children either. I guess her last marriage was happy enough. I never heard otherwise. Did you hear if her marriage was happy or not?

VERNON: No.

MILDRED: Did you ever know him?

VERNON: Who?

MILDRED: Her husband.

VERNON: No.

MILDRED: Did you know her first husband?

VERNON: No.

MILDRED: I can't even remember his name can you?

VERNON: No.

(A pause.)

MILDRED: It's nice to have you here for a change, Vernon. The phone hasn't rung once, can you believe it?

VERNON: No.

MILDRED: Do you remember the first time we met?

VERNON: No, I don't.

MILDRED: I do. Like yesterday. It was about a week before you asked me for a date. My cousin, Laura Vaughn, came by to take me for a ride and you were with her. I thought you were her steady as I'd heard she had one, and you looked so old to me. I thought you were Laura's age and I kept saying yessir to you and no sir and I barely said anything unless I was asked a question. Now do you remember that?

VERNON: Yes. Kind of.

MILDRED: I had long hair then tied with ribbons. I had on a middy blouse. I forgot what you wore. Those were the good old days. Carefree. (A pause.) And I was thinking too about one of the times when you were in New York for a doctors' convention, I don't know if it was your third convention or the fourth, anyway, I knew you were staying at the Pennsylvania Hotel. I went to be with you after you had been there a week and a friend of mine from the university was living in New York and I got in touch with him and he asked us out to dinner and he got very drunk and he said out of nowhere, "I ran into Richard Bennett in a bar. He was drunk and I was drunk and I said to him, 'How does it feel to be the father of three whores?'" And you swelled up like a pup and you wouldn't say a word the rest of the evening and after he left you said I was not to ever see him again, that you didn't ever want anyone that talked that way around me. And I said he was just showing off and I bet he doesn't even know Richard Bennett and then you said who is Richard Bennett and I said he is a famous Broadway actor and his daughters are, at least two of them, movie stars. Do you remember that?

VERNON: Kind of.

MILDRED: I'm so delighted you've decided to go on the cruise with me. I'm going into Houston tomorrow to buy a few things to wear on the cruise.

I don't need much. I'm going to get some things for you, too. I'll get some Bermuda shorts and some sport shirts. And I'd get some swimming trunks if I thought you would go swimming in the pool. Would you go swimming if I bought you a suit?

VERNON: No.

MILDRED: I didn't think so, but Vernon, just this once when we get to Bermuda go with me off the boat. It's so beautiful there. I know you would just love it and one day I would like us to spend a week or two there. But I won't pressure you. If you only want to stay on the boat I won't say a word. But promise me you'll at least think about leaving the boat just this once. Vernon, will you at least think about leaving the boat?

(Vernon has begun to cry.)

Vernon. Did you hear me? Vernon. *(She looks at him. She sees he is crying.)* Vernon, what's the matter?

(He doesn't answer. He continues crying.)

Vernon. Don't cry. You're just tired. We're going to have a wonderful time on the cruise. We'll rest and sleep and we'll have no worries. No phones. Just peace and quiet. Vernon, please don't cry. Please, please, don't cry.

(She pauses. He continues crying.)

Vernon. Vernon.

(She watches him not knowing what to say as the lights fade.)

END OF PLAY

GETTING FRANKIE MARRIED—
AND AFTERWARDS

CHARACTERS
Lavern
Constance
Mae
Isabel
Frankie
Fred
Georgia Dale
S.P.
Mrs. Willis
Helen Vaught
Bill Simmons
Carlton Gleason
Stanley and Douglas

PLACE
Harrison, Texas

TIME
1990

ACT I

SCENE I

A living room of the Willises house. It is a room furnished with no particular taste, the furnishings are fairly expensive, but with no distinction. Off the living room is one of the downstairs bedrooms. Laverne, forty, and Constance, thirty-nine, friends of the Willis's are there.

CONSTANCE: *(Whispering.)* How long have you been here?

LAVERNE: *(Whispering.)* About an hour.

CONSTANCE: Any change?

LAVERNE: I'm afraid not

CONSTANCE: How old is she?

LAVERNE: Let's see. Fred is forty-three. I've been told she had him when she was forty-two. So that would make her eighty-five.

CONSTANCE: I figured about that. Well, she's had a long life.

LAVERNE: Yes, she has.

CONSTANCE: Who is in there with her, Mae?

LAVERNE: I think that's her name.

CONSTANCE: And Fred and Frankie.

LAVERNE: I'm sure so.

(Mae, a large, black woman, comes out of the sick room.)

CONSTANCE: Mae?

(Mae looks up at her.)

Remember me?

MAE: Oh, yes, Miss Constance. How you been?

CONSTANCE: I'm well, thank you. You been all right?

MAE: Oh, yes ma'am.

CONSTANCE: Mae took such good care of Daddy the last years of his life.

MAE: I tried.

CONSTANCE: Mae is very religious. She used to read to Daddy from the Bible every morning when he first woke up and every evening just before he went to bed.

MAE: He knew his Bible.

CONSTANCE: That's what he said about you.

MAE: Yes, ma'am. That's one thing for sure, I know my Bible.

LAVERNE: Do you read the Bible to Mrs. Willis?

MAE: Oh, no ma'am. She's not one for the Bible. She says she goes to church on Easter and that's it.

LAVERNE: How is she?

MAE: About the same. The doctor will be back again later.

CONSTANCE: Do you think she'll last the night?

MAE: You never know. She is a fighter. I thought for sure she was gone for good last week, but nope, she fooled us all. She came right around. She may just get out of that bed yet.

CONSTANCE: Oh, do you think so?

MAE: No, ma'am, not really. I mostly says that to keep Mr. Fred's spirits up. He sure loves his mama. Miss Georgia Dale Ratliff called a little while ago. She says she's bringing over some soup.

LAVERNE: Oh, does she come over often?

MAE: No, ma'am, but she's started calling every day to inquire about Mrs. Willis.

LAVERNE: Does she?

CONSTANCE: Are Miss Frankie and Fred in there?

MAE: Both of them.

CONSTANCE: Tell Miss Frankie we're out here if she needs us.

MAE: Yes, ma'am. *(She goes into the room.)*

LAVERNE: Did you get that?

CONSTANCE: What?

LAVERNE: Georgia Dale Ratliff has been calling every day and is coming over here bringing soup.

CONSTANCE: Well? I'm sure a lot of people call. We do. I brought soup yesterday. Isabel will be here in a few minutes and she is going to bring soup.

LAVERNE: You and Isabel are not after what Georgia Dale Ratliff is after, and mark my word half the widows in this town are going to be after Fred to marry him as soon as his mother dies.

CONSTANCE: How is Georgia Dale Ratliff going to marry him? She has a husband...

LAVERNE: A husband as old as Mrs. Willis. A husband on his last legs.

CONSTANCE: Oh, come on. He's not nearly as old as Mrs. Willis. He's no more than seventy-four.

LAVERNE: He looks a hundred and seventy-four.

CONSTANCE: That's because he's dissipated.

LAVERNE: I'll say he's dissipated.

(Frankie, in her late thirties, comes out of the bedroom.)

FRANKIE: Hello. *(She kisses each of them.)*

LAVERNE: How are you doing?

FRANKIE: All right.

CONSTANCE: How is Mrs. Willis?

FRANKIE: Back and forth.

CONSTANCE: Isabel will be here in a few minutes. She's bringing some soup.

LAVERNE: I brought some cold chicken and potato salad earlier. I put them in the refrigerator.

FRANKIE: That's so sweet of you. Georgia Dale Ratliff called saying she was bringing some soup, too. I didn't know she was so fond of Mrs. Willis. Neither did Fred. Matter of fact, Mrs. Willis didn't even know who we were talking about at first. We had to explain who she was. *(Fred comes out.)*

FRED: Hello girls. Thank you for coming over.

LAVERNE: If you get hungry Fred, there is some cold chicken in the refrigerator.

FRED: Thank you. I'm not very hungry. Mae says Georgia Dale Ratliff is bringing over some soup. That's about all I want.

LAVERNE: Isabel is too.

FRED: That's very nice of her. *(The door bell rings.)*

LAVERNE: I'll answer it. *(She goes to the door and Georgia Dale and her husband, S.P., are there. She has a container of soup.)*

LAVERNE: Hello, Georgia Dale. Hello, S.P.

GEORGIA DALE: Hello, everybody. *(She goes over to Fred.)* Oh, Fred, I'm so sorry Mrs. Willis is so low.

FRED: Thank you for your concern, Georgia Dale, but she may fool us all yet. I'm not giving up on her. She still has a lot of fight in her.

GEORGIA DALE: Of course she has. Bless her heart and soul. I brought you some vegetable soup. Mae said it was your favorite.

FRED: Thank you. How are you, S.P.?

S.P.: Pretty fair. I'm sorry about your mama. I was in the hospital all last week.

FRED: Were you?

S.P.: It was my heart. I'm on my last legs, too, they tell me.

FRED: Shoot, you don't look like you're on your last legs to me.

S.P.: Well, thank you. I've had to give up everything. Whiskey, cigarettes. I take so many pills I can't keep them all straight. Georgia Dale has to read off to me what I'm supposed to take next.

GEORGIA DALE: S.P.

S.P.: What?

GEORGIA DALE: Will you stop burdening Fred with your troubles? He has a sick mama to worry about.

S.P.: I'm sorry Fred. Georgia Dale says all I do is worry about myself. She says half of it's in my mind, but I swear it's not. I just plain don't feel well. I get short of breath, my heart races...

GEORGIA DALE: S.P. Will you please change the subject.

S.P.: Yes, ma'am. I'm sorry. I know I talk too much. Georgia Dale is always having to tell me that.

GEORGIA DALE: S.P.

S.P.: Yes, ma'am.

(Mae comes into the room.)

MAE: Mr. Fred, your mama is asking for you.

FRED: Excuse me. *(He goes into the bedroom.)*

FRANKIE: Excuse me.

(She goes to the bedroom. Mae follows her.)

S.P.: How long have Fred and Frankie been going together?

GEORGIA DALE: At least twenty years.

LAVERNE: Twenty-five.

GEORGIA DALE: You're both close friends of Frankie's. Will you explain to me why they have never in all these years ever married?

LAVERNE: I've never discussed it with her.

CONSTANCE: Neither have I.

GEORGIA DALE: Now, come on...

LAVERNE: No, I never have. Have you, Constance?

CONSTANCE: No, I said I hadn't.

LAVERNE: Frankie is a very private person.

GEORGIA DALE: I used to think it was his mother that objected and since he was always so close to her, but lately she's over here all the time and goes everywhere with them, so Mrs. Willis isn't the reason they're not married. Is she?

LAVERNE: I have no idea, Georgia Dale.

GEORGIA DALE: Oh, it's just men. None of them would marry if you didn't make them. S.P. lived with Jackie Mae Gleason for how many years, S.P.?

S.P.: My God, Georgia Dale, I don't remember.

GEORGIA DALE: Long enough. A month after she died and he called me for a date I let him know right way if he wasn't interested in marriage not to come around. Of course, I know people in town say I had to get him drunk to marry me, but that's not true is it, Daddy?

S.P.: What?

GEORGIA DALE: You're not all that deaf. You just hear what you want to. *(She lifts her voice.)* I said you were sober when we got married. Weren't you?

S.P.: I guess so, if you say so.

GEORGIA DALE: I say so. *(She whispers.)* Of course Fred's daddy went with a woman on the sly, a married woman for years, and they say he promised to marry her when her old husband died.

LAVERNE: That was Jackie Mae's mother, wasn't it?

GEORGIA DALE: It was. We're talking about Jackie Mae's mother, S.P., that Fred's father went with all those years. What was Jackie Mae's mother's name? I forgot.

S.P.: Gloria Catherine.

GEORGIA DALE: Gloria Catherine.

S.P.: He called her Kitty.

GEORGIA DALE: Who did?

S.P.: Fred Willis's father. Lewis Willis.

GEORGIA DALE: Why didn't he marry her when her husband died?

S.P.: I don't know. I never asked him.

GEORGIA DALE: I heard that the night her old husband died, Mr. Willis rode into San Antonio and asked Mrs. Willis who was working in San Antonio then to marry him. Had he been going with her too?

S.P.: Who?

GEORGIA DALE: Fred's father and mother. Had they been going together at the same time he was going with Jackie Mae's mother?

S.P.: Kitty?

GEORGIA DALE: Yes.

S.P.: I guess so.

GEORGIA DALE: My God, you men are all just animals.

(The bedroom opens and Mrs. Willis, holding on to Fred and Frankie, comes slowly into the room.)

LAVERNE: Mrs. Willis. Bless your sweet heart.

MRS. WILLIS: I got sick of that bed, darling. I said to Fred I want to get out of bed and he said Mama the doctor says you're to stay in the bed and I said…

FRED: Mama don't talk too much. Just say hello to everybody and then you're going back into your room. We don't want you to get overexcited.

GEORGIA DALE: Hello, Mrs. Willis.

MRS. WILLIS: Who are you?

GEORGIA DALE: Georgia Ratliff.

MRS. WILLIS: Who?

GEORGIA DALE: Georgia Dale Ratliff.

MRS. WILLIS: Spell it.

FRED: G-E-O-R-G-I-A Georgia, D-A-L-E Dale. She's the one that Mae said was bringing some soup.

GEORGIA DALE: I have it right here.

FRED: And there are Laverne and Constance.

MRS. WILLIS: Oh, yes. Nice to see you both. You're looking well.

CONSTANCE: So are you, Mrs. Willis.

FRED: They call every day, Mama, to see what they can do to help. You remember Laverne is married to Dotson Lovell and Constance to Travis Baxter. We all went through school together here, Mama, remember?

CONSTANCE: Not me.

FRED: That's right. Constance met Travis in college. Isabel calls often, too. Where is Isabel?

CONSTANCE: She'll be along. She's bringing soup, too.

MRS. WILLIS: I'm tired, Son. All this company is tiring me out.

FRED: All right, Mama.

MRS. WILLIS: I was forty-two when I had this boy. I was forty when I married his daddy. Everybody said to me you're too old to have children. Not me, I said, I'm going to have a baby if it kills me. It didn't kill me. Look at him. His daddy died when he was five.

FRED: When I was seven, Mama.

MRS. WILLIS: When he was seven, and I raised him all by myself. I'm the last of my family, you know. My papa is dead, my mama, my brothers. *(A pause.)* I have some nieces and nephews somewhere, don't I, Son?

FRED: Yes, you do, Mama.

MRS. WILLIS: Where are they, Fred?

FRED: Two in Houston. One in New Orleans, one in Mississippi.

MRS. WILLIS: Where in Mississippi?

FRED: Biloxi, last I heard. Mama, come on now, you'll tire yourself.

MRS. WILLIS: *(Pointing to S.P.)* Who is that man there?

FRED: That's S.P., Mama.

S.P.: How are you, Mrs. Willis?

MRS. WILLIS: I'm here but being careful, as the old folks say. How are you getting along, S.P.?

S.P.: I'm making it.

MRS. WILLIS: Did you ever marry?

FRED: Yes, Mama. He's married to Georgia Dale.

MRS. WILLIS: Georgia Dale? I thought she had a husband.

GEORGIA DALE: Three, Mrs. Willis. One divorced, one died, and S.P. is my third.

MRS. WILLIS: Do you have any children?

GEORGIA DALE: No, ma'am.

MRS. WILLIS: Fred has never married. Of course, his papa never married until he was in his forties. Frankie has never married. They started going together in high school. Wasn't it in high school, Son?

FRED: Yes, Mama.

MRS. WILLIS: People ask me why they don't marry. I say don't ask me, ask them. Fred's father was in his forties when he married. Forty-five. How old are you Fred?

FRED: Forty-three.

MRS. WILLIS: Forty-three. My God, where have the years gone? I had him when I was in my forties.

FRED: You've told everybody that, Mama.

MRS. WILLIS: Did I? You start to repeat when you get my age.

S.P.: I'm getting dizzy, Georgia Dale.

GEORGIA DALE: Well, sit down.

(He does so.)

MRS. WILLIS: There were some cousins of ours who had this old nigra woman that worked for them. They had taken her in when she was twelve and after they moved away she stayed on here, and they would write to her and send her a check after they were gone, and she would go all over town with the letter and the check they sent her and she would say: "I got a letter from 'em," and she would read you the letter and she would tell you each time they taught her to read and write and the multiplication tables and she would start saying all the multiplication tables to you and I would say Corrine—that was her name wasn't it, Son?

FRED: Yes, ma'am.

MRS. WILLIS: I'd say Corrine, you have told me all this a hundred times, but she'd go right on. Now I've gotten like Corrine. I just repeat and repeat. Good night.

(She starts for her room. Frankie and Fred assist her through the door and close it after.)

S.P.: Georgia Dale, I'm getting short of breath.

GEORGIA DALE: Oh, Lord. Well, close your eyes and rest.

S.P.: When I close my eyes I get a buzzing in my head.

GEORGIA DALE: That's the first time I've heard of that.

S.P.: A buzzing in my head?

GEORGIA DALE: Yes.

S.P.: It happens to me all the time. Every time I close my eyes.

GEORGIA DALE: You never told me about it before.

S.P.: I don't tell you everything.

GEORGIA DALE: Well, you ought to tell me when you have something like a buzzing in your head. Did you tell the doctor?

S.P.: Yes.

GEORGIA DALE: What did he say?

S.P.: Nothing, except to try and close my eyes.

GEORGIA DALE: He didn't give you a pill for it?

S.P.: No.

GEORGIA DALE: That's the first thing he hasn't given you a pill for. God knows how many pills the poor soul has to take every morning just to get started.

S.P.: Afternoons and nights, too.

GEORGIA DALE: I'll say, afternoon and night, too.

S.P.: Maybe it's time for one of my pills now, Georgia Dale, maybe that's why I feel dizzy.

(She looks at her watch.)

GEORGIA DALE: No, the next one is in an hour.

S.P.: You're sure?

GEORGIA DALE: Yes, I'm sure.

S.P.: Georgia Dale, I'm still short of breath. I'd better get on home.

GEORGIA DALE: All right, let me take this soup out into the kitchen first.

LAVERNE: I'll take it for you, Georgia Dale. Thank you. *(Laverne takes the container and goes out to the kitchen.)*

GEORGIA DALE: Come on, S.P. *(She helps him up.)* So long.

CONSTANCE: So long.

(S.P. and Georgia Dale leave. Laverne comes back in.)

Maybe she doesn't want to marry him.

LAVERNE: What on earth are you talking about?

CONSTANCE: Frankie. Maybe she doesn't want to get married to Fred or anyone. Maybe she likes her independence.

LAVERNE: I don't believe it.

CONSTANCE: Has she ever told you she wanted to marry him?

LAVERNE: No.

CONSTANCE: Well.

(The door opens. Isabel appears with a container of soup.)

ISABEL: I met S.P. and Georgia Dale. They said you were still here. They said Mrs. Willis was walking around. I find that hard to believe.

LAVERNE: She was.

ISABEL: That's remarkable.

CONSTANCE: It is.

(Frankie comes into the room.)

FRANKIE: Oh, Isabel. When did you get here?

ISABEL: I just did. I brought some soup. Vegetable.

FRANKIE: Wonderful. I'll take some with Fred. He's hungry. I'm sure he'd prefer your soup to Georgia Dale's. I don't expect Georgia Dale is much of a cook.

LAVERNE: I wouldn't think so.

ISABEL: I'll heat it for you.

FRANKIE: Thank you.

ISABEL: Would you like some, too?

FRANKIE: Yes, thank you.

(Isabel goes to the kitchen.)

Isn't Mrs. Willis remarkable?

LAVERNE: Yes, she is.

FRANKIE: She's asleep now, but Fred won't leave her bedside. I told him he's going to have to get some rest. Thank God they let me take my vacation from my job at the courthouse.

LAVERNE: Why don't you spend the night at our house and get yourself a good rest.

FRANKIE: I don't think I'd better leave Fred.

LAVERNE: Come on. He can always call you if she takes a turn for the worse.

FRANKIE: Oh, I don't know.

(Fred appears.)

Isabel is heating you some soup.

FRED: Thanks. Lola Dickinson just called. She's sending over some fried chicken. I told her Mama was feeling better.

FRANKIE: People have been so kind.

LAVERNE: Fred, I want Frankie to spend the night at my house and get a good rest.

FRANKIE: Fred is the one that needs the rest.

FRED: I'm all right. I doze off on the couch in there from time to time. I think I should always be there when Mama wakes up, but you go to Laverne's tonight Frankie if you want to.

FRANKIE: No, I'm going to stay the night here. You might need me.

FRED: Suit yourself.

> (*He goes back into the bedroom. Isabel comes in with two bowls of soup on a tray.*)

FRANKIE: Thank you. (*She takes the tray and goes into the bedroom.*)

LAVERNE: Oh, I think it's terrible.

ISABEL: What?

LAVERNE: What Frankie is doing with her life. Just throwing it away. And I tell you this. Once Mrs. Willis dies, every free woman in town is going to start chasing him, and he's just liable to take off and leave Frankie for some eighteen-year-old girl.

CONSTANCE: Not Fred.

LAVERNE: What do you mean, not Fred?

CONSTANCE: I just don't think he's that kind. I'll bet you anything in this world he'd never do that.

LAVERNE: Then why in all these years hasn't he asked her to marry him?

CONSTANCE: Maybe he has. Maybe she doesn't want to marry him.

LAVERNE: My foot.

CONSTANCE: I've never known him to look at another woman, have you?

LAVERNE: No.

CONSTANCE: Well, then. (*A pause.*) What are you so quiet about, Isabel?

ISABEL: Nothing.

CONSTANCE: Are you feeling all right.

ISABEL: Yes.

> (*A pause.*)

CONSTANCE: Isabel.

ISABEL: Yes.

CONSTANCE: What is the matter?

ISABEL: I don't think I'd better discuss it. Not here anyway.

LAVERNE: What is it, Isabel?

ISABEL: I can't talk about it here.

LAVERNE: Why not? (*Isabel cries.*) What in the world is it, honey?

ISABEL: Oh, it's all so upsetting. I just can't talk about it.

CONSTANCE: Honey. Honey.

> (*Isabel wipes her eyes.*)

ISABEL: You must never say I told you any of this. Promise?

CONSTANCE: I promise.

LAVERNE: Promise.

ISABEL: Pete would kill me if he knew I was telling you any of this. (*A pause.*)

I answered the phone at noon at our house and a woman called to ask for Pete. I asked her name and she told me and it was no one I knew, so when Pete got through with the call I asked him who it was and he didn't want to tell me, and I kept after him and he said he would tell me if I never told another soul, preferably you two. He said it was a woman from Houston that Fred had been seeing for several months and she was calling to inquire how his mother was...

CONSTANCE: Oh, my God.

LAVERNE: I knew it. I knew something like this was going to happen.

ISABEL: And I said to Pete is it serious and he said he didn't know and he didn't want to discuss it any way.

LAVERNE: I'm going to tell Frankie.

ISABEL: You can't. I swore to Pete I wouldn't tell a soul.

LAVERNE: I won't tell her who told me.

CONSTANCE: Be careful, Laverne. Think about what you're doing.

(Frankie comes out with two soup bowls.)

FRANKIE: The soup was delicious.

ISABEL: Would you like some more?

FRANKIE: No, thank you.

ISABEL: Give me the bowls and I'll take them to the kitchen. *(She takes them and goes.)*

FRANKIE: What's the news in town?

CONSTANCE: Not much. It's been quiet.

FRANKIE: When did Georgia Dale leave?

CONSTANCE: Right after you took Mrs. Willis to bed. S.P. was getting short of breath.

FRANKIE: What was the name of her first husband? I can't remember and Mrs. Willis is about to drive me crazy asking me to remember his name.

LAVERNE: Ross. Ross something. He was with an oil crew. I don't think they were married more than eight months.

CONSTANCE: Ross Matthews?

LAVERNE: I think so.

(Isabel comes in.)

Was the name of Georgia Dale's first husband Ross?

ISABEL: No, Billy.

LAVERNE: Billy?

ISABEL: Yes, don't you remember? She was a little taller than he was and so she stopped wearing high heels whenever she went out with him.

LAVERNE: It wasn't Billy. It was Ross.

CONSTANCE: Ross Matthews.

ISABEL: Well, maybe so, but who was Billy?

LAVERNE: God knows.

ISABEL: Don't you remember how she stopped wearing high heels when she met him? I thought she married him.

LAVERNE: No, it was Ross.

CONSTANCE: I think so, too. Ross Matthews.

(Mae comes out.)

MAE: Mrs. Willis wants to know if you found out the name of Miss Georgia Dale's first husband?

FRANKIE: Yes, I have. I'll see you all later.

(She and Mae go into the bedroom.)

LAVERNE: I almost told her.

CONSTANCE: Oh, you didn't.

LAVERNE: Yes, I did.

ISABEL: You better never say I told you. Pete would have my neck.

LAVERNE: Don't worry. I'm not going back on my promise to you. But I know one thing, if Pete knows he has already told Dotson I'll bet anything he's told Travis, too. If he's told Dotson I'm going to get it out of him. Get Travis to tell you, Constance.

CONSTANCE: No, I'm staying out of it.

LAVERNE: Don't you have any loyalty to Frankie? Don't you think it's terrible after all these years he's seeing another woman?

CONSTANCE: Well, maybe that's all there is to it. He's just seeing her. Pete didn't say he was marrying her.

LAVERNE: What if he does?

CONSTANCE: That would be terrible.

LAVERNE: And we would be partly responsible.

CONSTANCE: How?

LAVERNE: By not warning her of what might happen so she could try and stop it.

CONSTANCE: How?

LAVERNE: I don't know how, but she could try some way.

ISABEL: Pete says he's never going to marry anybody. He says he's just like his father.

LAVERNE: His father finally did marry somebody. He married Fred's mother.

ISABEL: That's true. (A pause.) Oh, it's all so complicated. (A pause.) Do you think they live together like man and wife?

LAVERNE: Oh, come on.

ISABEL: Well, I don't know.

LAVERNE: This is 1990, honey. Of course they do.

ISABEL: I've never been really sure. Once we went on a trip out of town with them and our reservations got mixed up and when we arrived all that was available were two double rooms and I had to sleep with Frankie and Pete and Fred slept together.

CONSTANCE: Whenever we go with them out of town they make a point of getting separate rooms.

ISABEL: I said to Pete I have never seen him in public with his arm around her or do one affectionate thing. Have you?

CONSTANCE: No.

ISABEL: If they live together...

LAVERNE: If they live together. This is 1990. Of course they're living together.

ISABEL: I hate to even ask her. I asked Pete and he wouldn't answer me. Does that make Frankie his common-law-wife?

LAVERNE: It certainly does. But once he's married, she won't even be that. She will be only his ex-common-law-wife. I'm going home. I'm going to get the story out of Dotson.

ISABEL: And then are you going to tell her?

LAVERNE: I think I will. *(She goes.)*

ISABEL: I don't know about telling your friends things. I don't know if I'd want to be told if Pete were having an affair. Would you want to be told if...

CONSTANCE: I don't know.

(Frankie comes into the room.)

FRANKIE: Mrs. Willis says Ross Matthews wasn't the name of Georgia Dale's first husband it was Billy something.

ISABEL: I knew it. Laverne can be so positive. She makes me sick sometimes. She never can be wrong.

FRANKIE: Did you remember Billy's last name?

ISABEL: I don't.

CONSTANCE: I don't either.

(Mae comes out.)

MAE: Mrs. Willis says she remembers now. Billy Cunningham.

CONSTANCE: That's right, of course.

MAE: Mr. Fred says can you come back in. He needs you.

FRANKIE: All right. I'll be right there.

(Mae goes.)

Have you girls ever heard of Helen Vaught?

CONSTANCE: Helen Vaught?

FRANKIE: Yes.

CONSTANCE: No.

FRANKIE: Have you ever heard of her, Isabel?

ISABEL: Why no.

FRANKIE: She called Mae said, but Fred said he'd never heard of her and I hadn't…

(Fred comes out.)

I was just coming in, Fred.

FRED: Thank you. I want you to sit with Mama while I make a phone call.

FRANKIE: They never heard of Helen Vaught.

FRED: No. I'll be right back.

(He goes out. Frankie goes into the bedroom.)

ISABEL: Oh, my God.

CONSTANCE: What is it?

ISABEL: That's the name of the woman Pete says he's been seeing in Houston.

CONSTANCE: Don't tell me.

(Fred comes back in.)

Make your phone call?

FRED: No. The line was busy. I'll try again in a few minutes. (He goes into the bedroom.)

CONSTANCE: The dirty dog.

ISABEL: Constance…

CONSTANCE: The low-down dirty dog. That's all he is. He looks guilty as hell to me. Doesn't he to you? I bet he knows Pete told you about this woman. I hope now Laverne does tell Frankie. I'm mad enough to tell her myself.

(Frankie comes in.)

FRANKIE: Are you all free for lunch tomorrow?

CONSTANCE: I am.

ISABEL: I am, too.

FRANKIE: Well, let's have lunch together unless Mrs. Willis takes a turn for the worst.

CONSTANCE: Fine.

FRANKIE: How about you, Isabel?

(Isabel cries.)

What is it?

ISABEL: Oh, forgive me. I've been very emotional today. Seeing Mrs. Willis so frail and old has upset me.

FRANKIE: You know, she is liable to outlive us all. Everyone of us. Fred remembered who Helen Vaught was. She works in a Trust Company in Houston that's been handling some investments of Mrs. Willis's. People are so thoughtful. Imagine a woman as busy as that taking time off to inquire about an old woman's health. *(She starts back out of the room.)*

CONSTANCE: Frankie…

FRANKIE: *(Pausing.)* Yes?

CONSTANCE: Nothing. I forgot what I wanted to say.

ISABEL: I'll be going home now.

CONSTANCE: So will I.

FRANKIE: I'll see you tomorrow. Will you pick me up here? Around twelve?

CONSTANCE: We certainly will.

FRANKIE: And ask Laverne.

CONSTANCE: I will.

(They go. Frankie is alone for a moment. Fred comes out to her.)

FRED: I thought they would never leave.

FRANKIE: They mean to be helpful.

FRED: I suppose.

FRANKIE: If Mrs. Willis is still improving I'm going out for lunch tomorrow.

FRED: I think you should.

(She starts for the bedroom.)

Frankie…

FRANKIE: Yes?

FRED: Will you marry me?

FRANKIE: What?

FRED: Will you marry me?

FRANKIE: Yes.

FRED: Thank you. I'll tell Mama.

FRANKIE: Fred.

FRED: Yes?

FRANKIE: Why after all these years?

FRED: Let's don't look back. I want to get married right away.

FRANKIE: Right away?

FRED: Yes. Day after tomorrow. We can get married here so Mama can watch the ceremony.

FRANKIE: Have you told your mother?

FRED: Yes, I told her just now. She was pleased.

(Mae comes to the door.)

MAE: Mr. Fred, your mama is asking for you.

FRED: I'll be right there.

(Mae goes.)

FRANKIE: When do you want to marry?

FRED: Day after tomorrow. Tomorrow if I could arrange things in time, but I don't think I can. Late as it is now. There are blood tests and a license.

FRANKIE: I would like Laverne, Constance, and Isabel at the wedding.

FRED: All right.

FRANKIE: Will you invite anyone?

FRED: Just Mama. I'd like it as quiet as possible. There'll be talk you know, as it is.

FRANKIE: I know.

(Mae appears.)

MAE: Mr. Fred...

FRED: I'll be there right away, Mae.

(He goes back in. Mrs. Willis calls: "Fred.")

(Calling back.) In a minute, Mama. We're making plans about the wedding.

MRS. WILLIS: *(Calling.)* Well, make them in here.

FRANKIE: Where have the years gone? Why?

FRED: Now, let's don't even look back. *(He starts away.)*

FRANKIE: Fred.

FRED: Yes.

FRANKIE: There was a time I thought I would do anything if we would only marry, but now...I feel suddenly very insecure.

FRED: You love me?

FRANKIE: Yes. That's not it. I don't know what it is. All of a sudden...

FRED: Marry me, Frankie. Please marry me.

FRANKIE: Day after tomorrow.

FRED: Yes.

(From the bedroom Mrs. Willis calls: "Fred. Fred, where are you?")

I'll be right there, Mama.

FRANKIE: Why not next week, next month? We've waited this long.

FRED: Mama may not be here next week. Let's think of Mama and the pleasure it would give her. *(He starts away.)*

FRANKIE: Fred.

FRED: Yes.

FRANKIE: Who is Helen Vaught?

FRED: I told you all I know...

FRANKIE: Fred, tell me the truth. Who is Helen Vaught?

(From the bedroom Mrs. Willis calls: "Fred, Fred.")

FRED: Good God, Mama. Be patient. I told you I'd be there in a minute. *(A pause.)* Let me go into Mama. I'll come out when she's quiet.

FRANKIE: Who is Helen Vaught?

   (A pause.)

FRED: Helen Vaught. Is a woman.

FRANKIE: A young woman?

FRED: Yes.

FRANKIE: Younger than we are?

FRED: Yes.

FRANKIE: Why has she called here three times today?

FRED: How do you know she has called three times?

FRANKIE: Mae told me.

   (A pause.)

FRED: She's suing me for Breach of Promise.

FRANKIE: Breach of Promise?

FRED: Yes. I feel terrible about it. I've been seeing her every now and again in Houston the past two months. One night we went into Galveston and I got drunk and she says I proposed marriage and on the strength of that she quit her job at the Trust Company and now she's suing me for Breach of Promise.

FRANKIE: I see.

FRED: I don't want to marry her, Frankie. I'm not sure I even proposed, I was drunk. She said she can produce witnesses that heard me propose. *(A pause.)* I've been maybe drunk five times in my life. Please, marry me Frankie.

FRANKIE: What are you asking me to do? Everybody in town will say you're marrying me because of that woman's suit.

FRED: That's got nothing to do with it.

FRANKIE: Does your mama know about the Breach of Promise suit?

FRED: Yes.

   (Mae comes to the door.)

MAE: She's crying, Mr. Fred. She thinks you have gone off and left her.

FRED: Tell her I haven't.

MAE: I told her, but she don't believe me.

FRED: I'll be right there.

   (Mae goes. He goes to Frankie.)

   Will you marry me, Frankie?

FRANKIE: I don't know, Fred. Go on to your mama. She's crying in there.

   (He starts away.)

   How much is she suing you for?

FRED: I don't know yet.

(He goes. Frankie goes to the window and looks out. Mae comes in with a Bible.)

MAE: Excuse me. Mrs. Willis wants to be alone with Mr. Fred. She got very upset. Do you mind if I sit here and read?

FRANKIE: No.

(Mae opens a Bible and begins to read.)

You're reading the Bible?

MAE: Yes, ma'am. Every chance I get. It keeps me calm. I'm very nervous by nature.

(When Mae reads the Bible she does so by pointing to each word and silently sounding them out with her lips.)

FRANKIE: You couldn't tell it.

MAE: No'm.

(Fred comes to the door.)

FRED: Frankie, Mother wants to see you.

FRANKIE: I'll be in in a little while.

(He starts into the room.)

Fred…

FRED: Yes.

FRANKIE: I'm going for a walk.

FRED: Where to?

FRANKIE: No where in particular.

FRED: Will you be gone long?

FRANKIE: I don't think so.

FRED: Say hello to Mama before you go.

FRANKIE: No. I'll stop in when I get back.

(She goes. He goes back into the room. Mae continues reading the Bible. She begins to sing: "He leadeth me. He leadeth me. By His own hand He leadeth me" as the bedroom door opens and Fred appears again.)

FRED: Mae…

MAE: Yessir.

FRED: Mama says read your Bible all you want to, but hymns make her nervous.

MAE: Yessir.

(He goes. She goes back to reading her Bible as the lights fade.)

The lights are brought up. The next day. The Willises living room. Constance and Isabel are there. Laverne enters.

LAVERNE: Does Frankie know you're here?

CONSTANCE: Yes, Mae came out to say she'd be out in a little. They're bathing Mrs. Willis.

LAVERNE: Then you haven't seen her?

CONSTANCE: No.

LAVERNE: *(Whispering.)* I suppose you've heard Fred is being sued for Breach of Promise?

CONSTANCE: Yes. It's all over town, unfortunately.

ISABEL: Do you think it's true?

LAVERNE: I know it is for a gospel fact.

ISABEL: How do you know?

LAVERNE: Dotson is Fred's lawyer.

CONSTANCE: How much is the woman suing him for?

LAVERNE: Dotson wouldn't tell me. All he'd say was that it was a lot.

CONSTANCE: Do you think Frankie knows?

LAVERNE: We'll soon find out.

(The door bell rings and Laverne goes to answer it. Georgia Dale and S.P. are there. Georgia Dale has a container of gumbo.)

GEORGIA DALE: Hello. I brought some crab gumbo for Mrs. Willis's lunch. I called Fred and asked if he thought she could eat crab gumbo. He said if she couldn't, he could.

S.P.: Georgia Dale makes the best crab gumbo in Texas.

ISABEL: How do you make your gumbo, Georgia Dale?

GEORGIA DALE: Not like the cajuns let me tell you. Never any chicken or sausage and all that rue.

ISABEL: Don't you use rue?

GEORGIA DALE: Yes, honey. I use rue in moderation, not like the cajuns. I use okra, tomatoes, a little rue, and lots of crabs.

S.P.: Crabs are expensive now. Not cheap like they used to be. They're shipping all our crabs up north, because the Chesapeake Bay is so polluted they can't eat the crabs from there any longer.

GEORGIA DALE: Tell me about it.

LAVERNE: Well, we're doing a mighty good job of polluting our gulf, if you ask me.

S.P.: But we can still eat our crabs, if you can afford to buy them.

GEORGIA DALE: Don't expect to get crab gumbo in New Orleans. I went to Arnand's, to Galatoire's and to Antoine's and every time I asked for pure crab gumbo, they said we don't fix our gumbo that way, we put crab in it, along with oysters and shrimp, and God knows what else I thought to myself. I said then I'll pass on the gumbo. Bring me some fried oysters. They did. I never saw such funny looking oysters in my life. What is this I said. That's brochette they said. I don't care what you call it, I said, but are they fried in corn meal? Why they looked at me like I was crazy, like they'd never heard of frying oysters in corn meal. I told them they'd shoot you in Texas if you didn't fry them in corn meal. How's Mrs. Willis this morning?

LAVERNE: We haven't heard. We just got here.

S.P.: I had a terrible night. I had to sit up in bed two hours trying to get my breath.

GEORGIA DALE: Don't talk to me about that, S.P. You'll get no sympathy out of me. Do you know what he did at four this morning after he got his breath back? He snuck into the bathroom and smoked a cigarette.

S.P.: Just one.

GEORGIA DALE: I'll say just one. I took the rest of the pack and flushed them down the toilet.

S.P.: My wife is a mean woman, but I love her.

GEORGIA DALE: I hate to bring up unpleasant things, but have you heard the news about Fred?

LAVERNE: Yes, but I don't think we should discuss it here.

GEORGIA DALE: I'm not going to discuss it. Fred talks about it though. When I called up and asked about the gumbo I said I sincerely hope the rumors I've been hearing up town weren't true, and he said yes, they were, if you've heard I'm being sued for Breach of Promise. I've nothing to hide, he said. Well, good for you, I thought. I feel the only way to face things like that is just to be open about it. I know when people were spreading all over town that I got S.P. drunk to marry me, I just went to all my friends and I said I know what's being said, but here is the true story. He was not drunk. We both had one or two drinks before the ceremony, but he was certainly not drunk.

S.P.: When Jackie Mae Gleason was dying I asked her to marry me, but she said it was too late. I hadn't married her when she wanted to, and now that she was dying it was too late. And you know what people around town said? They said I only wanted to marry her so I could reclaim that house I had given her and had put in her name so her brother couldn't get it.

GEORGIA DALE: That was partly true, S.P.

S.P.: No, it wasn't partly true. I did want to marry the poor thing if it would make dying easier for her. But people don't give you credit for a blessed thing.

GEORGIA DALE: Well, you tried every way in the world after she died to keep those brothers from getting that house.

S.P.: Because I never cared for her brothers in the first place. That's only partly true. One I liked all right. The one that kind of drug his left foot when he walked.

GEORGIA DALE: Carlton.

S.P.: Carlton. I wouldn't have cared if he got the house, it was the older brother I couldn't stand. He didn't even come back for the funeral. He only came back when the will was probated.

(There is a knock on the door. Laverne goes. She opens it. Helen Vaught, in her early thirties, is there.)

LAVERNE: Yes.

HELEN: Is Fred Willis here?

LAVERNE: Yes, I believe he's in with his mother. She's been ill.

HELEN: I know. Would you ask please if I might speak with him?

LAVERNE: All right. Who shall I say is calling?

HELEN: Helen Vaught.

(Laverne goes to the bedroom door. She knocks. Georgia Dale goes to Helen.)

GEORGIA DALE: I'm Georgia Dale Calhoun. This is my husband, S.P.

HELEN: Hello.

(Fred comes to the door.)

LAVERNE: Fred, Helen Vaught's here to see you.

(Fred comes into the room, closing the door to the bedroom.)

HELEN: I was on my way to Corpus. I thought I'd stop by and see how your mother's feeling.

FRED: That was kind of you, Helen. She's a little stronger today. Have you all met?

GEORGIA DALE: I introduced S.P. and myself.

FRED: These are old friends. Laverne Lovell, Isabel Gallagher, and Constance Baxter. Helen Vaught.

HELEN: How do you do.

(The others nod their heads in greeting.)

S.P.: You live in Corpus?

HELEN: No, Houston. I'm going to Corpus on a visit.

(*Mae opens the door.*)

MAE: Mr. Fred, your mama is asking for you.

FRED: Excuse me.

S.P.: I like Corpus a whole lot. Except for the prevailing winds. I had a friend that lived in Corpus and wore a wig and he had to give up wearing it while he stayed there. The wind wouldn't let it stay on his head.

GEORGIA DALE: It mustn't have been much of a wig to begin with.

S.P.: Maybe not.

(*Frankie comes out of the bedroom.*)

FRANKIE: Hello, everybody.

(*They all greet her as she goes over to Helen.*)

I'm Frankie Lewis, Miss Vaught, a friend of the Willis's. Fred asked to be excused as his mother gets very frightened when he leaves her even for a moment and insists on his staying by her bedside.

HELEN: I understand. Tell him not to worry. I can't stay anyway. Would you be kind enough to give him this note? (*She hands a note to Frankie.*)

FRANKIE: Yes, certainly.

HELEN: Nice to have met you all.

(*The women and S.P. say goodbye almost in unison as she leaves.*)

ISABEL: Is Mrs. Willis worse?

FRANKIE: No, as a matter of fact she's much stronger. She just gets spells of wanting Fred right by her side.

GEORGIA DALE: I brought over some gumbo. There is enough for Fred, Mrs. Willis, you, and Mae. (*She turns to Laverne, Constance, and Isabel.*) Unfortunately I didn't know you all were going to be here or I would have made more.

LAVERNE: Thank you, but we're all going out to lunch.

(*Fred and Mrs. Willis come out.*)

MRS. WILLIS: Hello, everybody.

(*They all greet her.*)

I'm getting stronger by the minute.

ISABEL: Isn't that wonderful.

MRS. WILLIS: I thought there was a lady from Houston here.

FRANKIE: She's gone, Mrs. Willis. (*She goes to Fred and gives him the note.*) She left this for you.

(*He takes it and puts it in his pocket.*)

MRS. WILLIS: Aren't you going to read it?

FRED: No, I'll let Dotson read it.

MRS. WILLIS: Why Dotson?

FRED: He's my lawyer. I told you Mama, she's the lady that's suing me for Breach of Promise. I explained it all to you this morning.

MRS. WILLIS: Why is she suing you?

FRED: Because she said I promised to marry her.

MRS. WILLIS: Did you?

FRED: If I did, I was drunk. I didn't know what I was saying. I'm going to marry Frankie.

MRS. WILLIS: When did you decide that?

FRED: I told you, Mama. I asked her last night.

MRS. WILLIS: Is that why you all have been whispering so back and forth?

FRED: Yes, ma'am.

MRS. WILLIS: Well, congratulations.

FRED: Thank you.

S.P.: Who is getting married?

GEORGIA DALE: Fred and Frankie.

S.P.: When?

GEORGIA DALE: I don't know. When are you getting married, Fred?

FRED: Ask Frankie. She hasn't said yet if she'll marry me.

MRS. WILLIS: Well, make up your mind soon, Frankie. I want to be here still when you have the wedding.

(Frankie cries and goes out of the room.)

What's wrong with her?

FRED: She's very emotional, Mama. She's upset that I'm being sued for Breach of Promise.

MRS. WILLIS: Aren't you upset?

FRED: Yes, but that doesn't get you anywhere.

MRS. WILLIS: Why are you ladies so dressed up?

CONSTANCE: We're here to take Frankie out to lunch.

GEORGIA DALE: I brought you some gumbo, Mrs. Willis.

MRS. WILLIS: Bless you sweet heart. Do you think the doctor will let me eat gumbo, Fred?

FRED: We'll have to call him and see mama.

S.P.: I'm feeling dizzy, Georgia Dale.

GEORGIA DALE: Well, sit down and rest. I haven't a bit of sympathy for him, Mrs. Willis. He still smokes cigarettes.

MRS. WILLIS: Your first husband was named Billy Cunningham wasn't he, Georgia Dale?

GEORGIA DALE: No, ma'am.

MRS. WILLIS: Then what was his name?

GEORGIA DALE: Ross Matthews.

MRS. WILLIS: Then who in the world was Billy Cunningham?

GEORGIA DALE: He was a boy that came here on an oil crew. I went with him, but I didn't marry him. His sister wrote me that when he heard I'd married Ross Matthews he went outside in the backyard and blew his brains out.

MRS. WILLIS: Where was his backyard?

GEORGIA DALE: In Navasota.

MRS. WILLIS: Was that his house?

GEORGIA DALE: No, it was his sister's house. His sister said he left a note saying he couldn't face life without me and he would love me forever. She said she would send me the note, but she never did.

MRS. WILLIS: Whatever happened to your first husband?

GEORGIA DALE: I don't know whatever happened to Ross Matthews. He told me at the time I divorced him I'd never see him again. And sure enough, I haven't.

MRS. WILLIS: He didn't want the divorce?

GEORGIA DALE: No, Ma'am.

S.P.: Georgia Dale feel my pulse. I think it's racing.

(She takes his wrist and holds it.)

MRS. WILLIS: Why did you divorce him?

GEORGIA DALE: Lord, that's been so long ago, Mrs. Willis. Near as I can remember, we got into a fight over the charge account he took out for me at the drugstore. He said after the first month by the size of my bill I must be treating the whole town to Coca Colas, which I wasn't. My second husband, Gus Levett, just went to sleep one night and never woke up. He was an angel.

(Frankie comes out.)

FRANKIE: If you don't mind I'd like to take a rain check on our luncheon date.

CONSTANCE: Certainly, darling.

MRS. WILLIS: How much is that woman suing you for, Fred?

FRED: A lot, Mama.

MRS. WILLIS: How much?

FRED: I really don't want to talk about it, Mama.

S.P.: How's my pulse, Georgia Dale?

GEORGIA DALE: I think it's all right.

S.P.: It's not racing?

GEORGIA DALE: If it is, I can't tell it. I'm no doctor, of course.

s.p.: I'm short of breath, too, Georgia Dale.

GEORGIA DALE: Well, what do you want me to do about it?

s.p.: I feel dizzy as well.

GEORGIA DALE: Come on, then, I'll take you home as soon as I put the gumbo in the kitchen.

FRANKIE: I'll take it.

GEORGIA DALE: Thank you.

(Frankie takes the gumbo out to the kitchen.)

Come on, S.P.

s.p.: Help me up.

(She goes to him and does so.)

Now hold on to me, I'm dizzy.

GEORGIA DALE: Goodbye, you all. I hope you enjoy the gumbo.

FRED: I'm sure we will. Come back, Georgia Dale.

GEORGIA DALE: Thank you.

(They go out.)

CONSTANCE: I'm going to have to go, too.

LAVERNE: So do I.

ISABEL: I'll go with you.

(Frankie comes back into the room.)

MRS. WILLIS: You all come back soon.

LAVERNE: Thank you, we will.

CONSTANCE: Goodbye.

ISABEL: Goodbye.

FRANKIE: Goodbye.

(They leave.)

MRS. WILLIS: I think I'll out last S.P. the way he looked today.

(There is silence in the room. Frankie hums a bar or two of a song to herself.)

Well, of course it's none of my business, I know, but I hope you do get married. When I married your father, Fred, he had been going with that woman and she threatened a Breach of Promise suit.

FRED: It wasn't a Breach of Promise because she was married at the time.

MRS. WILLIS: Well, it was some kind of suit, I don't know what they called it, and she said he had promised to marry her when her husband died, but he married me instead. He had to settle twenty-five thousand dollars on her, which in those days was a lot of money. Maybe you should offer to settle some money on this woman, Fred, and she would call off the suit.

FRED: My lawyer did. She said nothing doing.

MRS. WILLIS: What did you offer her?

FRED: Thirty thousand dollars.

MRS. WILLIS: I think that's fair, don't you, Frankie?

(Frankie doesn't answer.)

Oh, Frankie, I know how you feel. Your pride's hurt. But I hope you can put all that behind you. You can still have a child, you know. Once you have a child you forget everything else.

(Mae comes out.)

MAE: Time for your medicine.

MRS. WILLIS: My God, I am so sick of medicine. Would you call the doctor and see if I can have some of that gumbo, Fred?

MAE: Now you know he won't let you have no gumbo. How are you gonna have gumbo when you're on a strict no salt diet? Come on with me.

MRS. WILLIS: I want Fred.

FRED: I'll be along in a minute, Mama. Go on with Mae now, please.

(Mae takes Mrs. Willis out.)

FRED: Frankie?

FRANKIE: Yes?

FRED: I have our marriage license. *(A pause.)* Frankie, did you hear me?

FRANKIE: Yes, I did.

FRED: Why don't we get married tomorrow? *(A pause.)* Please. Marry me, Frankie. *(A pause.)* Will you marry me, Frankie?

FRANKIE: I guess so. I don't know what else to do. Of course, I could not marry you…

FRED: We've been married in a way all these years. And I've been faithful to you, Frankie, except for this one time and I was drunk, I swear to you I was drunk…

FRANKIE: Don't Fred…

FRED: Don't you believe me?

FRANKIE: No.

FRED: Ask anybody. Ask Dotson, ask Travis. In all these years I've never looked at another woman. I don't know what got into me this time. It will never happen again. I swear to you. Frankie, I could ditch you now and marry this woman. It would save me a lot of money, but I want to marry you. We'll go on a regular honeymoon, too, go on a cruise, or to Europe. Anyplace you want to go as soon as Mama feels better.

FRANKIE: I was eighteen when I first remember seeing S.P. and Jackie Mae Gleason. I was riding around with a girlfriend and we passed them and she told me they were living together, had been for a number of years, and he wouldn't marry her, and then soon after someone told me about your father and the woman he lived with before he married your mother and I thought what was wrong with these women. That will never happen to me…

FRED: And it's not happening to you is it? Because we're going to get married and have children.

FRANKIE: The other day at the supermarket I was standing in line and I heard someone say as they pointed to me that's Fred Willis's woman.

FRED: Oh, you didn't.

FRANKIE: Yes, I did too. And it's not the first time.

FRED: I better never hear anybody talk about you that way…

FRANKIE: Why? That's what I have been. Your woman. Your common-law-wife.

FRED: Oh, my God, Frankie. Why are you talking this way?

FRANKIE: I don't know. I'm just talking. I feel like talking, Fred. I've never had anybody to talk to about this. Not you, not my girlfriends…
(A pause.)

FRED: What can I say to you. I'm sorry…

FRANKIE: What are you sorry for, Fred?

FRED: I don't know, Frankie. Whatever it is I've done wrong. *(A pause.)* Can we get married tomorrow?

FRANKIE: I suppose.

FRED: What time?

FRANKIE: Whatever time you want.

FRED: Five o'clock?

FRANKIE: All right. Five o'clock. Where have the years gone, Fred? Where in the world have they gone?

FRED: I'm going to make it all up to you, Frankie.

FRANKIE: I'm sure you will, Fred.

FRED: Do you want to go downtown and buy a dress for the wedding? I'll pay for it.

FRANKIE: No, thank you. I'll go to the apartment and find something suitable.

FRED: No, I want you to go downtown and get a dress. The most expensive you can find.

FRANKIE: I'll see… *(She starts to leave.)*

FRED: You'll never be sorry you married me, Frankie. I promise you that.

FRANKIE: I'm sure…
(She continues on out as the lights fade. The lights are brought up. It is the afternoon of the wedding. There are a few potted flowers in the room. Laverne is there arranging the flowers. Constance and Isabel come in from

the kitchen. They have trays with refreshments: finger sandwiches, stuffed eggs, etc.)

CONSTANCE: Oh, doesn't the room look nice?

(They put the refreshments on a table.)

LAVERNE: It will do. The florists here have nothing this time of year but chrysanthemums.

ISABEL: No time of the year except Christmas, Easter, and Valentine's Day. Is Frankie back yet?

LAVERNE: She called. She's still over at her place getting dressed. Oh, it's been something. The doctor came and said Mrs. Willis could not attend the ceremony and she said she would or know the reason why and so he gave in even though he said it was much against his better judgment, and then Fred called Brother Martin and asked if he would perform the ceremony and he said he couldn't as he was going to be out of town this afternoon and then he called Brother Jones and he said he wasn't available. So, he's getting the justice of the peace to marry them.

CONSTANCE: Do you really think those preachers were really busy or they didn't want to be involved because…

LAVERNE: Because of what?

CONSTANCE: Because of Fred and Frankie's past relationship…

LAVERNE: Oh, come on Constance. This is 1990. Every other person on a talk show tells about their live-in girlfriends and boyfriends. Half the movie stars never bother to get married. Who cares?

ISABEL: Where is Fred?

LAVERNE: He's off somewhere. I hope he remembers to get a ring.

CONSTANCE: I heard up town earlier this afternoon they were settling the Breach of Promise suit out of court.

LAVERNE: They are.

CONSTANCE: Do you know for how much?

LAVERNE: Yes, but I can't tell you.

CONSTANCE: Oh, come on, Laverne. I won't tell anybody.

ISABEL: I know how much.

LAVERNE: How do you know?

ISABEL: Dotson told Pete.

CONSTANCE: Then he'll have told Travis, so tell me.

LAVERNE: I'm not absolutely sure, but I think it's sixty thousand.

(Fred comes in.)

FRED: Heh, girls.

LAVERNE: Hello, Fred.

CONSTANCE: Hello there.

ISABEL: Hi, Fred.

FRED: Frankie back yet?

LAVERNE: No. Did you remember to get a ring, Fred?

FRED: Oh, my God. I didn't. I'll be right back.

LAVERNE: And get her a corsage, too.

> *(He goes.)*

ISABEL: Poor man. He's got a lot on his mind, a sick mother, a Breach of Promise suit, getting married.

CONSTANCE: Tell me about it.

> *(The door bell rings and Laverne answers it. Georgia Dale and S.P. are there. She has a container of soup.)*

GEORGIA DALE: Mae said they all enjoyed the gumbo so much I brought some more for their supper. S.P., take it out to the kitchen.

> *(He takes the container of gumbo and goes to the kitchen.)*

> Oh, how pretty everything looks. Are you having a party?

ISABEL: Fred and Frankie are getting married at five.

GEORGIA DALE: Are they?

> *(S.P. comes back in.)*

> S.P. you're wrong. S.P. said when he heard the Breach of Promise suit was settled that he bet the wedding would be called off.

LAVERNE: Why would they do that?

GEORGIA DALE: Well, you know. Who all is coming to the wedding?

LAVERNE: Just the three of us and Mrs. Willis.

GEORGIA DALE: Oh, well, can I do anything?

LAVERNE: I don't believe so.

GEORGIA DALE: May I speak to Fred and Frankie to wish them happiness?

LAVERNE: They're not here, Georgia Dale.

GEORGIA DALE: Oh, well, tell them I was here and I wish them happiness and S.P. does too.

> *(They go.)*

LAVERNE: Do you think we need a few more flowers?

ISABEL: I don't know. What do you think, Constance?

CONSTANCE: Everything looks all right to me.

> *(Mae comes out of the bedroom.)*

MAE: Mrs. Willis wants to know if Mr. Fred is back.

LAVERNE: No. He was here, but he had to go again.

MAE: Miss Frankie not back either?

LAVERNE: No. There's some crab gumbo in the kitchen Georgia Dale just brought.

MAE: Oh, my God. That gumbo she brought over yesterday was the worst tasting mess I ever tasted. One bite and Mr. Fred and I threw it all out. Don't ever tell her I said that though. *(She goes back into the bedroom.)*

ISABEL: Do you remember your wedding day?

CONSTANCE: Yes.

LAVERNE: I remember every step of mine. It was raining and I began to cry because I said to Mama no one will come because of the rain, but about an hour before we were to leave for the church the sun came out and it turned out to be a lovely day.

ISABEL: It was a lovely day, too, I remember. I was one of Laverne's bridesmaids and she was one of mine.

LAVERNE: Frankie was a bridesmaid for both of us.

ISABEL: I said to Pete this morning, and he got real mad at me for bringing it up, but I couldn't help wondering what if Pete and I had never married until now and went together all these years like Frankie and Fred in a town where our friends were all married and had children and lived very conventional lives and where everybody knew or thought they knew what was going on between us.

CONSTANCE: It must have been terrible on Frankie.

LAVERNE: The world is different. Movie stars…

CONSTANCE: But she's not a movie star. She's living in a small town where everybody is supposed to be married by the time they're twenty-five.

ISABEL: Well, however she lived. She was certainly always modest and ladylike and discreet about it.

(Frankie comes into the room.)

FRANKIE: Oh, how pretty everything looks.

CONSTANCE: Laverne did the whole thing by herself.

LAVERNE: Isabel and Constance brought some food for afterwards.

FRANKIE: That was certainly sweet of you all.

ISABEL: It's nothing much. Just finger sandwiches and dips.

FRANKIE: Is Fred back?

LAVERNE: No. He was here, but he forgot something and had to go again.

FRANKIE: The Breach of Promise suit was settled.

LAVERNE: We know.

FRANKIE: I said Fred now it's settled, if you don't want to marry me, you don't have to. But he said he still wanted to go ahead with the wedding. *(A pause.)* I'm sure you realize we've been together as man and wife all these years.

LAVERNE: Now come on, Frankie, now is not the time.

FRANKIE: I am his common-law-wife.

LAVERNE: Frankie, please. This is your wedding day. Let's make it a happy day.

FRANKIE: Neither of the preachers he called would marry us. He wanted to call the Episcopalian minister and I said don't bother. He won't marry us either.

ISABEL: Oh, sure he would have, Frankie. He's very broad-minded.

CONSTANCE: And I think the Baptist and the Methodist preachers were telling the truth when they said they were busy. After all, you gave them no notice. I talked to Brother Martin myself and he said he was sorry he couldn't perform the ceremony.

LAVERNE: This is 1990, Frankie. Everything's different today. Preachers are all very broad-minded.

(Fred comes in. He has a corsage.)

FRED: Here's a corsage to wear, Frankie.

FRANKIE: Thank you.

FRED: It's all they had at the florists. If you don't want to wear it, you won't hurt my feelings.

FRANKIE: It's kind of tacky, Fred. I don't think I will wear it. *(She puts it on the table.)*

FRED: The justice of the peace, Bill Simmons, will be here in a few minutes. I hope Mae has Mama ready. Who brought the food?

LAVERNE: Constance and Isabel.

FRED: That was thoughtful of you both.

LAVERNE: Georgia Dale brought gumbo. It's in the kitchen.

(He makes a face.)

FRED: I'm pouring it out. The gumbo she brought yesterday was the worst, I swear to you, I ever in this world tasted.

FRANKIE: Lil Jeffers said at the beauty parlor when I went to get my hair set that Georgia Dale said if I didn't marry you, she was going to set her cap for you. Lil Jeffers said how are you going to do that. You're married to S.P. And Georgia Dale said have you seen S.P. lately? He won't be here long.

ISABEL: Now why would some fool tell you something like that on your wedding day?

CONSTANCE: What a tacky thing to say.

LAVERNE: She's just common. You know how people are.

FRED: I'm going to see about Mama. *(He goes into the bedroom.)*

CONSTANCE: Fred seems very happy to me.

LAVERNE: Yes, he does, doesn't he?

ISABEL: He's such a sweet thing. I've always been so fond of Fred. I never understood…

FRANKIE: What?

ISABEL: Nothing.

(Fred and Mrs. Willis come out of the bedroom.)

LAVERNE: Hello, Mrs. Willis.

MRS. WILLIS: The flowers are lovely. Well, I've lived to see Fred married and I told the doctor today I'm determined to live to see their child. So better not wait too long, Frankie. Are we going to have a little music with the wedding?

LAVERNE: I'm afraid not.

MRS. WILLIS: The justice of the peace is marrying them. Fred's father and I were married by a justice of the peace. What was his name?

FRED: Whose name?

MRS. WILLIS: Your father's name.

FRED: Oh, come on, Mama.

MRS. WILLIS: I don't remember.

FRED: Lewis Willis.

MRS. WILLIS: That's right. He died when Fred was five.

FRED: Seven, Mama.

MRS. WILLIS: Seven. How long has he been dead?

FRED: Thirty-five years.

MRS. WILLIS: You know I can't for the life of me remember what he looked like. Do we have a picture of him?

FRED: Somewhere, Mama.

MRS. WILLIS: Find it and let me see it.

FRED: I will in a little, Mama.

MRS. WILLIS: I want to see it now.

(Fred calls: "Mae." Mae enters.)

FRED: Would you see if you could find that picture of my father that is, I think, in the top dresser drawer in Mama's bedroom.

MAE: Yes sir. *(She goes.)*

MRS. WILLIS: How old are you, Frankie?

FRANKIE: Thirty-nine.

MRS. WILLIS: A year younger than I was when I got married. How old were you, Constance, when you got married?

CONSTANCE: Twenty-two.

MRS. WILLIS: And you have children?

CONSTANCE: Two, both off at college.

MRS. WILLIS: How old were you, Laverne?

LAVERNE: Twenty.

ISABEL: I was eighteen.

(Mae comes in with a picture. She gives it to Mrs. Willis.)

MAE: Is this the one you wanted?

MRS. WILLIS: I guess so. Is this your father, Fred?

(He looks at it.)

FRED: Yes. That's the one.

MRS. WILLIS: You don't look a thing like him.

FRED: No?

MRS. WILLIS: You look like my people, not like me, but like my father. *(She hands the picture back to Mae.)* Are you going to watch them get married, Mae?

MAE: I don't know. So far I haven't been invited.

MRS. WILLIS: I invite you.

MAE: Thank you.

(The door bell rings. Mae goes to answer it. Bill Simmons, a man in his early thirties is there.)

BILL: Hello, Mae. Hello everybody.

(They all greet him. He goes to Mrs. Willis.)

How are you feeling, Mrs. Willis?

MRS. WILLIS: Some better, thank you. You're the justice of the peace, aren't you?

BILL: Yes, Ma'am.

MRS. WILLIS: I was married by the justice of the peace. It was on a Friday night. I had gone to bed early and around ten thirty there was a knock on the door and I thought who can that be, and I called out and I said who's there? And this voice called back and said your husband to be. Well I got out of bed and put a robe on. I peeked out the window and sure enough there was my husband to be. I opened the door and I said what in the world are you doing here at ten thirty at night. I've come to marry you, he said, why, I said, now, he said, now, I said, what's the big hurry. I always planned on having a church wedding. We've no time for that, he said, I'm going to the car and wait while you change your clothes. And I changed my clothes and I went out to the car, it was a Buick, a green Buick near as I remember, and I said who will marry us at this time of the night, and he said the justice of the peace, and I got into the car and off we went to God knows what part of San Antonio to this house where a justice of the peace lived and he married us.

BILL: Why was your husband in such a hurry?

MRS. WILLIS: I didn't find that out until later. He was mixed up with some married woman, who he had planned to marry when her husband died and he'd died at three that afternoon and my husband got somebody over at the courthouse to give him a marriage license and he came over to San Antonio to marry me.

BILL: That was quite an experience.

MRS. WILLIS: Yes, it was.

BILL: Where did you go on your honeymoon?

MRS. WILLIS: We didn't have one. My husband had to get back as soon as we were married because it was the middle of cotton season. He said we could have a honeymoon as soon as cotton season was over, but we never did.

BILL: Are you folks expecting anyone else?

FRED: That is all.

BILL: Frankie, none of your family are coming?

FRANKIE: I have no people.

CONSTANCE: Her mother and father are dead.

ISABEL: And she's an only child.

BILL: I'm an only child, too. My mother and father are still living though. Well, shall we get started? I'll stand here. Fred, are you and Frankie having anyone stand with you?

FRANKIE: I'm not.

FRED: I'm not either.

BILL: Then everybody here is just spectators?

FRED: Yes.

BILL: All right. You all sit at this end of the room.
    (*They all move to the far end of the room.*)
    Thank you, folks. Now Frankie and Fred stand here before me and repeat after me when I call your name.

ISABEL: Don't you think somebody should say a prayer or read Frankie's Bible first?

BILL: This is a civil ceremony, Isabel.

ISABEL: Oh, that's right.

BILL: A lot of people get married again later in a church ceremony. They never really feel they're married until they do.

MRS. WILLIS: I never did.

ISABEL: My mother and father say when they reach their fiftieth wedding anniversary they're going to renew their vows in church. I think that's so sweet. Don't you?

BILL: Shall we begin?

FRED: Yes, sir.

(He and Frankie take their places in front of Bill and are married.)

BILL: Now, sir, you may kiss the bride.

MRS. WILLIS: What did he say?

LAVERNE: He said he could kiss the bride.

(Fred kisses Frankie. Laverne, Constance, and Isabel go up to them and kiss them.)

I'm so happy for you both.

CONSTANCE: It's just a dream come true.

ISABEL: I wish you both all the happiness in the world.

BILL: May I kiss the bride?

FRED: Certainly.

(He kisses her.)

MAE: I'll serve the refreshments.

FRED: I have a bottle of champagne in the refrigerator, Mae.

MAE: Yessir. *(She goes.)*

LAVERNE: May I get you a finger sandwich, Mrs. Willis?

MRS. WILLIS: Just one.

(She gets one for her. The others go to the table and get food. Mae comes in with the champagne and glasses on a tray. She puts them down on the table.)

I'm tired, Son. I want to get back to bed. It's been a long day.

FRED: All right, Mama. Mae will take care of that. Mae come help Mama to her bed.

MAE: Yessir. Come on, Mrs. Willis.

(She takes Mrs. Willis back to her bedroom. Fred is pouring the champagne. He gives a glass to each of his guests.)

BILL: I want to make a toast. To Fred and Frankie, may they have many, many happy years together.

(They all take a swig of champagne.)

Where will you go on your honeymoon?

FRED: We can't have a honeymoon for awhile, I'm afraid, until Mama is stronger.

BILL: I was very surprised at how well she looked. I'd heard she was very low there for several days. You'll live on here with her?

FRED: Yes.

BILL: My wife and I lived with my parents when we first married.

(Mae comes to the door.)

MAE: Mr. Fred, your mama wants you.

FRED: Excuse me. *(He goes into the room after Mae.)*

BILL: Hasn't it been warm?

LAVERNE: Yes, it has. Very warm.

ISABEL: What would we do without air conditioning?

BILL: It's a wonderful age we live in: air-conditioning, television, V.C.R.'s, cable. I wonder how we ever got along without all those things?

(Mae comes out.)

MAE: Excuse me, Mr. Fred says his mother wants him to stay with her. He says you all go on with the party.

CONSTANCE: Thank you, Mae.

LAVERNE: Is there anything we can do to help?

MAE: No, not when she gets one of her spells. He wanted me to ask Miss Frankie to excuse herself and come and sit with him, but Mrs. Willis said she didn't want anyone in there but him. She won't even let me stay in there.

ISABEL: Have some champagne, Mae, and a sandwich.

MAE: Yes, ma'am. I don't care for any champagne. I will have a sandwich, thank you.

(Frankie begins to cry. Laverne goes to her.)

LAVERNE: Frankie, what is it?

CONSTANCE: It's just nerves. I cried too, right after I got married.

(Frankie is sobbing now. Isabel goes to her.)

ISABEL: Frankie, darling, have a little champagne. That will make you feel better.

(Frankie continues sobbing.)

CONSTANCE: Maybe we'd better get Fred.

LAVERNE: Maybe so.

(Constance goes to the bedroom door.)

CONSTANCE: Fred.

(He opens the door.)

Frankie is crying.

(He comes out of the room. He goes to her.)

FRED: Frankie. What's the matter? Please don't cry. This is your wedding day. Aren't you happy, Frankie?

MRS. WILLIS: *(Calling from the bedroom.)* Fred.

(He starts away.)

FRANKIE: Don't leave me, Fred, please don't leave me.

MRS. WILLIS: *(Calling.)* Fred…

FRED: All right, Mama. I'll be in in a second. Frankie just wipe your eyes now and give me a few minutes to get Mama calm once again. She did a very generous thing this morning. She insisted on giving me half the money to settle that suit.

MRS. WILLIS: *(Calling.)* Fred. Fred. I'm dying.

FRED: All right, Mama. I'll be right there.

(He hurries back into the bedroom. No sooner is the door closed than Frankie begins to scream.)

FRANKIE: *(Screaming.)* Fred come out of there. This is our wedding day. Come out of there at once.

(Laverne goes to her.)

LAVERNE: Frankie, honey, Frankie, get a hold of yourself.

(She continues screaming.)

Frankie, darling, keep calm.

FRANKIE: *(Screaming.)* Fred, come out of there. Come out at once. Do you hear me? Come out of there.

(Fred comes out of the room. He goes to her.)

FRED: Frankie, have you lost your mind. Control yourself.

(She is sobbing and crying again now.)

Frankie, Frankie.

MRS. WILLIS: *(Calling from the bedroom.)* Fred. Where are you? I'm dying. Don't leave me alone to die. Fred, Fred.

FRED: Oh, my God. Laverne, Constance, Isabel. Help me, take Frankie.

(They go to Frankie.)

MRS. WILLIS: Fred. Fred. Fred. Don't leave me. Fred. Fred. Fred.

(He goes to her. The women surround Frankie as she continues once again to scream as the lights fade.)

ACT II

SCENE I

Three months later. Frankie is there. Mrs. Willis and Fred enter. Mrs. Willis is dressed in a dark dress, and Fred in a dark suit. Frankie is in a house dress.

FRED: Frankie, you'd better hurry and get dressed. I'm a pall bearer, you know, and I have to be there early.

FRANKIE: I'm not going, Fred.

MRS. WILLIS: Fred is one of the pall bearers, Frankie.

FRANKIE: I know. I heard him.

FRED: Are you feeling all right?

FRANKIE: Not so hot, to tell you the truth.

MRS. WILLIS: Maybe you're pregnant, Frankie, and you're having morning sickness. I had morning sickness something terrible the whole time I was carrying Fred.

(Frankie leaves the room.)

What in the world gets into her, Fred?

FRED: I try to explain to you, Mama, she's emotional. She gets easily upset.

MRS. WILLIS: She didn't use to be so sensitive. Before she married you she was so easy to get along with. She was always happy and smiling.

FRED: How do you know that, Mama? You never spent twenty-four hours a day with her until we got married.

MRS. WILLIS: What in the name of God is she upset about now? Because S.P. is dead?

FRED: No. I don't think that's it at all. I think she's worrying that she might never get pregnant.

MRS. WILLIS: You've only been married three months. I didn't get pregnant until I was married six months.

(Mae comes in from the kitchen.)

Go tell her that, Fred.

(Fred goes out to find Frankie.)

Mae, I told you I was going to outlive S.P. Didn't I tell you that?

MAE: Yes, ma'am. You're an inspiration to us all.

MRS. WILLIS: I'm liable to outlive Frankie, the way she's moping around. She's in her room crying again.

MAE: Yes, ma'am. She's troubled.

MRS. WILLIS: What in the name of God does she have to be troubled about? She's married to one of the finest young men that God ever made.

MAE: Yes, ma'am.

MRS. WILLIS: I'm well off. Fred is well off. She could have anything within reason that she wants. But no, she has to sit around the house and mope. Fred says it's because she's afraid she can't have a baby. Well, she'll never have a baby if all she does is sit around and worry about it.

(Fred enters.)

FRED: Let's go.

MRS. WILLIS: Did you tell her it was six months after I got married before I got pregnant?

FRED: She knows that, Mama.

(They leave. Mae gets her Bible and begins to read from Psalms.)

MAE: *(Reading aloud in the manner of one who has not many reading skills.)* I love the Lord because he hath heard my voice and my supplications.

Because he hath inclined his ear unto me, therefore will I call upon him as long as I live.

The sorrow of death compressed me, and the pain of hell got hold of me. I found trouble and sorrow.

Then called I upon the house of the Lord, Oh, Lord, I beseech thee, deliver my soul.

Gracious the Lord, and righteous; yea, our God is merciful.

The Lord preserveth the simple: I was brought low and he helped me.

(The door bell rings. Mae answers it. Isabel is there.)

ISABEL: I met Fred and Mrs. Willis down the street. They said Frankie wasn't going to S.P.'s funeral. I said I'd come visit with her. Where is she?

MAE: In her room.

ISABEL: Will you tell her I'm here, Mae?

MAE: Yes, ma'am.

(She goes. Isabel sees the Bible and picks it up and puts it down again as the door bell rings. She goes to the door and opens it. Carlton Gleason, in his early fifties, is there.)

ISABEL: Yes?

CARLTON: I'm Carlton Gleason. I was born and raised here. Lived here until I was fifteen.

ISABEL: My, yes. I've heard of you. I knew your sister, Jackie Mae.

CARLTON: Did you?

ISABEL: Come in. I'm Isabel Gallagher.

CARLTON: How do you do. Nice to know you.

ISABEL: Nice to know you, too.

(When he comes in, we see that he walks dragging his left foot behind him.)

CARLTON: I came back for S.P.'s funeral, and I was passing by and I said I think this is the Willis house. I used to know Mr. Willis pretty well when I was a boy growing up. So I thought I'd just stop in and introduce myself. I had a picture of Mr. Willis that I brought here with me thinking his son—his name is Fred isn't it?

ISABEL: Yes.

CARLTON: Might like it. Is he here?

ISABEL: No, he's gone to the funeral too.

CARLTON: Oh, well I'll see him there then, I suppose. I'll leave the picture here if I may.

ISABEL: Certainly.

(He puts the picture on a table.)

CARLTON: I came here to say goodbye to old S.P. I'm sure everybody here thinks he ruined my sister's life by not marrying her. But that's not exactly how it was. I was there in the room when she was dying and S.P. got down on his knees to her and begged her to marry him, but she said no. I don't want to marry you now. My brother says he only wanted to marry her so he could claim the house he gave her to live in. But S.P. told me himself that that wasn't so, he said he tried to keep my brother from getting the house because he never cared for my brother. He said he would have been happy for me to have the house. S.P. was always good to me. He sent me twenty-five dollars every Christmas and on my birthday the whole time he was going with my sister, and he kept on after she died. He never missed a Christmas and he never missed a birthday, which is more than my own brother ever done. Do you know what time S.P.'s funeral service is?

ISABEL: I think it's about to begin. It's being held at the Harrison Funeral Home. Do you know where that is?

CARLTON: Yes, ma'am. Nice to have met you.

ISABEL: Nice to have met you.

(He leaves. She takes the picture and looks at it. Frankie comes into the room.)

FRANKIE: Who were you talking to?

ISABEL: Carlton Gleason.

FRANKIE: Carlton Gleason?

ISABEL: Yes, he came to town for S.P.'s funeral. He brought a picture by of Fred's father. He said Fred could have it.

(Frankie looks at the picture and then puts it back down.)

FRANKIE: Did Constance and Laverne go to the funeral?

ISABEL: Yes, and Dotson and Travis and Pete. I was supposed to meet them there, but I decided instead to come and visit with you.

FRANKIE: How did you know I wasn't going to the funeral?

ISABEL: I met Fred and Mrs. Willis and they told me.

FRANKIE: Some people think Carlton Gleason is Fred's half brother. Did you ever hear that?

ISABEL: Yes, I have.

FRANKIE: I've heard he's the exact image of Fred's father.

ISABEL: Of course, I don't remember Fred's father. I was two when he died.

FRANKIE: Well, there's his picture. Does he look like his picture?

(She looks at it.)

ISABEL: Well, this is a much younger looking man than Carlton. This man is not more than thirty.

FRANKIE: *(Calling.)* Mae.

MAE: *(Calling back from one of the bedrooms.)* Yes'm.

FRANKIE: Would you see if you can find that picture of Fred's father. The one that's kept some place in Mrs. Willis's dresser.

MAE: *(Offstage.)* Yes ma'am.

FRANKIE: Do you know what I overheard last night? That woman, Helen Vaught, is going to have a baby.

ISABEL: Who told you?

FRANKIE: I overheard Fred telling his mother. She claims the baby's Fred's.

ISABEL: Does Fred think it is?

FRANKIE: He told his mother he can't be sure. His mother wants him to deny it.

(Mae comes in with the picture and gives it to Frankie, who gives it to Isabel.)

Mr. Willis was fifty when this was taken. Does Carlton look like him?

ISABEL: I suppose. A little bit.

(She hands the picture back to Frankie who gives the picture to Mae, who takes it back to Mrs. Willis' bedroom. Frankie takes another look at the younger picture of Mr. Willis.)

FRANKIE: He doesn't look a thing like Fred, does he?

ISABEL: No.

(Frankie puts the picture back on the table.)

FRANKIE: I'm going to have a baby, Isabel.

ISABEL: That's wonderful. When?

FRANKIE: The doctor isn't exactly sure. I just found out yesterday. I haven't told Fred or anyone, so please don't say a thing. Not even to Laverne or Constance or Fred.

ISABEL: I won't, but why haven't you told Fred?

FRANKIE: I was about to tell him when I heard him telling his mother about Helen Vaught. And I just couldn't tell him after that. It made me feel so funny. If it is true and Fred is the father of Helen Vaught's child then my child will have a half-brother or sister.

ISABEL: But it may not be true. Helen Vaught is probably promiscuous.

FRANKIE: Fred said not.

ISABEL: How would Fred know.

FRANKIE: I don't know. But he seems to feel she isn't. He discussed with his mother the possibility of settling some more money on Helen Vaught, so she can go away some place and have the baby. His mother is opposing that. She says if he does that there will be no end to Helen Vaught's demands.

(Fred and Mrs. Willis enter.)

ISABEL: Is the funeral over already?

FRED: No, Mama overdid, I'm afraid. I had to bring her home.

MRS. WILLIS: I'm going to have a stroke. I swear to you, I'm going to have a stroke.

FRED: Now, Mama. Just keep calm. You just got a little over excited. *(Calling.)* Mae.

(Mae enters.)

MAE: Yes sir?

FRED: Help Mama get undressed.

MRS. WILLIS: I'm going to have a stroke, I know it. Mae ask God to take me before I have a stroke. I don't want to lie in that bed helpless, not able to talk, or to move even my toes. Ask God, Mae.

MAE: Ask him yourself, Mrs. Willis. He hears you as well as me.

MRS. WILLIS: But you read your Bible, Mae. I don't read the Bible, or even put my foot in church except at Easter time.

MAE: You can still ask him for help. He's a very present help in trouble.

MRS. WILLIS: How do I do that, Mae?

MAE: Just say Lord help me.

MRS. WILLIS: What if I said Lord help me from having a stroke.

MAE: That's all right. Lord help me from whatever.

FRED: Come on, Mama. Let Mae take you to your room.

MRS. WILLIS: Lord help me.

MAE: That's it.

MRS. WILLIS: Lord help me.

MAE: God be praised.

MRS. WILLIS: Why did you say that?

MAE: Because I felt like it.

MRS. WILLIS: Would it help if I said that, too?

MAE: Do you feel it in your heart?

(Mrs. Willis cries.)

MRS. WILLIS: I'm afraid.

FRED: Now, Mama…

MRS. WILLIS: I don't want to die, Fred.

FRED: You're not going to die. Now, come on. Help me, Mae.

MAE: Yessir.

(Together they take Mrs. Willis into her bedroom.)

ISABEL: I'd better be going. I know Constance and Laverne are going to Georgia Dale's after the funeral. I think I'll join them there.

FRANKIE: Thank you for coming and don't forget what I told you is a sworn secret.

ISABEL: I know.

(She starts out. Mae comes in.)

Goodbye, Mae.

MAE: Goodbye.

(Isabel leaves.)

FRANKIE: How is she?

MAE: Resting. That funeral was just too much for her.

FRANKIE: Did you call the doctor?

MAE: Yes, ma'am. He said to just keep her resting.

FRANKIE: Mae.

MAE: Yes, ma'am.

FRANKIE: Don't tell Mrs. Willis or Fred, but I'm going to have a baby…

MAE: God bless you. When?

FRANKIE: The doctor's not exactly sure. He'll know better next week.

MAE: I'm so happy for you.

FRANKIE: Thank you. How many children do you have?

MAE: Three living. I had five in all. Two died at birth. I had all my children except the last one at home. We couldn't afford to go to the hospital.

FRANKIE: Do you think the two that died would have lived if you'd gone to the hospital?

MAE: I got the money to go to the hospital for the last one, but he was born dead anyway.

FRANKIE: He? Was it a boy?

MAE: Yes ma'am. Both of my dead babies were boys.

FRANKIE: What were their names?

MAE: I didn't name them; you don't name babies that are born dead.

FRANKIE: You don't?

MAE: No, ma'am. No sense to it. I got a boy in the army about ready for retirement. He'll come out with a nice pension. His poor daddy has been working in the rice fields all these years until he's gotten too old to work and he has no pension at all. I got a girl teaching in a Junior College in North Carolina and my baby boy is working in construction in Houston.

(Fred comes into the room.)

FRED: She's asleep. I don't think we have to call the doctor again. Do you?

MAE: No, sir. She just got all nervous at the funeral. I'll go sit with her. *(She goes.)*

FRED: Frankie, something has come up that I have to tell you about. I would spare you if I could, but I'm sure you'll hear about it sooner or later.

FRANKIE: Is this about Helen Vaught?

FRED: Yes.

FRANKIE: I know about it, Fred. I heard you telling your mother last night.

FRED: I don't know if the child is mine, of course. Still…It could be. Mama doesn't want me to give Helen anything, still if there is any chance the child is mine, I just can't abandon it, or her…

FRANKIE: No. How did you hear about this?

FRED: Her lawyer wrote me. Then I went to Dotson and we arranged to meet with her and her lawyer.

FRANKIE: When is she expecting the child?

FRED: In six months.

(A pause.)

FRANKIE: Fred.

FRED: Yes.

FRANKIE: I'm going to have a baby, too.

FRED: When?

FRANKIE: The doctor isn't exactly sure.

FRED: I'm very happy, Frankie. Mama will be happy too.

(Mae and Mrs. Willis come out of the bedroom.)

MRS. WILLIS: Why did you leave me, Fred?

FRED: You were asleep, Mama. Come on, I'll take you back to bed.

MRS. WILLIS: No, I'm awake now.

FRED: I know, but let's go back to bed and rest.

MRS. WILLIS: I don't want to go back to bed. You know I think I saw Carlton Gleason at the funeral. Did you see him?

FRED: No. He could have been there. Dotson says S.P. left him some money in his will.

MRS. WILLIS: Why did he do that?

FRED: I have no idea, Mama.

FRANKIE: He was here earlier.

FRED: What did he want?

FRANKIE: I didn't talk to him; Isabel did. He told her he wanted to give you a picture of your father that he had. He left it there.

(Fred picks it up. He looks at it and hands it to his mother.)

FRED: It's an earlier picture than the one we have.

(She looks at it. She puts the picture down.)

Mama, Frankie has some news for you.

MRS. WILLIS: What is it, Frankie?

FRANKIE: You tell her, Fred.

FRED: Frankie is going to have a baby.

MRS. WILLIS: Oh, that's wonderful. I'm going to live to see my grandchild. I told you, I would. Didn't I tell you I would?

FRED: Yes, you did Mama.

MRS. WILLIS: When are you expecting?

FRANKIE: I won't know exactly until next week.

(The door bell rings. Mae answers it. Constance and Laverne are there. They enter the room.)

LAVERNE: Are you all right, Mrs. Willis? We saw you leave the funeral parlor just as the eulogy was beginning.

MRS. WILLIS: I'm all right now. I overdid.

CONSTANCE: You mustn't do that.

LAVERNE: You're sure you're all right now?

MRS. WILLIS: Yes, I'm sure.

LAVERNE: Well, you look all right. Doesn't she look fine to you, Constance?

CONSTANCE: Just fine.

MRS. WILLIS: Have you heard Frankie's news?

CONSTANCE: No, what?

FRANKIE: I'm having a baby.

LAVERNE: When Frankie?

MRS. WILLIS: She won't know for sure until next week.

CONSTANCE: Oh, I'm just thrilled. I'm going to be the first to give you a baby shower. What dates do you have open for next week?

LAVERNE: Constance, you don't want to give her a baby shower this early. God forbid, what if something happened?

CONSTANCE: Like what?

LAVERNE: Like a miscarriage. There is always danger of a miscarriage during early pregnancy. A shower is never appropriate in my opinion this early. I think you'd better wait until she's at least four months pregnant.

CONSTANCE: I guess you're right. But I still want to be the first. I'm giving your baby shower, Frankie, four months from today. I'll write it down in my engagement book as soon as I get home, and you write it down in yours. Aren't you thrilled, Frankie? And I know you are, Fred. Oh, I'd love to have another baby. Wouldn't you, Laverne?

LAVERNE: Well, I guess I would, but Dotson would kill me if I got pregnant after all these years, and I bet Travis wouldn't be all that thrilled, either. And my children would die. Imagine having a baby brother or sister when you're nineteen and twenty.

CONSTANCE: Oh, they'd get over it.

MRS. WILLIS: Is that how old your children are, Laverne? Nineteen and twenty?

LAVERNE: Yes, ma'am.

MRS. WILLIS: How old are your children, Constance?

CONSTANCE: The same.

MRS. WILLIS: How old were you when you had your children?

CONSTANCE: I was nineteen.

MRS. WILLIS: Were you in college when you had your children?

CONSTANCE: No, ma'am. I left college in my freshman year when I married Travis. He was in college though. He was in college when we had both the children. It was a struggle let me tell you.

MRS. WILLIS: I was in my forties when I had Fred.

FRED: They know that, Mama.

MRS. WILLIS: I didn't marry until I was forty.

FRED: They all know that, Mama.

MRS. WILLIS: There's a picture of my husband there that Carlton Gleason had and brought it over here today. (She shows the picture to the women.)

CONSTANCE: He's handsome. Isn't he handsome?

LAVERNE: Yes, he is. He is so good looking. How old was he when this picture was taken?

MRS. WILLIS: I don't know. I never saw it before until today. I wouldn't have known who it was if Frankie hadn't told me Carlton left it here. I have a picture in my bedroom of my husband as I can remember him. Would you like to see that picture?

FRED: I don't think they would, Mama.

MRS. WILLIS: How long has he been dead, Fred?

FRED: Well, I'm forty-two and I was seven when he died. So, he's been gone thirty-five years.

MRS. WILLIS: We were married nine years. If he had lived we would have been married how long, Fred?

FRED: Forty-four years, Mama.

MRS. WILLIS: Fred is good with figures. I used to be. I read the *Wall Street Journal* and *Forbes Magazine* every day of my life until last year and then I just lost interest. I called my broker and bought and sold stocks, too, until last year. And I lost interest. I turned it all over to Fred. It's going to all be his someday, anyway.

(Isabel comes in.)

ISABEL: Why didn't you go to Georgia Dale's after the funeral?

LAVERNE: Because we saw Fred take his mother out of the funeral parlor early and we got to worrying about her.

CONSTANCE: Frankie tell Isabel your wonderful news.

FRANKIE: I've already told her.

CONSTANCE: Isn't it thrilling, Isabel?

ISABEL: Yes, it is.

CONSTANCE: I'm giving her the first baby shower four months from today.

LAVERNE: Did you go to Georgia Dale's?

ISABEL: Briefly, when I saw you all weren't there I left.

CONSTANCE: How did you know we were here?

ISABEL: I saw your car parked in front.

CONSTANCE: Was there a big crowd at Georgia Dale's?

ISABEL: Not too big. About the same as at the funeral.

CONSTANCE: Well, I thought the crowd at the funeral parlor was kind of pitiful.

ISABEL: Well, it was kind of pitiful at the house too.

LAVERNE: Did they have much food?

ISABEL: Yes, a lot of food.

CONSTANCE: What all did they have?

ISABEL: Everything. You name it. They had it. Shrimp, crab meat, roast beef, fried chicken, coleslaw, fruit salad, potato salad, all kinds of pies and cakes, cheese straws.

CONSTANCE: That was a feast.

LAVERNE: Did you eat any of it?

ISABEL: I had a deviled egg and a piece of fried chicken, but when I saw you weren't there I just went over to Georgia Dale and paid my respects and left.

LAVERNE: She didn't shed a tear during the service at the funeral home. Did she seem grieved when you talked to her?

ISABEL: No. Not a bit of it. She was laughing and talking and having the best old time. There was a man by her side that I wouldn't have known only he came by here earlier bringing a picture of Mr. Willis. Did you all see the picture?

FRED: Yes, we did.

CONSTANCE: Who was the man?

ISABEL: Carlton Gleason.

CONSTANCE: I wouldn't recognize him either.

LAVERNE: I would if I saw him walk. He drags one leg behind the other.

ISABEL: He still does. Anyway, he was by her side and she had him by the arm.

LAVERNE: I wonder if she cried at the grave when they were lowering the casket.

ISABEL: I doubt it.

LAVERNE: S.P. left Carlton Gleason a thousand dollars in his will.

CONSTANCE: How do you know?

LAVERNE: Because Dotson is S.P.'s lawyer and drew up the will.

CONSTANCE: Did he leave Georgia Dale well fixed?

LAVERNE: Yes, he did. He left everything he had except for the thousand dollars to Carlton.

CONSTANCE: How much?

LAVERNE: It's hard to tell until the taxes are all paid and they'll be tremendous let me tell you. Dotson thinks conservatively seven hundred thousand dollars.

CONSTANCE: Mercy.

LAVERNE: Of course, you're not to repeat that.

ISABEL: And S.P. left Carlton how much?

LAVERNE: A thousand dollars. Dotson says it says in the will "for old time's sake."

CONSTANCE: I wonder what that means.

LAVERNE: God knows.

ISABEL: For old time's sake.

LAVERNE: Carlton was the brother of Jackie Mae that he lived with for so long. Poor thing had a terrible death. So much suffering. People were so narrow minded back in those days, they said that suffering was God's punishment to her for living in sin all those years.

MRS. WILLIS: I think I better go to my room now, Son.

FRED: All right, Mama.

(He and Mae take her to the room.)

FRANKIE: I'll go with you and help. I'll be right back.

(The four of them go into Mrs. Willis' room.)

ISABEL: Laverne, do you realize what you just said about living in sin?

LAVERNE: I know it. I know it. I thought I would die. I don't know what I was thinking of. I got started and didn't know how to stop. How did Frankie take it?

ISABEL: I was too embarrassed to look at her.

LAVERNE: *(Whispering.)* Helen Vaught is going to have a baby. She is claiming Fred is the father, Dotson says.

CONSTANCE: Do you think Frankie knows?

ISABEL: Yes, she does.

CONSTANCE: How do you know?

ISABEL: She told me she did.

(Frankie comes out of the bedroom.)

LAVERNE: How is she?

FRANKIE: She'll be all right. She just gets tired easily.

LAVERNE: Of course she's all right. She's determined now to live to see your baby. I'm going to start knitting a robe for your baby crib tomorrow. I'll knit two. One pink and one blue.

ISABEL: Maybe you'll have twins.

CONSTANCE: Wouldn't that be something. Twins. You remember Grace Anne Summers. She had triplets. She knew in advance that she was going to and whenever she went to a party, she'd say here comes the old mother cat. Of course, one of the three little babies was born afflicted and they had to keep it in a nursing home all its life. That's so sad, I think, when something like that happens.

FRANKIE: Girls. I'm scared.

ISABEL: Oh, Frankie.

FRANKIE: But I shouldn't be having a child. Maybe I should have had my children when I was your age.

LAVERNE: Don't be silly. Look at Mrs. Willis. Everybody is afraid when they first hear they are having a child. I was.

ISABEL: I was too. Now come on, Frankie. Cheer up now. You're going to love having a baby. There is nothing in this world like it. Is there girls?

CONSTANCE AND LAVERNE: No, nothing.

(The door bell rings. Isabel goes to the door. Carlton Gleason is there. He has a container of food.)

CARLTON: Hello.

ISABEL: Hello, again.

CARLTON: Georgia Dale asked me to bring this food to the Willis's. She saw they had to leave early.

(Isabel takes the food.)

ISABEL: Thank you. Tell Georgia Dale I'm sure they'll appreciate it.

(Fred comes out of the bedroom. Isabel goes to him.)

Fred, Georgia Dale sent this food over to you and your mother.

FRED: That was kind.

(Carlton comes in.)

CARLTON: Fred Willis?

FRED: Yes.

CARLTON: Carlton Gleason.

FRED: How do you do.

(They shake hands.)

Thank you for my father's picture.

CARLTON: That's all right. I came across it just the other day when I was fixing to come here. I figured you'd like it.

FRED: Where do you live now?

CARLTON: Colorado. I'm not used to the climate here now anymore. The humidity is about to kill me. I thought on my way here, I might just stay here to live and work, but now I'm not so sure I can take it. How do you folks stand the humidity?

ISABEL: I guess we're used to it.

LAVERNE: It's something. Of course, air-conditioning helps. Everything is air-conditioned. Our cars, our houses, our churches, our schools.

CARLTON: Wasn't so when I went to school here.

LAVERNE: Well, no. Air-conditioned schools are a fairly recent thing.

CARLTON: A man came up to me at S.P.'s funeral and said are you kin to Fred Willis. You look enough like him to be his brother. But now I see you, I don't think we look a thing alike. Do you ladies think we look alike?

ISABEL: No, not exactly.

LAVERNE: No, not at all.

(Carlton turns to Constance and Frankie.)

CARLTON: What do you ladies think?

CONSTANCE: No, I can't say you do.

(Frankie is silent.)

CARLTON: And what about you little lady?

FRANKIE: No, I don't.

CARLTON: Well, I'll say goodbye to you.

(*He extends his hand to Fred. Fred shakes his hand.*)

FRED: Goodbye, and thank Georgia Dale for the food.

(*Carlton leaves. Mrs. Willis calls: "Fred." Fred goes into his mother's room as the lights fade.*)

SCENE II

The lights are brought up. It is four months later, the day of Constance's baby shower. Mrs. Willis and Mae are in the living room. Mrs. Willis is dressed in a new dress. Fred comes in.

FRED: Mama, why didn't you go to the shower?

MRS. WILLIS: After I got dressed I felt so tired I just thought it wisdom if I stayed home. Bought a new dress, too.

MAE: Are you going to be home for awhile, Mr. Fred?

FRED: Yes.

MAE: Then I'm going to wash out a few things. (*She goes.*)

MRS. WILLIS: Helen Vaught called. (*A pause.*) Did you hear me, Fred? Helen Vaught called and asked for you.

FRED: Did she say it was Helen Vaught?

MRS. WILLIS: No, but I recognized her voice. I almost hung up on her, but I decided to act like a lady, and so I was real polite and I just said you weren't here as you had to go out to the farms to see how our crops were coming along and if she'd tell me her name, I would have you call her back. That's all right, she said, just as sweet as pie, I'll call him later. (*A pause.*) I hope you're not considering paying for her having that baby?

FRED: Yes, Mama. I've arranged to pay all the costs.

MRS. WILLIS: Oh, my God. Do you know what you're letting yourself in for? By doing this, you're as good as admitting this baby is yours. She'll bleed you the rest of your life. When your papa died Mrs. Gleason had a lawyer get in touch with me to inform me that Carlton was your papa's child and they wanted a share of the estate.

FRED: Was Carlton his son?

MRS. WILLIS: He never said and I never asked him. I know a lot of people thought so. He just told me he felt sorry for Carlton because he was lame and he used to send her money from time to time for Carlton, but he never saw any of it. She'd just get drunk and spend it all. She used to beat the boy, too, when she was drunk. Your father told me that. That's why he's lame, your father said, because of her beatings. Anyway, I didn't ever consider giving Carlton anything, because he would never have seen a penny of it. She would have spent it all herself, and that's what will happen if you start giving money to this baby. The baby will never see it. The mother will spend it all.

FRED: You don't know that, Mama.

MRS. WILLIS: I know what happened when your papa gave money to Mrs. Gleason for Carlton.

FRED: Well, Helen is not Mrs. Gleason. *(A pause.)* I've been seeing her again, Mama. I know I shouldn't, but I have.

MRS. WILLIS: Oh, my God. I don't want to hear this. I'm too old to hear this. *(Frankie enters followed by Laverne and Isabel. They are carrying some of Frankie's gifts from the shower.)*

FRANKIE: I'm sorry you couldn't have been at the party, Mrs. Willis. We had a wonderful time. The baby and I got some gifts.

MRS. WILLIS: That's nice.

LAVERNE: Where shall we put them?

FRANKIE: In my room.

(Laverne and Isabel go out.)

FRED: Who all was there?

FRANKIE: She invited twenty people and all of them came but Mrs. Willis.

MRS. WILLIS: I got overtired.

FRANKIE: I know. I think you were wise staying home. Would you like to see the gifts?

MRS. WILLIS: I'll look at them later.

FRANKIE: That was just part of the gifts. Constance and Georgia Dale are bringing the rest over later. We won't have to buy a thing for the baby, Fred. Except a baby crib.

MRS. WILLIS: I want to get that for you. And a baby carriage and a car seat.

FRANKIE: Well, thank you.

(Laverne and Isabel come back in.)

ISABEL: Constance had such a darling party. She's so clever. She had pink and blue decorations everywhere. All the cut flowers she used for decorations were pink and blue, her table cloths and napkins were pink and blue, and even the dress she wore was pink and blue.

MRS. WILLIS: *(Calling.)* Mae.

(Mae comes in.)

MRS. WILLIS: I want to go to my room.

(Mae helps her out of her chair.)

FRANKIE: Are you all right, Mrs. Willis?

MRS. WILLIS: Yes, I'm all right. I get tired is all.

LAVERNE: Don't overdo Mrs. Willis. You've got to keep well and strong for the new baby.

MRS. WILLIS: I'll do my best.

(She and Mae leave.)

ISABEL: And then, Fred, we all took a vote whether it was going to be a boy or a girl. And who do you think won?

FRED: I have no idea, Isabel.

ISABEL: Two to one you're going to have a boy. So you had better start thinking of boys' names. Have you thought of any names?

FRANKIE: No, not really. Have you, Fred?

FRED: No, not really.

(Constance and Georgia Dale come in with more presents.)

CONSTANCE: Where do you want these?

FRANKIE: In my bedroom.

(They go out.)

Did you ever see so many presents in your life, Fred?

FRED: No, I doubt if I have.

FRANKIE: Come on, let me show them to you.

FRED: I'll look at them later.

(Constance and Georgia Dale come back in.)

CONSTANCE: I thought it was a wonderful party, if I do say so myself.

LAVERNE: I was trying to remember last night who all gave me my baby showers. I know I had three for the first baby and two for the second.

CONSTANCE: Didn't you write it down in your baby book?

LAVERNE: I don't know where either of my children's baby books are.

ISABEL: Did somebody give you a baby book, Frankie?

FRANKIE: I don't believe so.

LAVERNE: Oh, I don't think people do that anymore.

GEORGIA DALE: What in the world is a baby book?

CONSTANCE: It's a book where you keep all your baby's records. How much they weighed at birth, the hour they were born, who gave them presents, when they got their first tooth, a lock of their hair if they have any, when they take their first step. You know it's a variation of a bridal book. You had a bridal book when you got married, didn't you?

GEORGIA DALE: No.

CONSTANCE: I had four given me at different bridal showers.

GEORGIA DALE: I didn't have a bridal shower either time when I got married. Fred, Carlton Gleason is working for me now. S.P. left him something in his will.

FRED: I heard that.

GEORGIA DALE: I've given him a job looking after the farms S.P. left me. Two of them, I believe, border farms of yours.

FRED: That's right.

GEORGIA DALE: I told Carlton to ask you to ride out one day and show him where our boundaries are exactly. Would you mind doing that?

FRED: No.

LAVERNE: How many farms did S.P. leave you, Georgia Dale?

GEORGIA DALE: Seven.

CONSTANCE: All in cotton?

GEORGIA DALE: No, only two in cotton, I've been told. Two in rice and one in corn and soy beans and I forget what the others grow. I can't even find them. Thank God Carlton knows where they are.

LAVERNE: How does he know?

GEORGIA DALE: He used to ride out with S.P. and his sister. He knows every-one of them. He said he's going to take me out one day.

LAVERNE: You should go.

GEORGIA DALE: No, thank you. I'll pay Carlton to go look at them. I can't stand the country. I don't know cotton from Irish potatoes and I don't care to learn. Do you know how Carlton got that limp? He said his mother used to get drunk and beat him.

FRED: Excuse me. I think I'll go look at the presents. *(He leaves.)*

ISABEL: Poor thing.

LAVERNE: Where is Carlton's brother?

GEORGIA DALE: In Colorado. Carlton has been living out there too.

CONSTANCE: I'm suddenly so tired. I've been working on this shower night and day for three days.

ISABEL: Well, it was certainly a success.

FRANKIE: It certainly was. I can't tell you how much it meant to me. Everyone has been so sweet. I'll never forget it.

CONSTANCE: I'd better get back home.

ISABEL: Me, too. I have to think about supper, not that I can eat a bite after all those lovely refreshments. Are you coming with me, Laverne?

LAVERNE: Yes, I will.

ISABEL: We'll see you.

(They all say their goodbyes and leave.)

GEORGIA DALE: I'll be going in a little while, too. I know you must be tired after such a party.

FRANKIE: No, I'm fine.

GEORGIA DALE: I don't mind telling you, I get lonesome. I miss old S.P. Constance, Laverne and Isabel will all go home to husbands. I'm going home to an empty house, and I don't like it at all. How did you stand all those years of being single? I was thinking the other night I'd get married again, if I could, but who in the world would I marry? Nobody around here I'd want. Well, I'm thinking of going on a cruise. Now, Carlton is here and looking after things. I hear a cruise is a wonderful place to meet men. Unattached men. Have you heard that?

FRANKIE: No, not really. I suppose it would be though.

GEORGIA DALE: Have you ever been on a cruise?

FRANKIE: Twice. Once Fred and I went with Constance and Travis to the Bahamas and another time through the Panama Canal.

GEORGIA DALE: Was it fun?

FRANKIE: Yes, it was.

GEORGIA DALE: Did you see a lot of unattached men?

FRANKIE: I'm sure there were, but I was with Fred.

(Fred enters.)

GEORGIA DALE: How did you like all those presents?

FRED: They were something else.

GEORGIA DALE: I was telling Frankie I'm thinking of going on a cruise now that Carlton's here to look out for things. *(She gets up.)* Well, so long.

FRED: Goodbye, Georgia Dale.

FRANKIE: Come back, Georgia Dale.

(She leaves.)

FRANKIE: I'd better be thinking about your supper.

(She starts away.)

FRED: Frankie…

FRANKIE: Yes.

FRED: I'm moving out. I'm going to Houston to live.

FRANKIE: Why, Fred?

FRED: Because I'd like a divorce once the baby is born.

FRANKIE: You can have a divorce now if that's what you want.

FRED: No, I think we should wait until after the baby is born. *(A pause.)* I'm in love with someone else. *(A pause.)* Helen Vaught.

FRANKIE: I'm supposed to stay here with your mother while you live in Houston with Helen Vaught.

FRED: I won't be living with her. I'll be seeing her but I won't be living with her. She's living with her mother and her brothers now.

FRANKIE: This is very cruel of you, Fred.

FRED: I know, and I'm sorry.

FRANKIE: That doesn't help much, Fred.

FRED: You and the baby are to have half of all I have and after Mother goes I'll give you half of what she leaves.

FRANKIE: I don't want your money, Fred.

FRED: Then I'll leave it to our child.

FRANKIE: Is this how it's going to end? I don't blame you, really. I blame myself. I am a conventional person living in a conventional town. I knew the consequences of how we lived.

FRED: It could have happened anytime, Frankie. Even if we'd been married for years. Look at the couples we know that have been married for years and then one or the other meets someone else and falls in love and they get divorced. That's how life is today. I promise to be a good father to the baby, as good as you'll let me be. I'll visit the baby as often as you let me and I'll…

FRANKIE: I am so mortified. Why did you marry me? Why in the name of God did you ever marry me if you loved her?

FRED: I was confused. I didn't think I loved her. It wasn't until afterwards when she was having the baby.

FRANKIE: Is it your baby?

FRED: I think so. She says so.

FRANKIE: What if it's not?

FRED: Then it's not. I still love her.

FRANKIE: I don't want to stay on here, Fred, with your mother.

FRED: Where do you want to go?

FRANKIE: God knows. I'll have to think.

(Mae comes out.)

MAE: Mr. Fred, your mama's crying in there.

FRED: Oh, my God.

FRANKIE: I think I want to leave and you stay here with your mother.

FRED: We'll see. (He goes.)

FRANKIE: He wants a divorce, Mae. He wants to marry another woman.

MAE: Yes, ma'am. Are you going to give him a divorce?

FRANKIE: Yes, I am.

MAE: Bless your heart. Why?

FRANKIE: Because I don't want to live with him if he wants to divorce me.

MAE: What about your baby?

FRANKIE: What good will he be to the baby if he doesn't want to live with us. Who could be happy or content then? You know what I feel like, Mae? Hager in the Bible.

MAE: Hager. She wasn't Abraham's lawful wife. You're his lawful wife.

FRANKIE: I know, but he sent her away out into the wilderness alone with her baby, because his wife was having a baby.

MAE: But the Lord took care of Hager. In the wilderness...

FRANKIE: I pray he takes care of me and my baby. *(She cries.)* Mae. I've got no one to turn to and I'm so mortified. I am so mortified. How will I face my friends?

(The door bell rings. Mae goes. Carlton is there.)

CARLTON: Is Mr. Willis home?

MAE: Yes, sir.

CARLTON: Would you ask if I could see him, please?

MAE: Yes, sir.

(Carlton comes into the room.)

CARLTON: Mrs. Willis?

FRANKIE: Yes.

CARLTON: I'm Carlton Gleason.

FRANKIE: How do you do?

CARLTON: I'm pretty well, thank you. I'm working for Georgia Dale.

FRANKIE: She told us.

CARLTON: Two of her farms join two of your husbands. I have most of the boundaries figured out, but there is a line on the parcel of the land which according to the survey I have isn't clear where our line stops and his begins.

FRANKIE: I'm sure my husband can help you.

CARLTON: Yes, ma'am. *(A pause.)* Warm for this time of the year, isn't it? I've been living in Colorado. We sleep under blankets there every night all summer long. My brother said you ought to have your head examined going back to that heat and humidity. Well, I always think of it as home, I said. I like it where it is flat and you can see what's around you. I never took to the mountains at all. Have you ever been to Colorado?

FRANKIE: Twice. In the winter time.

CARLTON: Skiing?

FRANKIE: I went with people that ski. I don't ski.

CARLTON: I don't either on account of my leg. Of course, a handicap like mine never stops some people. I knew a man once with only one leg and he could ski as well as anybody. They called him the one-legged wonder. Did you ever see him on T.V.?

FRANKIE: No.

CARLTON: He was on T.V. a couple times.

(Mae comes out.)

MAE: He'll be out in a minute.

CARLTON: Thank you.

(She goes.)

Georgia Dale says you and Fred just got married.

FRANKIE: Not just. We've been married almost a year.

CARLTON: And you're expecting a child?

FRANKIE: Yes.

CARLTON: That's nice. I used to live here, you know.

FRANKIE: Yes, you said.

CARLTON: Did you know my sister?

FRANKIE: Oh, yes. Very well.

CARLTON: She was quite a bit older than you.

FRANKIE: Yes.

CARLTON: She was eight years older than me, and I don't know how old you are, but I'm eight or nine years older than Fred. After we left here and moved to Houston to live, Fred's daddy every now and again used to bring him to Houston when he came to see us.

(Fred enters.)

I was just telling your wife that after we moved to Houston your daddy used to bring you by our house every now and again. But you weren't more than four or five, so I don't guess you'd remember it.

FRED: No, I don't.

CARLTON: I remember the day he died. Mama came in and said Carlton I have sad news for you. Your Uncle Lewis has died. I always called him Uncle, though he wasn't my uncle, of course.

FRED: You wanted to ask me something?

CARLTON: Yessir. I've been studying the map of two of Georgia Dale's farms. I think I have the boundaries all figured out except for these two. See here, on the map.

(He shows the map to Fred as Mae comes in.)

MAE: Mr. Fred I called the doctor. I think your mama has had a stroke. A bad stroke.

FRED: Oh, my heavens.

(He goes into the bedroom. Mae follows.)

CARLTON: I guess I picked a bad time. I hope everything turns out all right.

FRANKIE: Thank you.

(He goes as Mae comes in the room.)

How is she?

MAE: She's pitiful. She can't move. She can't talk.

FRANKIE: Is she dying?

MAE: I don't know.

(Mae gets her Bible. She sits in a chair and begins to read as the lights fade. The lights are brought up—a year later. Mrs. Willis is in a wheelchair. Her paralysis has left her unable to speak, and it is not apparent if she can hear. She sits motionless and is very passive. Helen is there with Georgia Dale. They are having drinks.)

GEORGIA DALE: I just want to take a look at your baby again. *(She goes over to the bassinet and picks up the baby.)* He's darling, Helen.

HELEN: Thank you. I think he's pretty cute, myself.

(Georgia Dale takes the baby over to Mrs. Willis.)

GEORGIA DALE: Mrs. Willis, I think your grandson is just precious. I bet you're proud of him.

HELEN: You can save your breath, Georgia Dale. I don't think she understands a thing anybody says. Fred doesn't agree with me. He'll sit right there and talk to her like she knows every word he says.

GEORGIA DALE: Mrs. Willis, isn't Stanley cute? See he's smiling at you. Smile at your grandma, Stanley.

HELEN: You're wasting your breath, Georgia Dale.

GEORGIA DALE: Maybe so. Poor thing. I'd hate to end up that way in a wheel chair, not able to know what was going on. *(She takes the baby back to the bassinet.)* Who is Stanley named for?

HELEN: My grandfather. I'm going to go crazy, Georgia Dale, cooped up here with this old woman.

GEORGIA DALE: What happened to Mae?

HELEN: She quit. Fred said she was tired and had to rest, but I hear she is working for Frankie. I don't think she was tired at all. I think she quit when she heard I was coming here to live. Oh, there has been so much gossip it makes me sick. I know everybody is speculating whether this is really Fred's baby or not. Well, I swear to you and to my maker it is Fred's baby, but I pray to God it turns out to look like Fred, or no one here will believe it's his baby. You and Carlton are the only ones that will come to see us even. None of Fred's other friends will, not even Laverne. Dotson will come on business, but he's uncomfortable the whole time, because Laverne told him not to be nice and friendly to me. I said to Fred as soon as his mama dies we are leaving this town for good.

GEORGIA DALE: Oh, they'll all get over it. Give them time. They carried on something terrible when I married S.P. Said I had to get him drunk to marry me, that I married him just for his money and I don't know what all. Gradually, it quieted down. I heard Fred gave the two farms next to mine to Frankie as part of his divorce settlement.

HELEN: Yes, he did and God knows what else.

(Fred comes in.)

FRED: Hello, Georgia Dale.

GEORGIA DALE: Hi.

HELEN: Want a drink, Fred?

FRED: Not right now.

HELEN: Georgia Dale is going to have dinner with us.

FRED: Fine.

GEORGIA DALE: I'm going to have to make some crab gumbo for you all one of these days. Fred loves my crab gumbo.

FRED: That's right.

GEORGIA DALE: I think your baby is precious, Fred.

FRED: Thank you. I'm certainly proud of him. *(He goes to the bassinet.)* Hello, Son. *(He goes over to his mother. He kisses her on the forehead.)* Hello, Mama. How are you doing?
(Mrs. Willis makes no response. He watches her for a moment and then goes back to Helen and Georgia Dale.)
Frankie is bringing her baby over to see Mama in a few minutes.

HELEN: You're not serious?

FRED: Yes, I am.

HELEN: Well, thank you for telling me. I'm not going to be here, Fred.

FRED: Now, listen Helen, we have to be civilized about this. I'm the father of two children. We all live in the same town. We are bound to meet. I want my other son to know his grandmother, too, and for her to know him.

HELEN: She doesn't know anything, Fred. She never will again.

FRED: Now you don't know that. I wish you please wouldn't keep saying that. Not in front of Mama anyway. You don't know at all what she understands and what she doesn't understand. Personally, just in case she can understand, I want her to have the pleasure of seeing both my sons.

GEORGIA DALE: Maybe I'd better go. I can have dinner with you another time.

FRED: No, don't go. Let's try and make this as normal as possible. Let's all just relax.

HELEN: Jesus Christ, I don't want to live in this town, Fred. I hate this town. Everybody but Georgia Dale just treats me like dirt.

FRED: They'll change. You'll see.

GEORGIA DALE: That's what I told her. In another year or two everything will be forgotten.

HELEN: Another year or two? We're leaving the minute his mother dies.

FRED: Helen.

HELEN: I mean it, Fred.

FRED: Don't talk about dying in front of Mama.

HELEN: I'm sorry. Have you found someone to stay with your mother?

FRED: Not yet.

GEORGIA DALE: I know a Mexican woman that is very reliable. Lupe something.

FRED: No, thank you. Mama doesn't like Mexicans. She wants a Negro.

HELEN: How do you know what she wants?

FRED: She would always only have Negro help.

HELEN: Jesus Christ. I could ring that Mae's neck. She lied to you, Fred. When she said she was tired and didn't want to work any longer. She's working right now for Frankie.

FRED: I don't believe that.

(The door bell rings. Fred goes. Frankie is there with Carlton, who holds their baby.)

Hello, Frankie. Hello, Carlton.

FRANKIE: Hello, Fred.

CARLTON: Hi, Fred.

FRANKIE: I asked Carlton to ride over with me to help me with the baby.

FRED: Come on in.

CARLTON: I'm kind of dirty so forgive my appearance. I've been tramping throughout the woods all day trying to figure out the line between the farms you gave Frankie and Georgia Dale's farms.

FRED: I explained to you...

CARLTON: I know you did, but I took a surveyor out there the other day and he said you had gotten it all wrong.

FRED: I haven't gotten it all wrong. I walked that line many a time with my father.

CARLTON: I know he had me out there once or twice, too.

FRED: My father did?

CARLTON: Yes, once before you were born, and the next time I remember you were just two years old.

FRANKIE: Hello, Helen. Georgia Dale.

GEORGIA DALE: Hi, Frankie.

HELEN: Hello, Frankie.

FRANKIE: Hello, Mrs. Willis.

(There is no answer from Mrs. Willis.)

How is she, Fred?

FRED: About the same.

HELEN: Frankie, I hear Mae is working for you.

FRANKIE: Yes, she started yesterday.

HELEN: I told you, Fred.

FRED: What can I do about it?

HELEN: You can call her a liar the next time you see her.

GEORGIA DALE: Let me see your baby. *(She goes to Carlton to look at the baby.)* Oh, he's just precious. I just regret so not having children. They're so sweet. How old is he now?

FRANKIE: Three months.

GEORGIA DALE: Three months. His name is Douglas?

FRANKIE: Yes, after my father. Douglas Johnson Willis.

GEORGIA DALE: What do you call him? Doug?

FRANKIE: No, I call him Douglas.

FRED: Let me hold the baby, Carlton.

(Carlton gives him the baby.)

FRED: I want to show the baby to Mama. *(He takes the baby over to his mother.)* Mama, you know who this is? This is my son by Frankie. His name is Douglas.

HELEN: She don't know a thing he's saying. Look at her.

FRED: How old is he, Frankie?

FRANKIE: Three months.

FRED: He's three months old, Mama. Helen, bring Stanley over there so Mama can see the two of them together.

HELEN: I will not, Fred. She doesn't know a thing that's going on.

FRED: Stop saying that, will you? She knows more than you think she does. Carlton bring Stanley over here for Mama to see.

CARLTON: Who is Stanley?

GEORGIA DALE: His baby by Helen. He's in the bassinet.

(Carlton goes to the bassinet and picks up Stanley and brings him over to Fred and Mrs. Willis.)

FRED: See, Mama. Your two grandsons. Douglas and Stanley. Sons, this is your grandmother.

GEORGIA DALE: Isn't that precious.

HELEN: Precious. I swear to you she doesn't know a thing that's going on. *(She goes to Carlton.)* Give me my baby. *(She takes the baby and puts it in the bassinet.)*

(Fred holds Douglas up close to Mrs. Willis.)

FRED: This is your Grandmother Willis, Douglas.

GEORGIA DALE: How are you feeling, Frankie?

FRANKIE: All right.

GEORGIA DALE: I heard you were sick for awhile.

FRANKIE: I was for a week or so, but I'm all right now.

(Fred comes back with the baby.)

FRED: He's growing.

FRANKIE: Yes, everyday.

FRED: Can I fix you a drink?

FRANKIE: No, I think not. I've things to do at home. We're expecting Constance and Travis for dinner.

FRED: We?

FRANKIE: Carlton and I. We're getting married next week, Fred.

FRED: Congratulations, Carlton.

CARLTON: Thank you.

FRANKIE: Carlton has been helpful to me in so many ways while I was getting settled after the baby came and seeing to my farms.

GEORGIA DALE: He's good at that. He's done a grand job with my farms, too. I hope you're not going to leave me Carlton, now you're marrying Frankie.

CARLTON: No, ma'am.

FRANKIE: Let me know next week when you would like me to bring the baby over again, Fred.

FRED: I will. Thank you.

(She and Carlton leave.)

GEORGIA DALE: Well, what do you know about that? Well, their getting married has come as no surprise to me—not at all. Were you surprised, Fred?

FRED: I suppose—in a way…

HELEN: Still water runs deep.

FRED: What?

HELEN: I said still water runs deep.

FRED: Oh.

GEORGIA DALE: I went off on the cruise thinking I could meet someone unattached, but there was not a soul on that cruise over twenty-five without a wife. And those under twenty-five that were unattached look at me like I was an old woman. I called Carlton and asked him to meet me at the airport and I thought to myself—Carlton isn't all that bad. Maybe I'll take him on when I get back, but Lord, if he didn't have Frankie and the baby in the car with him when he came to meet me. I saw right away she got there first.

HELEN: A woman the other day, a perfect stranger, came up to me at Wynn Dixie…

GEORGIA DALE: Wynn Dixie?

HELEN: You know the supermarket.

GEORGIA DALE: Oh, ours it not called Wynn Dixie. It's the Apple Tree, or H.E.B.

HELEN: Whatever. And this woman proceeded to tell me some long story about your father, being Carlton's father and Carlton was really your half-brother.

FRED: Forget it, Helen.

HELEN: Is it true?

FRED: Who knows. Mama says it wasn't.

HELEN: She said he looks just like your father. Does he? And she said Carlton's mother sued when your father died for a share of the estate.

FRED: Well, he didn't get it.

(He goes to the bassinet. He takes the baby and goes back to his mama.)

GEORGIA DALE: I think people are so tacky telling you things like that.

HELEN: You never heard that?

GEORGIA DALE: Yes, I heard it, but it would never occur to me to tell it to you.

FRED: *(Holding the baby out to his mother.)* Mama. Here is your oldest grandson. He's mine and Helen's baby son. This is your Grandmother Willis.

GEORGIA DALE: Of course, if you think about it, if Carlton marries Frankie he's going to get part of Mr. Willis's estate after all. At least he'll share in Frankie's part of it. Did those two farms you gave Frankie belong to your daddy, Fred?

FRED: Yes.

GEORGIA DALE: See?

MRS. WILLIS: *(Slowly and almost inaudibly.)* Mae.

FRED: What did you say, Mama? What did you say? Frankie…

HELEN: What did you say?

FRED: I'm sorry, I meant Helen.

HELEN: That's better. I better never catch you calling me Frankie again.

FRED: For God's sake, Helen, I didn't know what I was saying. I was so excited. Mama spoke a word. Didn't you hear her?

HELEN: No.

FRED: Didn't you hear her, Georgia Dale?

GEORGIA DALE: I heard something.

FRED: She said Mae. Mae. Oh, that's wonderful, Mama. Mae. Say it again, Mama. Mae. Mae. Mae.

HELEN: Are you getting hungry, Georgia Dale?

GEORGIA DALE: Not particularly.

HELEN: Do you want to listen to the evening news?

GEORGIA DALE: What for? Just get depressed. I wonder if Carlton is marrying Frankie for her farms? Well, if he had married me I have twice as many farms as Frankie. How many farms did you give Frankie, Fred?

FRED: Two.

GEORGIA DALE: I've got seven. I wish to God now I'd never gone on that silly cruise.

HELEN: Come talk to us, Fred.

FRED: I want to stay here in case Mama speaks again.

HELEN: He gave Frankie half of everything he had.

GEORGIA DALE: You told me.

HELEN: Guilt.

GEORGIA DALE: And now Carlton is marrying her and half of what she has will be his unless they sign a prenuptial agreement of some kind.

HELEN: How does that make you feel, Fred? Carlton ending up with half of what you gave Frankie.

FRED: It's hers to do with what she wants.

HELEN: When his mama dies half of what she leaves goes to my boy and half to Frankie's. So Frankie's boy will always be taken care of, and my boy, well, of course he'll get the rest of what his daddy has when he dies. If Mrs. Willis ever dies…

MRS. WILLIS: Mae.

GEORGIA DALE: I heard that.

HELEN: So did I. *(A pause.)* If Mrs. Willis ever dies—which doesn't look like now she ever will.

MRS. WILLIS: Mae.

HELEN: Why is she calling Mae? For God's sake, Fred, tell her Mae is gone. She is a liar and she's gone.

(Fred has begun to cry.)

GEORGIA DALE: Helen, look there. Fred is crying. Bless his heart.

MRS. WILLIS: Mae.

(Helen goes to him.)

HELEN: Fred, don't cry. It ought to make you happy that your mother is speaking. Fred. Fred.

(But Fred is sobbing uncontrollably now as Mrs. Willis continues calling: "Mae. Mae. Mae." as the lights fade.)

END OF PLAY

HORTON FOOTE has had plays produced on Broadway, Off-Broadway, Off-Off-Broadway, and at many regional theaters. They include *The Chase; The Traveling Lady; The Trip to Bountiful; The Habitation of Dragons; Night Seasons; A Coffin in Egypt; Tomorrow; The Orphan's Home Cycle: Roots in a Parched Ground, Convicts, Lily Dale, The Widow Claire, Courtship, Valentine's Day, Death of Papa; Dividing the Estate; Talking Pictures; Getting Frankie Married — and Afterwards; The Roads to Home; Laura Dennis; Vernon Early* and many one-act plays. His films include: *Baby the Rain Must Fall; Tomorrow; Courtship; On Valentine's Day; 1918; Convicts; The Trip to Bountiful; Of Mice and Men* and *Lily Dale.* Mr. Foote received an Academy Award for Best Screenplay and the Writers Guild of America Screen Award for his screenplay *To Kill a Mockingbird;* his original screenplay, *Tender Mercies,* won an Academy Award for Best Screenplay. He received The William Inge Lifetime Achievement Award and was presented with both the Evelyn Burkey Award and the Screen Laurel Award from the Writers Guild of America. In 1995 he received the Pulitzer Prize for Drama for *The Young Man from Atlanta* presented as part of Signature Theater's entire season devoted to his plays. *The Young Man from Atlanta* was also done at the Alley and On Broadway in New York and was nominated for a Tony. The same year he was awarded the Lucille Lortel Award for Outstanding Achievement for the Signature Series of his plays and an Academy Award in Literature from the Academy Arts and Letters. In 1996 he was elected to the Theatre Hall of Fame. In 1998 he received an Emmy for his dramatization of Faulkner's "The Old Man" and was elected to membership in American Academy of Arts and Letters, and at the same time received the Gold Medal for Drama for the entire body of his work from the Academy.